A Brief Orientation to Counseling

Professional Identity, History, and Standards

A BRIEF ORIENTATION TO COUNSELING

Professional Identity, History, and Standards

Ed Neukrug

BROOKS/COLE
CENGAGE Learning

Australia • Brazil • Japan • Korea • Mexico • Singapore • Spain • United Kingdom • United States

BROOKS/COLE
CENGAGE Learning·

A Brief Orientation to Counseling: Professional Identity, History, and Standards
Ed Neukrug

Editor in Chief: Linda Ganster

Publisher: Jon-David Hague

Executive Editor: Jaime Perkins

Acquisitions Editor: Seth Dobrin

Assistant Editor: Naomi Dreyer

Associate Media Editor: Elizabeth Momb

Executive Brand Manager: Liz Rhoden

Art and Cover Direction, Design, Production Management, and Composition: PreMediaGlobal

Manufacturing Planner: Judy Inouye

Rights Acquisitions Specialist: Don Shlotman

Cover Image: Sergey Shlyaev/Shutterstock

For product information and technology assistance, contact us at **Cengage Learning Customer & Sales Support, 1-800-354-9706**

For permission to use material from this text or product, submit all requests online at **www.cengage.com/permissions**

Further permissions questions can be e-mailed to **permissionrequest@cengage.com**

Library of Congress Control Number: 2012940980

Student Edition:

ISBN-13: 978-1-111-52122-6

ISBN-10: 1-111-52122-0

Brooks/Cole
20 Davis Drive
Belmont, CA 94002-3098
USA

Cengage Learning is a leading provider of customized learning solutions with office locations around the globe, including Singapore, the United Kingdom, Australia, Mexico, Brazil, and Japan. Locate your local office at **www.cengage.com/global**

Cengage Learning products are represented in Canada by Nelson Education, Ltd.

To learn more about Brooks/Cole, visit **www.cengage.com/brookscole**

Purchase any of our products at your local college store or at our preferred online store **www.cengagebrain.com**

Printed in the United States of America
1 2 3 4 5 6 7 16 15 14 13 12

Dedicated to All Counseling Professionals

CONTENTS

CHAPTER 5

History of the Counseling Profession   63

CHAPTER 6

Current Issues and Future Trends in the Counseling Profession   81

SECTION III

STANDARDS IN THE COUNSELING PROFESSION   97

CHAPTER 7

Accreditation in Counseling and Related Fields   99

CHAPTER 8

Credentialing in Counseling and Related Fields   109

APPENDIX   A

Multicultural Counseling Competencies   167

APPENDIX   B

Advocacy Competencies   171

PREFACE

Welcome to the book *A Brief Orientation to Counseling: Professional Identity, History, and Standards*. The purpose of this book is to highlight those aspects of counseling most important in developing a counseling perspective and in building an affiliation with the field. The book is separated into three sections, the first of which focuses on professional identity, the second of which looks at history and trends, and the last of which examines standards in the profession. An afterword provides information on applying to graduate school and on applying for a job. Let's take a quick look at these sections and the afterword and describe some of the special features of the book.

SECTION I: PROFESSIONAL IDENTITY OF THE COUNSELOR

Chapter 1: What Is Counseling and Who Is the Counselor? begins by offering a historical perspective on the words *guidance, counseling,* and *psychotherapy* and describes the difference between these three words. After acknowledging that some counselors do all three, the chapter moves on to offer a recent definition of *counseling* that embraces guidance, counseling, and psychotherapy. Next in the chapter, we discuss different types of counselors while noting their respective types of accreditation, credentialing, and professional associations. We briefly do the same for a number of related non-counseling mental health professionals so that you are familiar with those individuals with whom you will likely work.

Chapter 2: Professional Associations in Counseling and Related Fields examines the importance of professional associations and then describes, in a fair amount of detail, the American Counseling Association (ACA) as well as its 19 divisions, 56 branches, and 6 professional partnerships. In addition, specific membership benefits are relayed. As in Chapter 1, we offer information about our non-counseling professional colleagues by providing a brief overview of a number of professorial associations for non-counseling mental health professionals. These include: the American Art Therapy Association (AATA), the American Association of Marriage and Family Therapy (AAMFT), the American Association of Pastoral Counselors (AAPC), the American Psychiatric Association (APA), the American Psychiatric Nurses Association (APNA), the American Psychological Association (APA), the National Association of School Psychologists (NASP), the National Association of Social Workers (NASW), the National Organization of Human Services (NOHS), and the National Rehabilitation Counseling Association (NRCA).

The last chapter in this section is called *Chapter 3: Characteristics of the Effective Counselor* and examines a number of qualities that are embraced by effective counselors. We begin this chapter by offering a quick review of some of the research that has examined the effectiveness of counseling. Then we suggest there are nine factors that collectively work toward increasing counselor effectiveness, including six that jointly describe the working alliance: empathy, acceptance, genuineness, embracing a wellness perspective, cultural competence, and the "it factor," and three that together are related to the counselor's ability to deliver his or her theoretical approach: belief in your theory, competence, and cognitive complexity.

SECTION II: HISTORY AND CURRENT TRENDS IN THE COUNSELING PROFESSION

The first chapter of this section, *Chapter 4: Predecessors to the Counseling Profession: From Early Antiquity to Early Social Work, Psychology, and Psychiatry,* begins by identifying and discussing antecedents to the development of the mental health professions. The rest of the chapter gives a relatively brief history of social work, of psychology, and of psychiatry. In particular, how the early beginnings of these fields impacted the counseling profession is discussed. A summary table is provided at the end of the chapter to highlight points and help you remember salient events.

Chapter 5: History of the Counseling Profession focuses solely on the 100-year history of counseling. The chapter takes us through the early history of vocational guidance and the impact testing and early methods of psychotherapy had on counseling. It then moves on to cover the emergence, diversification, and proliferation of the field during the second half of the twentieth century. In addition, new issues that have arisen within the past twenty years that will likely impact the counseling profession in the future are discussed. As in Chapter 4, a summary table is provided at the end of the chapter to highlight points and help you remember salient events.

Because the past is intimately connected with the future, the last chapter in this section is *Chapter 6: Current Issues and Future Trends in the Counseling Profession.* In this chapter we highlight a number of new approaches to counseling that are being emphasized today; the impact that technology is having and will have on counseling; how trends in health management, such as managed care, medications, and diagnosis will affect the profession; the many new codes and other standards that will change the way counselors practice; and professional issues related to division expansion, division autonomy, and recent efforts to create greater unity amongst the many different counseling organizations.

SECTION III: STANDARDS IN THE COUNSELING PROFESSION

We begin this section with *Chapter 7: Accreditation in Counseling and Related Fields*. Here we describe the history of the Council for Accreditation of Counseling and Related Educational Professions (CACREP). Next, we discuss the many benefits of accreditation. We then offer an overview of the CACREP standards that includes a quick look at the master's- and doctoral-level standards. The chapter concludes with a brief description of accrediting bodies in related mental health fields.

Chapter 8: Credentialing in Counseling and Related Fields begins with a history of credentialing in counseling and related fields. We then discuss the benefits of credentialing and distinguish three types of credentialing: registration, certification, and licensing. We next describe, in some depth, different kinds of counselor licensure and certification and how credentialing can serve as a unifying force for the counseling profession. The chapter concludes with a brief overview of credentialing in related mental health professions and a short discussion of the importance of lobbying for credentialing and other counseling-related concerns.

Chapter 9: Ethics in Counseling and Related Fields begins by defining values and morality and discussing their relationship to the law. We then go on to discuss the development of and need for ethical codes. After describing the ACA code in some detail, we next identify ethical "hot spots" and describe four models of ethical decision-making: problem solving, moral, social constructionist, and developmental. A case example is offered so that students can practice the models. How to report ethical violations is discussed next, followed by legal issues related to ethical violations, the importance of malpractice insurance, and using best practices to avoid malpractice suits.

The last chapter of this section is *Chapter 10: Multicultural Counseling and Social Justice Work: The Fourth and Fifth Forces*. This chapter first defines multicultural counseling and social justice work and then goes on to offer some reasons why counseling is not working for many individuals from nondominant groups. After offering definitions for a number of common terms related to multicultural counseling, we go on to describe three conceptual models to help us understand ourselves and our clients: the RESPECTFUL acronym, the Tripartite Model, and Developmental Models of Cultural/Racial Identity. The chapter concludes with a description of the Multicultural Counseling Competencies and the Advocacy Competencies and how multicultural counseling and social justice work are considered the fourth and fifth forces in the history of the counseling profession.

AFTERWORD: APPLYING TO GRADUATE SCHOOL AND FINDING A JOB

At some point, most students who read this book will be applying to graduate school and/or applying for a job in the counseling profession. The afterword was developed to make this process easier. In the afterword you will find items to consider when choosing a graduate program and/or finding a job, some pointers to remember in the application process, how to develop your resume and portfolio, specific resources to help you find a graduate program or a job, and how to deal with being chosen by or being denied entrance to your favorite school or your dream job.

Activities to Enhance Learning

You will find a number of items throughout the book that will add to the learning process. For instance, on a number of occasions I refer students to websites to gain additional information. In some cases they are websites of professional associations. Other times, they are websites to enhance the learning of a subject area. For instance, when I talk about counseling theory, I refer students to an interactive website where students can learn more about counseling theorists. Another time I refer students to the positive psychology website, where they can see their "positivity ratio." In addition, a number of tables can be found throughout the text that highlight points and enhance learning, such as the definitions Meyers and Sweeney use in their 5-factor Indivisible Self wellness inventory, which students can use to assess their wellness levels. Finally, I have included experiential activities throughout the text to enhance the understanding of subject areas. These are usually fun, short exercises that students can share in class.

Ancillaries

A number of ancillaries to the text that might be helpful are available. Search for this book under its title or under the name of the author Neukrug.

For the Instructor:
1. *Syllabus:* A sample syllabus is provided, which can be adapted to the instructor's liking.
2. *Test questions.* Questions on the content of each chapter are available.
3. *Teaching tips:* Ideas about novel ways of teaching this course offered.
4. *PowerPoints:* PPTs for each chapter are available.
5. *Experiencing the World of the Counselor:* If you want additional experiential exercises to enhance learning, please obtain a desk copy from Brooks/Cole of the workbook, *Experiencing the World of the Counselor: A Workbook for Counselor Educators and, from Cengage Learning.* Each chapter is filled with experiential activities and includes about 15 ethical, professional, and legal scenarios to discuss. The workbook not only provides a wealth of practical exercises related to all the chapters in this text but also to other areas of the counseling profession.

ACKNOWLEDGEMENTS

I'd like to thank Seth Dobrin, Acquisitions Editor for Brooks/Cole, for the foresight to publish this text. And my thanks to all the others from Brooks/Cole that have helped in the publication of this text. I'd also like to thank my copy editor Ali Landreau, and a big "cheers" and thanks to Jared Sterzer and Soumya Nair, Project Co-Managers at PreMedia Global. Finally, a special thanks to all those who reviewed the initial version of this text, including: Michael Altekruse, Northern Kentucky University; Steve Bradshaw, Richmont Graduate University; Conrad Brombach, Christian Brothers University; Rhonda Bryant, Albany State University; Katrina Cook, Texas A&M University; Mary Ann Coupland, Sinte Gleska University; Jamie Edwards, Forsyth Technical Community College; Melissa Freeburg, Bridgewater State College; Malik Henfield, University of Iowa; Evelyn Lyles, University of Maryland; Christopher Maglio, Truman State University; Sangeeta Singg, Angelo State University; Jennifer Ann Walker, Northern Arizona University; and Judith Warchal, Alvernia University. I would also like to thank Daniel Baggarly for his hard work and diligence on the subject index.

Finally, a good-bye to my oldest daughter, Hannah, who is about to go off to college, and who, in her own way, is already a counselor.

FINAL THOUGHTS

This book is streamlined and covers the most essential elements needed to help you build your professional identity and to assist you on your journey to becoming a professional counselor. It is filled with critical information that is known by only a chosen few—those who become counselors! The knowledge in this book makes us special and gives us a sense of purpose. Throughout the book you will find short exercises and some vignettes to highlight points. These are meant to be interesting, fun, and placed in the text to expand your knowledge base. My hope is that by the time you finish this book, you will be a changed person in the sense that you will have crossed over into the world of the counselor and have a new and important professional identity and affiliation.

PROFESSIONAL IDENTITY OF THE COUNSELOR

The first section of the text describes the professional identity of the counselor. Although professional identity can be described in multiple ways, in these chapters we zero in on the kinds of degrees obtained and specialty areas focused upon by counselors, define the word counseling, highlight the purposes of professional associations, identify the professional associations of counselors, list credentials of counselors, and note the kinds of accreditation processes in the counseling field. In addition, to contrast the counselor with other professionals in the mental health field, we briefly identify related mental health professions and list their types of credentials and accreditation processes. Finally, to gain a perspective on the qualities that most counselors view as critical to a successful counseling relationship, we delineate nine personal and professional characteristics that lead toward counselor effectiveness.

What Is Counseling and Who Is the Counselor?

CHAPTER I

... counseling has proven to be a difficult concept to explain. The public's lack of clarity is due, in part, to the proliferation of modern-day services that have adopted the counselor label. They range from credit counselors to investment counselors, and from camp counselors to retirement counselors. Although their services share the common ingredient of verbal communication and possibly the intention to be helpful, those services have little in common with ... [psychological counseling]. (Hackney & Cormier, 2013, p. 2)

How come when I tell people I am a counselor, they often seem to look at me sideways—as if they are asking me to repeat what I said? Maybe it's because they are ill-informed about counselors, or maybe it's because there are so many different types of counselors (e.g., school, mental health, rehabilitation, college, and so forth). Perhaps it's because some people view the word *counselor* generically—a word that encompasses a number of mental health professionals such as psychologists, social workers, or human service professionals. Whatever the reason, I know that as a counselor my identity is unique and different from those of other related professionals. This chapter will help us define counseling, describe who the counselor is, and distinguish counselors from related mental health professionals.

DEFINING COUNSELING

When I hear the word *counseling*, I think of the following: "facilitative, here-and-now, short-term, change, problem-solving, being heard, and awareness." Distinguish this from the word *psychotherapy*, which I associate with "deep, dark, secretive, sexual, unconscious, pain, hidden, long-term, and reconstructive." And lastly, the word *guidance* makes me think of "advice-giving, direction, on-the-surface, advocacy, and support." However, not all people make similar distinctions. In fact, over the years some have suggested counseling could be anything from a problem-solving, directive, and rational approach to helping normal people—an approach that is distinguishable from psychotherapy (Williamson, 1950, 1958); to a process that is similar to but less intensive than psychotherapy (Nugent & Jones, 2009); to an approach that suggests there is no essential difference between the two (Corey, 2013; Neukrug, 2011; Patterson, 1986).

Some confusion in distinguishing counseling from guidance and psychotherapy rests in the related history of the three words. The word guidance first appeared around the 1600s and was defined as "the process of guiding an individual." Early guidance work involved individuals acting as moral compasses and giving advice. This definition continued into the twentieth century when vocational guidance counselors used the word to describe the act of "guiding" an individual into a profession and offering suggestions for life skills. Meanwhile, with the development of psychoanalysis near the end of the nineteenth century came the word *psychotherapy*. Derived from the Greek words *psyche*, which means spirit or soul, and *therapeutikos*, which means caring for another, psychotherapy literally translates to "caring for the soul" (Kleinke, 1994).

During the early part of the twentieth century, vocational guidance counselors became increasingly dissatisfied with the word guidance and its heavy emphasis on advice-giving and morality. Consequently, the word counseling was adopted to indicate that vocational counselors, like the psychoanalysts who practiced psychotherapy, dealt with social and emotional issues. As mental health workers became more prevalent during the mid-1900s, they too adopted the word counseling, rather than use the word guidance with its moralistic implications, or psychotherapy, which was increasingly associated with psychoanalysis. Tyler (1969) stated that "those who participated in the mental health movement and had no connection with vocational guidance used the word counseling to refer to what others were calling [psycho]therapy ..." (p. 12).

Today, most lay people, many counseling students, and a fair number of counselor educators view some counselors and related mental health professionals as practicing what traditionally have been called guidance activities, others as conducting counseling, and still others as doing psychotherapy (see Figure 1.1). And perhaps they are right. For example, many school counselors probably use techniques that place them on the left of the continuum in Figure 1.1, while a fair number of clinical mental health counselors likely use skills that place them on the right side of the figure. Where do you think rehabilitation counselors, college counselors, pastoral counselors, and addiction counselors might fall? And what about social workers and counseling and clinical psychologists: where do you think they fall?

Despite the fact that different kinds of counselors sometimes practice in different ways, their training is remarkably similar. In fact, it has always been argued that a person with a master's degree in counseling is primarily a counselor and secondarily a school counselor, clinical mental health counselor, college counselor, or other type of counseling specialist. Thus, in an effort to unify the many counseling specialty areas, in 2010 a committee that included 30 counseling organizations came up with a definition that embraces a wide range of views regarding how one might define the word counseling:

> Counseling is a professional relationship that empowers diverse individuals, families, and groups to accomplish mental health, wellness, education, and career goals. (American Counseling Association. (2010). 20/20: A Vision For the Future of Counseling: Consensus Definition of Counseling. Reprinted by permission.)

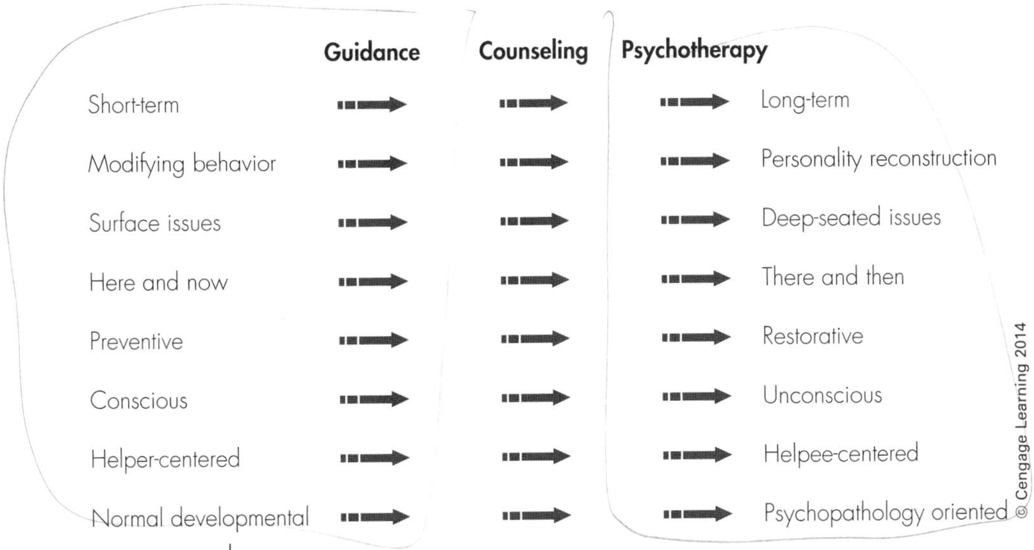

	Guidance	Counseling	Psychotherapy	
Short-term	▪▪➡	▪▪➡	▪▪➡	Long-term
Modifying behavior	▪▪➡	▪▪➡	▪▪➡	Personality reconstruction
Surface issues	▪▪➡	▪▪➡	▪▪➡	Deep-seated issues
Here and now	▪▪➡	▪▪➡	▪▪➡	There and then
Preventive	▪▪➡	▪▪➡	▪▪➡	Restorative
Conscious	▪▪➡	▪▪➡	▪▪➡	Unconscious
Helper-centered	▪▪➡	▪▪➡	▪▪➡	Helpee-centered
Normal developmental	▪▪➡	▪▪➡	▪▪➡	Psychopathology oriented

© Cengage Learning 2014

FIGURE 1.1 | GUIDANCE, COUNSELING, AND PSYCHOTHERAPY CONTINUUM

This definition places us under one umbrella—where we all are counselors, practicing counseling, and empowering our clients to accomplish their "mental health, wellness, education, and career goals." Now that we have defined the word counseling, this chapter will start us on our journey of examining the counseling profession, distinguishing specialty areas from one another, and differentiating the counseling profession from related mental health professions (see Box 1.1).

COUNSELORS AND RELATED MENTAL HEALTH PROFESSIONALS

Although we tend to find a fair amount of overlap in the ways that various mental health professionals are taught, there also exist huge differences (Feldman, 2010; Johnson, 2009; Todd & Bohart, 2006). This section of the chapter will first describe the kinds of degrees, credentials, and professional associations associated with counselors, including school counselors; clinical mental health counselors; marriage, couple, and family counselors; addiction counselors; student affairs and college counselors; rehabilitation counselors; and pastoral counselors. Then we will offer brief descriptions of related mental health professionals including social workers, psychologists (clinical, counseling, and school), psychiatrists, psychoanalysts, psychiatric-mental health nurses, expressive therapists, human service

BOX 1.1	DEFINING COUNSELING

Are you satisfied with the definition above? Come up with your own definition of *counseling* and share it in class. Then have the class come up with its own definition. Consider doing the same for the words *guidance* and *psychotherapy*.

practitioners, and psychotherapists. Table 1.1, which compares counselors and related mental health professions, will conclude the chapter. Chapter 2 will go on to further describe the professional identities of counselors and related professionals by describing their professional associations. In Chapter 2, we will pay particular attention to the American Counseling Association (ACA) and its divisions. Prior to moving on in the chapter, you might want to complete Box 1.2.

COUNSELORS

In the past, the word counselor referred to any mental health professional who practiced counseling (Chaplin, 1975). However, counselors are now generally seen as those who hold a master's degree in counseling. Today, we find a wide variety of counselors, such as school counselors, college counselors, mental health counselors, counselors in private practice, pastoral counselors, rehabilitation counselors, counselors in business and industry, and more. The counselor's training is broad and includes expertise in individual, group, and family counseling; administering and interpreting educational and psychological assessments; offering career counseling; administering grants and conducting research; consulting on a broad range of educational and psychological matters; supervising others; and presenting developmentally appropriate guidance activities for individuals of all ages. Although not all counselors have in-depth expertise in psychopathology, they all have knowledge of mental disorders and know when to refer individuals who might need more in-depth treatment.

Today, counselors tend to have had coursework in common areas defined by the professional accreditation body the Council for Accreditation of Counseling and Related Educational Programs (CACREP, 2009). Although not all programs are CACREP accredited, most follow their guidelines. These include knowledge in the following eight content areas (for more details, see Chapter 7):

1. professional orientation and ethical practice
2. social and cultural diversity

| BOX 1.2 | COMPARING MENTAL HEALTH PROFESSIONALS |

Prior to reading this section, compare school counselors; clinical mental health counselors; college counselors; addiction counselors; rehabilitation counselors; and marriage, couple, and family counselors in the areas listed below. When you have finished do the same with related mental health professions (e.g., psychologists, social workers, psychotherapists, psychiatrists, and so forth). Based on your responses, discuss your current level of knowledge of these professions.

	Education	Accreditation	Credentials	Professional Associations	Amount Earned
Type of Counselor					

3. human growth and development
4. career development
5. the helping relationship
6. group work
7. assessment
8. research and program evaluation

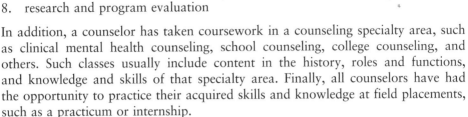

In addition, a counselor has taken coursework in a counseling specialty area, such as clinical mental health counseling, school counseling, college counseling, and others. Such classes usually include content in the history, roles and functions, and knowledge and skills of that specialty area. Finally, all counselors have had the opportunity to practice their acquired skills and knowledge at field placements, such as a practicum or internship.

Master's level counseling programs accredited by CACREP include programs in school counseling; *clinical mental health counseling*; *marriage, couple, and family counseling*; *addiction counseling*; *career counseling*; and *student affairs and college counseling*. *Rehabilitation counseling* is accredited by a separate accreditation body, the Council on Rehabilitation Education (CORE, 2011). CORE follows similar curriculum guidelines as those offered by CACREP and those guidelines include an emphasis on courses related to working with individuals with disabilities. Not all programs use the exact names that CACREP suggests and some programs offer specialty areas outside of those delineated by CACREP.

A master's level counselor can become a National Certified Counselor (NCC) by passing the National Counselor Exam (NCE); also students from CACREP-accredited programs are certified upon passing the exam and graduating from their program, while others have to obtain post-master's clinical experience (National Board for Certified Counselors [NBCC], 2011a). NBCC also offers subspecialty certifications as Certified Clinical Mental Health Counselor (CCMHC), National Certified School Counselor (NCSC), and Master Addictions Counselor (MAC). In addition, today all 50 states, Puerto Rico, and the District of Columbia have established licensing laws that allow a counselor who has a master's degree, additional training, and supervision to practice as a Licensed Professional Counselor (LPC) (some states use a different term) (ACA, 2011a). Whereas certification is generally seen as mastery of a content area, licensure allows counselors to practice independently and obtain *third-party reimbursement* for their practice. (An in-depth discussion of credentialing can be found in Chapter 8.) The professional association for counselors, called the American Counseling Association (ACA), currently has 19 divisions that focus on a variety of counseling concerns (see Chapter 2).

SCHOOL COUNSELORS *School counselors* have received their master's degrees in counseling with a specialty in school counseling. Some states credential school counselors on the elementary, middle, and secondary levels, while other states offer credentialing that covers kindergarten through twelfth grade (K–12). Today, the majority of school counseling programs are CACREP accredited, which requires a minimum of 48-credit hours for the degree. The professional association for school counselors is the American School Counselor Association (ASCA), which is a division of ACA, although one can become a member of ASCA without joining ACA.

In recent years, the *ASCA National Model* has been used as a model for the training of school counselors. In addition, over the past few decades, there has been a push by professional training programs, professional associations, and many in the field to replace the term *guidance counselor* with *school counselor*, as the latter term is seen as de-emphasizing the guidance activities of the school counselor (Baker & Gerler, 2008).

School counselors are certified or licensed by their state boards of education, usually directly after having graduated from a state-approved school counseling program. If they so choose, school counselors can also become National Certified Counselors (NCCs), National Certified School Counselors (NCSCs), and, in most states, Licensed Professional Counselors (LPCs). Other certifications are also available if the school counselor chooses to specialize (e.g., addiction counseling).

CLINICAL MENTAL HEALTH COUNSELORS (AGENCY COUNSELORS)   *Clinical mental health counselors* are individuals who have obtained their degrees in clinical mental health counseling, or a closely related degree in counseling (e.g., agency counseling). Although in the past CACREP had included standards for 48-credit agency (or community counseling) programs, CACREP's 2009 standards have eliminated those specialty areas. Programs accredited by the 2009 standards require a minimum of 54 credits until the year 2013, at which point all programs must have a minimum of 60 credits. Keep in mind, however, that some master's programs may still be accredited and operating under the older 48-credit standards. As these programs' accreditation periods expire, they will have to either expand their master's degrees to the new credit requirements or disband their programs. Although not all programs are CACREP accredited, those who obtain a degree in clinical mental health counseling, or related degrees, are generally trained to conduct counseling for those who are struggling with life problems, emotional issues, or mental health disorders. They are usually found working in a wide variety of agencies or in private practice conducting counseling and psychotherapy.

The clinical mental health counselors' professional association is the American Mental Health Counselors Association (AMHCA), which is a division of ACA, although one can now be a member of AMHCA without joining ACA. If they so choose, clinical mental health counselors can become NCCs and LPCs. Other certifications are also available if the clinical mental health counselors chooses to specialize (e.g., Certified Clinical Mental Health Counselor (CCMHC), Master Addictions Counselor (MAC), and more).

MARRIAGE, COUPLE, AND FAMILY COUNSELORS   *Marriage, couple, and family counselors* are specifically trained to work with couples and with families and can be found in a vast array of agency settings and in private practice. These counselors tend to have specialty coursework in systems dynamics, couples counseling, family therapy, family life stages, and human sexuality, along with the more traditional coursework in the helping professions. The International Association of Marriage and Family Counselors (IAMFC, n.d.a), a division of ACA, is one professional association these counselors can join; another is the American Association of Marriage and Family Therapy (AAMFT). These days, one can join IAMFC without joining ACA.

Although all 50 states have some requirement for marriage and family licensure, the requirements can vary dramatically (Occupational Outlook Handbook [OOH], 2010–2011). Generally, these individuals have the title Licensed Marriage and Family Therapist (LMFT). While some states license marriage and family counselors who have studied from programs that follow the 60-credit CACREP guidelines, other states prefer licensing counselors who have studied from programs that follow the guidelines set forth by AAMFT's Commission on Accreditation for Marriage and Family Therapy Education (COAMFTE), and still others have set their own curriculum guidelines for credentialing. Most states that offer marriage and family counselor credentialing allow licensed helping professionals with related degrees (e.g., counseling, social work, psychology) to also practice marriage and family counseling as long as they have expertise in this area. Often, couple, marriage, and family counselors can become NCCs, LPCs, and obtain other specialty certifications, if they so choose.

ADDICTION COUNSELORS *Addiction counselors* study a wide range of addiction disorders, such as substance abuse (drugs and alcohol), eating disorders, and sexual addiction. They are familiar with diagnosis and treatment planning and understand the importance of psychopharmacology in working with these populations. Today, CACREP offers a 60-credit accreditation in addiction counseling. Many addiction counselors can become certified through their state. In addition, NBCC offers a certification as a Master Addictions Counselor (MAC). Often addiction counselors can become NCCs, LPCs, and obtain other specialty certifications, if they so choose. In addition to AMHCA, addiction counselors often belong to the International Association of Addictions and Offender Counselors (IAAOC), which is also a division of ACA.

STUDENT AFFAIRS AND COLLEGE COUNSELORS *Student affairs and college counselors* work in a variety of settings in higher education, including college counseling centers, offices of educational accessibility, career centers, residence life, advising, multicultural student services, and other campus settings where counseling-related activities occur. Usually, these counselors will have taken specialty coursework in college student development and student affairs practices and may have attended a 48-credit CACREP-accredited program. Often counselors who work in college settings can become NCCs, LPCs, and obtain other specialty certifications (e.g., MAC), if they so choose. There are two main professional associations of counselors in higher education settings: College Student Educators International (this organization was formerly the American College Personnel Association and has kept the acronym ACPA), which tends to focus on administration of student services; and the American College Counseling Association (ACCA), which is a division of ACA and tends to focus on counseling issues in college settings. Today, one can join ACCA without joining ACA.

REHABILITATION COUNSELORS *Rehabilitation counselors* offer a wide range of services to people with physical, emotional, and/or developmental disabilities. "Rehab" counselors work in state vocational rehabilitation agencies, unemployment offices, or private rehabilitation agencies. The Council on Rehabilitation Education (CORE) is the accrediting body for rehabilitation counseling programs. Much of the curricula in rehabilitation counseling programs parallels that which you would find in CACREP-approved programs, although such programs also include coursework on vocational evaluation, occupational analysis, medical and psychosocial aspects of disability, legal and ethical issues in rehabilitation, and the history of rehabilitation counseling. Despite the fact that CORE and CACREP attempted to merge in the mid-2000s, these efforts failed and the possibility of a merger has, for now, been placed on hold (Keferl, 2011; The CACREP Connection, 2007). The Commission on Rehabilitation Counselor Certification (CRCC) credentials rehabilitation counselors as Certified Rehabilitation Counselors (CRCs), and rehabilitation counselors can usually obtain other related credentials, if they so choose (NCC, LPC, MAC). Many rehabilitation counselors join the National Rehabilitation Counseling Association (NRCA) and/or the American Rehabilitation Counseling Association (ARCA), a division of ACA. Today, one can join ARCA without joining ACA.

PASTORAL COUNSELORS *Pastoral counselors* sometimes have a degree in counseling but can also have a degree in a related social service field or even just a master's degree in religion or divinity. Pastoral counselors sometimes work in private practice or within a religious association. Pastoral counselors, religious counselors, or counselors with spiritual orientations might join the Association for Spiritual, Ethical, and Religious Values in Counseling (ASERVIC), a division of ACA, and/or the American Association of Pastoral Counselors (AAPC, 2005–2012a). AAPC offers a certification process for those who are interested in becoming Certified Pastoral Counselors (CPCs). Although there is no CACREP accreditation in pastoral counseling, counselors who obtain a master's degree from a CACREP-accredited program can go on to obtain certification as pastoral counselors and can become LPCs or NCCs.

RELATED NON-COUNSELING PROFESSIONALS

SOCIAL WORKERS Although the term *social worker* can apply to those who have an undergraduate or a graduate degree in social work or a related field (e.g., human services), more recently the term has become associated with those who have acquired a *master's degree in social work* (MSW). Traditionally found working with the underprivileged and with family and social systems, today's social workers provide counseling and psychotherapy for all types of clients in a wide variety of settings, including child welfare services, government-supported social service agencies, family service agencies, private practices, and hospitals. Social workers usually have extensive training in counseling techniques but less preparation in career counseling, assessment techniques, and quantitative research methods.

Even though theoretical distinctions exist between the MSW and the master's degree in counseling, the two degrees have many similarities (Keferl, 2011). With additional training and supervision, social workers can become nationally certified by the Academy of Certified Social Workers (ACSW). In addition, all states have specific requirements for becoming a Licensed Clinical Social Worker (LCSW). Two other, more advanced credentials include the Qualified Clinical Social Worker

(QCSW) and the Diplomate in Clinical Social Work (DCSW). Social work programs are accredited by the Council on Social Work Education (CSWE), and the professional association for social workers is the National Association of Social Workers (NASW).

PSYCHOLOGISTS Many different types of *psychologists* practice in a wide range of settings, including agencies, private practice, health maintenance organizations, universities, business and industry, prisons, and schools. Psychologists are often found running agencies, consulting with business and industry, or serving in supervisory roles for all types of mental health professionals. Some of the many different kinds of psychologists include clinical, cognitive, community, counseling, developmental, educational, engineering, environmental, evolutionary, experimental, forensic, health, industrial/organizational, neuro, quantitative, rehabilitation, school, social, and sports (American Psychological Association [APA], 2011). Today, each state determines the types of psychology licenses it authorizes as well as the requirements for obtaining those licenses.

Relative to the practice of psychotherapy, there are three degrees that can be pursued to become a *licensed counseling or clinical psychologist*—Ph.D. in Counseling Psychology, Ph.D. in Clinical Psychology, and the Doctor of Psychology, or "*Psy.D.*" In addition to obtaining the doctorate, to become a licensed counseling or clinical psychologist requires extensive post-doctoral supervised experience and the passing of a national licensing exam, although passing scores vary by state. Today, many states offer hospital privileges for *licensed psychologists*, which afford psychologists the right to treat those who have been hospitalized with serious mental illness. Not surprisingly, psychologists have recently sought, with very limited success, the right to prescribe medication for emotional disorders (Johnson, 2009). In contrast to counseling and clinical psychologists, *school psychologists* are credentialed by state boards of education and can also become certified as Nationally Certified School Psychologists (NCSP). The APA Commission on Accreditation (APA-CoA) accredits psychology programs, and APA is the professional association for psychologists.

Counselors are likely to have more contact with clinical and counseling psychologists and with school psychologists than with other types of psychologists. These specialty areas are described below.

Clinical Psychologists, Counseling Psychologists, and Doctorates in Psychology (Psy.D.) *Clinical and counseling psychologists* tend to have a particularly strong background in research and practice and work with a wide range of clients. Historically, clinical psychologists have focused somewhat more on psychopathology and individuals with chronic mental health problems, although these differences have lessened over the years (APA, 2011). The *Psy.D.*, a degree established in 1973, tends to have a stronger clinical focus, although less of a research focus, than either of Ph.Ds. To obtain a license as a psychologist, one must graduate from an APA-accredited doctoral program in one of these three areas and complete additional requirements identified by state licensing boards. Graduates with these degrees will often join Division 12 of the APA—the Society of Clinical Psychology, or Division 17 of the APA—the Society of Counseling Psychology.

School Psychologists   *School psychologists* have a master's degree or more in school psychology and are licensed by state boards of education. Their work involves children, families, and the schooling process, and their training tends to focus on consultation, evaluation and assessment, intervention, prevention, and research and planning (National Association of School Psychologists [NASP], n.d.a). Many school psychologists today are found working with students with learning problems, their parents, and their teachers. Although most school psychologists work in schools, you can sometimes also find them in private practice, in agencies, and in hospital settings. The professional associations for school psychologists are the National Association of School Psychologists (NASP) and Division 16 of the APA.

PSYCHIATRISTS   Generally, a *psychiatrist* is a licensed physician who has completed a residency in psychiatry, meaning that in addition to medical school, he or she has completed extensive field placement training in a mental health setting. In addition, most psychiatrists have passed an exam to become board certified in psychiatry. Being a physician, the psychiatrist has expertise in diagnosing organic disorders, identifying and treating psychopathology, and prescribing medication for psychiatric conditions. Although some states have granted psychologists prescription privileges for psychotropic medication (Johnson, 2009), currently it is psychiatrists, and in some cases psychiatric nurses, who take the lead in this important treatment approach.

Because psychiatrists often have minimal training in techniques of individual and group counseling, assessment techniques, human development, and career counseling, they are sometimes not seen as experts in the delivery of counseling and psychotherapeutic services. Psychiatrists are employed in mental health agencies, hospitals, private practice settings, and health maintenance organizations. The professional association for psychiatrists is the American Psychiatric Association (APA).

PSYCHOANALYSTS   *Psychoanalysts* are professionals who have received training in psychoanalysis from a number of recognized psychoanalytical institutes. Although, in past years, the American Psychoanalytic Association (APsaA), the professional association of psychoanalysts, would only endorse psychiatrists for training at psychoanalytical institutes (Turkington, 1985), they now allow other mental health professionals to undergo such training (APsaA, 2008). Because states do not tend to license psychoanalysts, clients who are seeing a psychoanalyst should make sure that the analyst was trained at an institute sanctioned by the American Psychoanalytic Association and that he or she has a license in a mental health field (e.g., psychiatrist, psychologist, licensed professional counselor, or licensed clinical social worker). The American Board for Accreditation in Psychoanalysis (ABAP) accredits psychoanalytic institutes.

PSYCHIATRIC-MENTAL HEALTH NURSES   Primarily trained as medical professionals, *psychiatric-mental health nurses* are also skilled in the delivery of mental health services (American Psychiatric Nurses Association [APNA], n.d.). Most psychiatric-mental health nurses work in hospital settings, with fewer numbers working in community agencies, private practice, and educational settings. Psychiatric-mental health nursing is practiced at two levels. The *RN psychiatric-mental health nurse* does basic mental health work related to nursing diagnosis and nursing care. The *Advanced practice registered nurse (APRN)* has a master's degree in psychiatric-mental health nursing and assesses, diagnoses, and treats individuals with mental health problems. Currently holding prescriptive privileges in all 50 states (Phillips, 2007), APRNs provide an important service in many mental health settings. Because of their training in both medicine and basic counseling skills, they hold a unique position in the mental health profession. Psychiatric-mental health nurses can acquire certification in a number of mental health areas based on their education and experience (see American Nurses Credentialing Center, 2012). The professional association of psychiatric-mental health nurses is the American Psychiatric Nurses Association (APNA). The American Association of Colleges of Nursing (AACN) and the National League for Nursing accredit psychiatric-mental health nursing programs.

EXPRESSIVE THERAPISTS *Expressive therapists* include art therapists, play therapists, dance/movement therapists, poetry therapists, music therapists, and others who use creative tools to work with individuals who experience trauma or emotional problems in their lives (Malchiodi, 2005). Through the use of expressive therapies, it is hoped that individuals can gain a deeper understanding of themselves and work through some of their symptoms. Expressive therapists work with individuals of all ages and provide individual, group, and family counseling. They can be found in many settings and are often hired specifically for their ability to reach individuals through a medium other than language. Many expressive therapists obtain degrees in counseling or social work and later pick up additional coursework. However, some programs do offer master's degrees in expressive therapy, such as those approved by the American Art Therapy Association (AATA).

In addition to AATA, other expressive therapy associations include the Association for Creativity in Counseling (ACC), a division of ACA; the American Dance Therapy Association (ADTA); the American Music Therapy Association (AMTA); and the Association for Play Therapy (APT). Although certification exists for some kinds of expressive therapies (e.g., see Art Therapy Credentials Board, 2007), states generally do not license expressive therapists. However, these individuals can become licensed if their degrees are in fields credentialed by the states in which they want to practice (e.g., counseling, social work) and sometimes can become licensed if they take additional courses so their degree coursework matches the curriculum requirements of the existing state licenses (Wadeson, 2004). Although no broad-based accreditation of expressive therapy programs exists, some expressive therapy programs do have an accreditation or approval process (e.g., the American Art Therapy Association approves art therapy programs).

HUMAN SERVICE PRACTITIONERS *Human service practitioners* have generally obtained an associate's or bachelor's degree in human services. These programs are accredited by the Council for Standards in Human Service Education (CSHSE), which sets specific curriculum guidelines for the development of human service programs. Individuals who hold these degrees are often found in entry-level support and counseling jobs and serve an important role in assisting counselors and other mental health professionals. Recently, CSHSE, in consultation with the National Organization for Human Services (NOHS) and the Center for Credentialing and Education (CCE), created a certification in human services called the Human Services Board Certified Practitioner (HS-BCP) (Hinkle & O'Brien, 2010).

PSYCHOTHERAPISTS Because the word *psychotherapist* is not associated with any particular field of mental health practice, most states do not offer legislation that would create a license for "psychotherapists." One result of this lack of legislation is that in most states, individuals who have no mental health training can call themselves psychotherapists. However, legislatures generally limit the scope of psychotherapeutic practice to those individuals who are licensed mental health professionals within the state (e.g., psychologists, LPCs, LCSWs). The bottom line is that in most states anyone can claim to be a psychotherapist, but only licensed practitioners can practice psychotherapy.

OVERVIEW OF COUNSELORS AND RELATED MENTAL HEALTH PROFESSIONALS

There are many different kinds of counselors and a variety of mental health professionals. Although we sometimes find ourselves pitted against each other as we vie for similar jobs or try to obtain our share of third-party reimbursements, we all serve a similar purpose—to help individuals with their mental health concerns. And, although our training is different in many ways, we probably share more similarities than differences. Table 1.1 provides an overview of the chapter and lists some of the different degrees, accrediting bodies, and credentials that one can obtain in the varying mental health professions.

SUMMARY

This chapter began by explaining the historical differences in the words guidance, counseling, and psychotherapy and by suggesting their current common usage. We then noted that delegates from a number of counseling organizations came together in an effort to unify the counseling profession and to capture the words guidance, counseling, and psychotherapy under one definition of counseling.

The chapter then went on to describe a number of mental health professionals. Starting with counselors, we explained the kinds of training counselors receive in CACREP-accredited programs and noted that CACREP accredits programs in clinical mental health counseling; marriage, couple, and family counseling; addiction counseling; career counseling; and student affairs and college counseling. We then went on to offer descriptions of a number of different kinds of counselors, including school counselors; clinical mental health counselors; marriage, couple, and family counselors; addiction counselors; student affairs and college counselors; rehabilitation counselors; and pastoral counselors.

The rest of the chapter gave brief descriptions of related mental health professionals including social workers, psychologists (clinical, counseling, Psy.D., and school), psychiatrists, psychoanalysts, psychiatric-mental health nurses, expressive therapists, human service practitioners, and psychotherapists. The chapter concluded with a table that elucidated the different types of professionals, along with their degrees, accreditation bodies, and possible credentials to obtain.

TABLE 1.1 | COMPARING THE VARYING MENTAL HEALTH PROFESSIONALS*

Professional	Degree	Accrediting Body	Most Common Credential**
Counselor			
school counselor	master's in counseling	CACREP	State board of education credential\NCC\National Certified School Counselor
clinical mental health counselor	master's in counseling	CACREP	LPC\NCC\Certified Clinical Mental Health Counselor (CCMHC)
marriage, couple, & family counselor	master's in counseling or couples and family therapy	CACREP COAMFTE	LMFT\LPC\NCC
addiction counselor	master's in counseling	CACREP	MAC\LPC\NCC
student affairs and college counselor	master's in counseling	CACREP	LPC\NCC
rehabilitation counselor	master's in counseling	CORE	CRC\LPC\NCC
pastoral counselor	master's in counseling, related field, or religion/spirituality	None	LPC\NCC (if degree is in counseling)
Social Worker	master's in social work	Council on Social Work Education	ACSW\LSCW\QCSW\DCSW
Psychologist			
clinical	doctorate in psychology	Commission on Accreditation of the American Psychological Association	Licensed psychologist
counseling	doctorate in psychology	Commission on Accreditation of the American Psychological Association	Licensed psychologist

(continued)

TABLE 1.1 | COMPARING THE VARYING MENTAL HEALTH PROFESSIONALS*

Professional	Degree	Accrediting Body	Most Common Credential**
school	master's or more in psychology	Commission on Accreditation of the American Psychological Association	State board of education credential\National Certified School Psychologist (NCSP)
Psychiatrist	medical degree	Association of American Medical Colleges	Licensed physician\Board certification in psychiatry
Psychoanalyst	graduate degree in helping profession	American Board for Accreditation in Psychoanalysis (ABAP)	Credential in specific mental health profession (e.g., LPC\ LMFT\Licensed psychologist)
Psychiatric-Mental Health Nurse	bachelor's or master's degree in psychiatric-mental health nursing	American Association of Colleges of Nursing (AACN) and the National League for Nursing	Advanced Practice Registered Nurse (APRN)
Expressive Therapist	usually, master's degree in helping profession	no broad-based accreditation; some accreditation in specific expressive therapy areas	None specific, although can become credentialed in many states (e.g., LPC)
Human Service Practitioner	associate's or bachelor's in human services	Council on Human Service Education (CHSE)	Human Services Board Certified Practitioner (HS-BCP)
Psychotherapist	no degree needed	None	

*For additional information on accreditation, see Chapter 7. For additional information on credentialing, see Chapter 8.

**Many professionals can obtain additional credentials. For instance, with experience, most counselors can become Certified Clinical Mental Health Counselors (CMHCs), Master Addictions Counselors (MACs), Licensed Professional Counselors (LPCs) and obtain state-specific certifications. For additional information on credentialing, see Chapter 8.

© Cengage Learning 2014

KEY TERMS

Academy of Certified Social Workers (ACSW)

Addiction counseling

Addiction counselors

Advanced practice registered nurse (APRN)

American Art Therapy Association (AATA)

American Association of Colleges of Nursing (AACN)

American Association of Marriage and Family Therapy (AAMFT)

American Association of Pastoral Counselors (AAPC)

American Board for Accreditation in Psychoanalysis (ABAP)

American College Counseling Association (ACCA)

American Counseling Association (ACA)

American Dance Therapy Association (ADTA)

American Mental Health Counselors Association (AMHCA)

American Music Therapy Association (AMTA)

American Psychiatric Association (APA)

American Psychiatric Nurses Association (APNA)

American Psychoanalytic Association (APsaA)

American Rehabilitation Counseling Association (ARCA)

American School Counselor Association (ASCA)

APA Commission on Accreditation (APA-CoA)

ASCA National Model

Association for Creativity in Counseling (ACC)

Association for Play Therapy (APT)

Association for Spiritual, Ethical, and Religious Values in Counseling (ASERVIC)

Career counseling

Center for Credentialing and Education (CCE)

Certified Clinical Mental Health Counselor (CCMHC)

Certified Rehabilitation Counselors (CRCs)

Clinical mental health counseling

Clinical mental health counselors

Clinical psychologists

College counselors

College Student Educators International

Commission on Rehabilitation Counselor Certification (CRCC)

Commission on Accreditation for Marriage and Family Therapy Education (COAMFTE)

Council for Standards in Human Service Education (CSHSE)

Council for Accreditation of Counseling and Related Educational Programs (CACREP)

Council on Rehabilitation Education (CORE)

Council on Social Work Education (CSWE)

Counseling

Counseling psychologists

Diplomate in Clinical Social Work (DCSW)

Division 12 of APA (Society of Clinical Psychology)

Division 16 of the APA (School Psychology)

Division 17 of the APA (Society of Counseling Psychology)

Expressive therapists

Guidance

Human service practitioners

Human Services Board Certified Practitioner (HS-BCP)

International Association of Addictions and Offender Counselors (IAAOC)

International Association of Marriage and Family Counselors (IAMFC)

Licensed clinical psychologist

Licensed Clinical Social Worker (LCSW)

Licensed counseling psychologist

Licensed Marriage and Family Therapist (LMFT)

Licensed Professional Counselor (LPC)

Licensed psychologist

Marriage, couple, and family counseling

Marriage, couple, and family counselors

Master Addictions Counselor (MAC)

Master's degree in social work (MSW)

National Association of School Psychologists (NASP)

National Association of Social Workers (NASW)

National Certified Counselor (NCC)

National Certified School Counselor (NCSC)

Nationally Certified School Psychologists (NCSP)

National Counselor Exam (NCE)

National League for Nursing

National Organization for Human Services (NOHS)

National Rehabilitation Counseling Association (NRCA)

Pastoral counselors

Psy.D.

Psychiatric-mental health nurses

Psychiatrist

Psychoanalysts

Psychologists

Psychotherapist

Psychotherapy

Qualified Clinical Social Worker (QCSW)

Rehabilitation counseling

Rehabilitation counselors

RN psychiatric-mental health nurse

School counselors

School psychologists

Social worker

Student affairs and college counseling

Student affairs and college counselors

Third-party reimbursement

CHAPTER 2

PROFESSIONAL ASSOCIATIONS IN COUNSELING AND RELATED FIELDS

So, I've added it all up, and this year I've spent about $500 on professional memberships. I sometimes think that maybe I should give them up—save a little money. But reason always wins out. Despite the fact that students can obtain pretty low student membership rates, when I teach my classes, I often hear students complain about how much they cost. I try, usually successfully, to explain why it's important to belong. There are some fundamental reasons to join professional associations, despite their cost, and this chapter will highlight these and provide you with information about some of the different associations out there.

The chapter will begin by describing a number of purposes for professional associations. Then, we will describe, in some detail, the American Counseling Association (ACA), the benefits it offers, and its divisions, branches, regions, and professional partners. We will conclude the chapter with a brief overview of other professional associations in mental health fields.

IMPORTANCE OF PROFESSIONAL ASSOCIATIONS

> Therefore, by virtue of the authority vested in me by the Universitatus
> Committeeatum e plurbis unum, I hereby confer upon you the honorary degree
> of Th.D.... Yeah—that ... that's Dr. of Thinkology! (The Wizard of Oz)

Our professional associations are our homes. They are where we go to learn, grow, and find friendship, collegiality, and mentoring. They are a place where we help others grow and learn, and they are a place where awards are conferred. Like the

Wizard who bestows the diploma upon the Scarecrow who has shown his ability to think wisely, we have bestowed upon us awards by our professional associations when we have shown our colleagues our greatness. And each of us has greatness. We sometimes just need to find a place where it can shine. Our professional associations can allow us to shine brightly.

I find that new students entering the counseling profession generally have some vague sense of the purposes that professional associations serve. For instance, they often correctly assume that such organizations run a yearly conference, maybe publish a journal, and might be good for networking. Although these are three important reasons for the existence of professional associations, there are many more. For instance, professional organizations provide members with the following (Bauman, 2008; Dodgen, Fowler, & Williams-Nichelson, 2003; "The Benefits of ...," 2010; Pope, 2004, Visconti, n.d., "Your Investment," 2009):

- *A Sense of Belonging:* Counselors are a unique group of people who share many of the same values. Professional associations provide us with a mechanism for being around others who share a similar understanding of the world and provide us with a sense of collegiality, support, and friendship.
- *Workshops and Conferences:* One major role of organizations is to provide local, regional, and national conferences so that we can learn new techniques and continue to offer cutting edge counseling services.
- *Mentoring and Networking Opportunities:* Mentoring and networking allows us to develop new friendships, find better ways of working with our clients, develop our research and scholarship, find individuals who can mentor and/or supervise us, and find new consulting and job opportunities.
- *Job Fairs:* Some conferences, especially the larger ones (e.g., ACA's national conference), have job fairs that enable individuals to apply and even interview for jobs at a conference.
- *Lobbying Efforts:* One of the most important aspects of professional organizations is to lobby for and influence important policy issues that impact the counseling profession. For instance, the expansion of school counseling to the middle and elementary levels, the licensing of counselors in all fifty states, and the increased parity that private practitioners have in third-party billing are the result of lobbying efforts. Where do organizations obtain the money to help in these efforts that serve each of our interests? From us, of course, when we pay our dues!
- *Scholarly Publications:* Whether it's a local professional organization's newsletter, a state-wide journal, a national magazine, or a national journal, our professional organizations provide us with important publications that generally focus on how we can best serve our clients. Usually, these publications are reviewed, edited, and put together by teams of volunteer members who spend their time ensuring the publications are worthwhile and cutting edge.
- *Standards in the Profession:* Professional organizations are generally the focal points for the development of important professional standards. For instance, ACA developed the first ethical code for counselors during the early 1960s, embraced the Multicultural Counseling Competencies in the 1990s, and recently endorsed the Advocacy Competencies. ACA and other professional

associations were also key to the development of the Council for Accreditation of Counseling and Related Educational Programs (CACREP), which accredits counseling programs, as well as the National Board for Certified Counselors (NBCC), which offers a number of credentials for counselors.

- *Ways to Build Your Professional Portfolio:* Professional organizations allow individuals to build their professional portfolios and develop areas of expertise. This occurs when members offer workshops, submit articles to professional publications, develop programs through the organization for national consumption (e.g., crisis counseling), volunteer for important professional development committees (e.g., revision of the ethical code), and, of course, list the organizations on their resumes.

- *Scholarships and Grants:* Most professional organizations provide scholarships and grants: for example, some state organizations provide support for graduate students to come to their conferences, and some national organizations provide money for researchers to work on projects.

- *Awards:* If you work hard you are rewarded by obtaining an award. Who gives the award? The professional organizations, through a careful selection process. Awards are symbols that what we have done, we have done well.

- *Needed Services for Members:* Many associations provide a wide-range of needed services for their individual members, including: malpractice insurance, credit cards at reduced interest rates, legal services, consultation on ethical issues, and more.

- *A Place Where We Can Become Famous:* I went to teach one evening, and in my classroom was an environmental engineer instructor finishing up his class. I greeted him, and quickly added that my brother, Howard Neukrug, was an environmental engineer. He said, "Oh, he's famous!" Later that evening I called my brother and told him the news! My brother said, "Yea, we're all famous in our own little worlds." What a gem of wisdom—which leads me to the last purpose of professional associations: they allow us to become famous. Professional associations provide places where people get to know who we are and how we work, and where we can be encouraged for our abilities. And, if we're lucky, perhaps we'll even get nominated for an award and become acknowledged. So yes, they provide us an opportunity to become famous— well, at least famous in our own little world.

Now that you have reviewed a list of a few of the many benefits that most professional organizations offer, you might be wondering which organization you should belong to. Some of you may have already joined or are thinking of joining the American Counseling Association (ACA) and/or one of its divisions, such as the American School Counseling Association (ASCA) or the American Mental Health Counseling Association (AMHCA). To help you in your decision, the following offers a description of the American Counseling Association, its benefits, and its divisions, branches, regions, and professional partners. This is followed by short descriptions of other professional associations in the mental health field. As you read about the many organizations in our field, consider which ones would be important to you. Keep in mind that there are dozens of professional organizations in the social services, and this section only features some of the more well-known ones.

THE AMERICAN COUNSELING ASSOCIATION

The beginnings of the American Counseling Association (ACA) can be traced back to the founding, in 1913, of the National Vocational Guidance Association (NVGA). After undergoing many changes of name and structure over the years, today's ACA is the world's largest counseling association. This 50,000-member not-for-profit association serves the needs of all types of counselors in an effort to "enhance the quality of life in society by promoting the development of professional counselors, advancing the counseling profession, and using the profession and practice of counseling to promote respect for human dignity and diversity" (ACA, 2012a, ACA Mission Statement section, para.1).

MEMBERSHIP BENEFITS OF ACA

Membership in ACA provides a number of unique opportunities and benefits, including the following:

- Professional development programs, such as podcasts, conferences, and continuing education workshops
- Counseling resources, including books, ethical codes, video- and audiotapes, electronic news, journals, and weblogs
- Computer-assisted job search services
- Professional liability insurance
- Consultation on ethical issues and ethical dilemmas
- Assistance in lobbying efforts at the local, state, and national levels
- A counselor directory
- Networking and mentoring opportunities
- Graduate student scholarships
- Subscriptions to the *Journal of Counseling and Development*, its scholarly journal, as well as to *Counseling Today*, a monthly professional magazine; in addition, other professional newspapers, magazines, and journals are available based on which division you join
- A variety of discount and specialty programs (e.g., credit cards, rental cars, auto insurance, medical insurance, hotels)
- Links to ACA electronic mailing lists for graduate students (*COUNSGRADS*) and those interested in diversity issues (*Diverse grad-L*)
- Links to ACA divisions, branches, regions, professional partners, and other relevant professional associations
- Legislative updates and policy setting for counselors

Want more benefit information? Go to www.counseling.org to find it.

DIVISIONS OF ACA

ACA currently sponsors 19 divisions, all of which maintain newsletters and most of which provide a wide variety of professional development activities. Many of these divisions also publish journals. Table 2.1 offers the name of each association, the year it was chartered, a brief purpose of the association, and the journal the association publishes.

BOX 2.1	CREATING YOUR OWN DIVISION

Create your own division of ACA. Include the following:

1. Requirements to be a member (e.g., student member, degree in counseling, membership in ACA, other?)
2. Purpose statement
3. Benefits
4. Cost of membership

© Cengage Learning 2014

Each division provides a number of specialized member benefits. Want more information about a division? Go to www.counseling.org and click "divisions, regions, and branches."

Many of ACA's divisions can now be joined separately from ACA, as they have moved to semi-independent status from their parent association. However, we believe that the most benefit for you and the profession comes from joining the parent association *and* one or more divisions (see Box 2.1).

BRANCHES AND REGIONS OF ACA

In addition to its 19 divisions, ACA has 56 branches, which consist of state associations and associations in Latin America and Europe. Branches often house other associations that mimic the national divisions. For instance, most state branches have a state school counseling and a state clinical mental health counseling association. Additionally, four *regional associations* support counselors throughout the United States: the North Atlantic Region, Western Region, Midwest Region, and Southern Region. These regions generally support the branches with which they are affiliated and sometimes offer a yearly regional conference. Want more information about the branches and regions? Go to www.counseling.org and click "divisions, regions, and branches."

PROFESSIONAL PARTNERS TO ACA

ACA supports a number of affiliates and organizations that contribute to the betterment of the counseling profession in unique ways. Brief descriptions follow.

- *The ACA Insurance Trust* (ACAIT). This organization provides liability insurance as well as a wide range of other kinds of insurance for its members (see http://www.acait.com/).
- *The American Counseling Association Foundation* (ACAF). ACAF offers support and recognition for a wide range of projects including scholarships for graduate students, recognition of outstanding professionals, enhancement of the counseling profession, and support for those in need (see http://www.acafoundation.org/).
- *The Council for Accreditation of Counseling and Related Educational Programs* (CACREP). CACREP is an independent organization that develops standards and provides accreditation processes for counseling programs (see http://www.cacrep.org/).

TABLE 2.1 | ACA's DIVISIONS

Acronym/ Chartered	Name	Purpose*	Name of Journal
AACE/1965	Association for Assessment in Counseling and Education	"… to promote the effective use of assessment in the counseling profession."	*Measurement and Evaluation in Counseling and Development*
AADA/1986	Association for Adult Development and Aging	"… serves as a focal point for information sharing, professional development, and advocacy related to adult development and aging issues; addresses counseling concerns across the lifespan."	*Adultspan*
ACC/2004	The Association for Creativity in Counseling	"… to promote greater awareness, advocacy, and understanding of diverse and creative approaches to counseling."	*Journal of Creativity Mental Health*
ACCA/1991	American College Counseling Association	"… to foster student development in colleges, universities, and community colleges."	*Journal of College Counseling*
ACEG/1984	Association for Counselors and Educators in Government	"… dedicated to counseling clients and their families in local, state, and federal government or in military-related agencies."	None
ACES/1952	Association for Counselor Education and Supervision	"… emphasizes the need for quality education and supervision of counselors for all work settings."	*Counselor Education and Supervision*
ACH/1952	Association for Humanistic Counseling	"… provides a forum for the exchange of information about humanistically-oriented counseling practices and promotes	*Journal of Humanistic Counseling*

(continued)

TABLE 2.1 | ACA's DIVISIONS

Acronym/ Chartered	Name	Purpose*	Name of Journal
		changes that reflect the growing body of knowledge about humanistic principles applied to human development and potential."	
ALGBTIC/1997	Association for Lesbian, Gay, Bisexual and Transgender Issues in Counseling	"Educates counselors to the unique needs of client identity development; and a non-threatening counseling environment by aiding in the reduction of stereotypical thinking and homoprejudice."	*Journal of LGBT Issues in Counseling*
AMCD/1972	Association for Multicultural Counseling and Development	"... strives to improve cultural, ethnic and racial empathy and understanding by programs to advance and sustain personal growth."	*Journal of Multicultural Counseling and Development*
AMHCA/1978	American Mental Health Counselors Association	"... represents mental health counselors, advocating for client-access to quality services within the health care industry."	*Journal of Mental Health Counseling*
ARCA/1958	American Rehabilitation Counseling Association	"... enhancing the development of people with disabilities throughout their life span and in promoting excellence in the rehabilitation counseling profession's practice, research, consultation, and professional development."	*Rehabilitation Counseling Bulletin*

(continued)

TABLE 2.1 | ACA's DIVISIONS

Acronym/ Chartered	Name	Purpose*	Name of Journal
ASCA/1953	American School Counselor Association	"… promotes school counseling professionals and interest in activities that affect the personal, educational, and career development of students. ASCA members also work with parents, educators, and community members to provide a positive learning environment."	*Professional School Counseling*
ASERVIC/1974	Association for Spiritual, Ethical, and Religious Values in Counseling	"… devoted to professionals who believe that spiritual, ethical, religious, and other human values are essential to the full development of the person and to the discipline of counseling."	*Counseling and Values*
ASGW/1973	Association for Specialists in Group Work	"… provides professional leadership in the field of group work, establishes standards for professional training, and supports research and the dissemination of knowledge."	*Journal for Specialists in Group Work*
CSJ/2002	Counselors for Social Justice	"… seek equity and an end to oppression and injustice affecting clients, students, counselors, families, communities, schools, workplaces, governments, and other social and institutional systems."	*Journal for Social Action in Counseling and Psychology*

(*continued*)

TABLE 2.1 | ACA's DIVISIONS

Acronym/ Chartered	Name	Purpose*	Name of Journal
IAAOC/1974	International Association of Addictions and Offender Counselors	"... advocate the development of effective counseling and rehabilitation programs for people with substance abuse problems, other addictions, and adult and/or juvenile public offenders."	*The Journal of Addictions and Offender Counseling*
IAMFC/1989	International Association of Marriage and Family Counselors	"... help develop healthy family systems through prevention, education, and therapy."	*The Family Journal: Counseling & Therapy for Couples & Families*
NCDA/1952	National Career Development Association	"... inspires and empowers the achievement of career and life goals by providing professional development, resources, standards, scientific research, and advocacy."	*The Career Development Quarterly*
NECA/1964	National Employment Counseling Association	"... to offer professional leadership to people who counsel in employment and/or career development settings."	*The Journal of Employment Counseling*

*American Counseling Association (2012b). *ACA divisions*. Based on information retrieved from http://www.counseling. org/About Us/DivisionsBranchesAndRegions/TP/Divisions/CT2.aspx.

- *The Council on Rehabilitation Education* (CORE). CORE develops standards and provides accreditation processes for rehabilitation counseling programs (see http://www.core-rehab.org/).
- *The National Board for Certified Counselors* (NBCC). NBCC provides national certification for counselors (National Certified Counselor, NCC); mental health counselors (Certified Clinical Mental Health Counselor, CCMHC), school counselors (National Certified School Counselor; NCSC) and substance abuse counselors (Master Addictions Counselor; MAC).
- *Chi Sigma Iota* (CSI). CSI, an honor society, promotes and recognizes scholarly activities, leadership, professionalism, and excellence in the profession of counseling.

© Cengage Learning 2014

FIGURE 2.1 | ACA AND ITS PROFESSIONAL PARTNERS

Want more information about the professional partners? Go to www.counseling.org, click "Students," and then click on "Related Organizations" (see Figure 2.1).

PROFESSIONAL ASSOCIATIONS IN RELATED MENTAL HEALTH PROFESSIONS

The following represent some of the more popular professional associations in fields related to counseling. Although most counselors join ACA or its divisions, counselors can sometimes join a few of these associations. For instance, although some rehabilitation counselors will join the American Rehabilitation Counseling Association (ARCA), which is a division of ACA, others will join the National Rehabilitation Counseling Association (NRCA), which is a standalone association. Others will join both. Similarly, counselors who have an interest in art therapy might join the American Art Therapy Association (AATA), while counselors who have an interest in pastoral counseling might join the American Association of Pastoral Counselors (AAPC). On the other hand, it is extremely unlikely that counselors will join the National Association of Social Workers (NASW), as a degree in social work is required for membership to this organization and the organization clearly focuses on issues somewhat askew to counseling. However, knowledge of this association and others is also included in this section so that you are familiar with the backgrounds and associations of colleagues with whom we often share clients and next to whom we often work.

THE AMERICAN ART THERAPY ASSOCIATION (AATA)

The American Art Therapy Association (AATA) was founded in 1969 and is open to any individual interested in art therapy. AATA is "dedicated to the belief that making art is healing and life enhancing. Its mission is to serve its members and the general public by providing standards of professional competence, and developing and promoting knowledge in, and of, the field of art therapy" (AATA, 2011, The Association's Mission section). The association establishes criteria for the training of art therapists, supports licensing for art therapists, maintains job banks, sponsors conferences, and publishes a newsletter and one journal: *Art Therapy*.

THE AMERICAN ASSOCIATION OF MARRIAGE AND FAMILY THERAPY (AAMFT)

If you have a counseling degree, you may be interested in joining the International Association of Marriage and Family Counselors (IAMFC), which is a division of ACA. However, in recent years the American Association of Marriage and Family Therapy (AAMFT), with its 24,000 members, has become a major association in the field of marriage and family counseling. Founded in 1942 as the American Association of Marriage and Family Counselors, AAMFT was established by family therapy and communication theorists. Today, AAMFT provides a wide range of services for its members, including the promotion of research and theory development, the development of standards of graduate training, the provision of an ethical code, legal and career resources, the sponsoring of yearly conferences, professional activities for couples and family counselors, and much more (AAMFT, 2002-2011a). AAMFT publishes the *Journal of Marital and Family Therapy*.

THE AMERICAN ASSOCIATION OF PASTORAL COUNSELORS (AAPC)

The purpose of AAPC is "to bring healing, hope, and wholeness to individuals, families, and communities by expanding and equipping spiritually grounded and psychologically informed care, counseling, and psychotherapy" (AAPC, 2005-2012b, para. 1). The association provides an annual conference, a code of ethics, employment opportunities, information about publications in pastoral counseling, ways of finding pastoral counselors, a list of accredited centers in pastoral counseling, and much more. It also supports certification of pastoral counseling that includes a three-year degree from a seminary, a graduate degree in a mental health discipline, supervision, and an assessment process (AAPC, 2005-2012c). AAPC publishes *Reflective Practice: Supervision and Formation in Ministry* and a new e-journal: *Sacred Spaces*.

THE AMERICAN PSYCHIATRIC ASSOCIATION (APA)

Founded in 1844 as the Association of Medical Superintendents of American Institutions for the Insane, today the American Psychiatric Association (which has the same acronym as the American Psychological Association, "APA") has over 36,000 members. The association's main purpose is to "ensure humane care and effective treatment for all persons with mental disorder, including mental retardation and substance-related disorders" (American Psychiatric Association, 2012, para. 1). The association offers workshops on psychiatric disorders, evaluates and publishes statistical data related to psychiatric disorders, supports educational and research activities in the field of psychiatry, and advocates for mental health issues. The APA publishes journals in the field of psychiatry and is responsible for the development and publication of the *Diagnostic and Statistical Manual* (currently DSM-IV-Text Revision; in 2013: DSM-5).

THE AMERICAN PSYCHIATRIC NURSES ASSOCIATION (APNA)

Founded in 1986 with 600 members, today the American Psychiatric Nurses Association (APNA) has over 7,500 members. APNA today is "committed to the specialty practice of psychiatric mental health nursing, health and wellness promotion through identification of mental health issues, prevention of mental health problems and the care and treatment of persons with psychiatric disorders" (APNA, n.d., Welcome to APNA section). APNA offers a number of continuing education and professional development activities and publishes the *Journal of the American Psychiatric Nurses Association.* The association provides advocacy for psychiatric nurses to improve the quality of mental health care delivery.

THE AMERICAN PSYCHOLOGICAL ASSOCIATION (APA)

Founded in 1892 by *G. Stanley Hall,* the American Psychological Association (APA) started with 31 members and now maintains a membership of 154,000. The main purpose of this association is to "advance the creation, communication and application of psychological knowledge to benefit society and improve people's lives" (APA, 2012a, Mission Statement section). The association has 54 divisions in various specialty areas and publishes numerous psychological journals. The Counseling Psychology Division (Division 17) of the APA shares many of the same goals and purposes of some divisions of the American Counseling Association. APA offers a particularly wide range of services to its members, including all that were noted earlier in this chapter.

THE NATIONAL ASSOCIATION OF SCHOOL PSYCHOLOGISTS (NASP)

In 1969, the National Association of School Psychologists (NASP) was formed with its mission being to "support school psychologists to enhance the learning and mental health of all children" (NASP, 2007, Mission section). Today, this association has 26,000 members and offers workshops and conferences, supports public policies for school psychologists, provides a career center, develops training standards, and sponsors a national certification for school psychologists (Nationally Certified School Psychologists [NCSP]). NASP publishes the journal *School Psychology Review* and numerous other types of publications for parents, educators, and school psychologists.

THE NATIONAL ASSOCIATION OF SOCIAL WORKERS (NASW)

The National Association of Social Workers (NASW) was founded in 1955 as a merger of seven membership associations in the field of social work. Serving both undergraduate- and graduate-level social workers, NASW has about 145,000 members. NASW seeks "to enhance the professional growth and development of its members, to create and maintain professional standards, and to advance sound social policies" (NASW, 2012a, About NASW section). The association publishes five journals and other professional publications. It has 56 chapters which include every state as well as additional chapters in New York City, District of Columbia,

Puerto Rico, Virgin Islands, Guam, and an International chapter. As does APA, NASW offers a particularly wide range of services to its members, including all that were noted earlier in this chapter.

THE NATIONAL ORGANIZATION FOR HUMAN SERVICES (NOHS)

Founded in 1975, the mission of the National Organization for Human Services (NOHS) is to "strengthen the community of human services by: expanding professional development opportunities, promoting professional and organizational identity through certification, enhancing internal and external communications, advocating and implementing a social policy and agenda, and nurturing the financial sustainability and growth of the organization" (NOHS, 2009, Our Mission section). NOHS is mostly geared toward undergraduate students in human services or related fields, faculty in human services or related programs, and human service practitioners. NOHS publishes one journal, *The Journal of Human Services*.

THE NATIONAL REHABILITATION COUNSELING ASSOCIATION (NRCA)

The largest association representing rehabilitation counselors, NRCA was founded in 1958. Developed to "represent the unique concerns of practicing rehabilitation counselors" (NRCA, 2012, para. 1), NRCA offers a process for maintenance of one's credential as a Certified Rehabilitation Counselor (CRC), provides employment opportunities, offers awards of practitioners, publishes the *Journal of Applied Rehabilitation Counseling,* and more.

SUMMARY

This chapter began by highlighting a number of common benefits professional organizations offer to their members, including providing a sense of belonging, offering workshops and conferences, providing mentoring and networking opportunities, offering job fairs, supporting lobbying efforts, publishing scholarly materials, developing standards for the profession, providing a vehicle for building professional portfolios, making available scholarships and grants, giving awards, and offering a number of other needed services.

The chapter next discussed specific professional associations. Beginning with ACA, we noted that this large association for counselors offers a wide range of benefits for its members and has 19 divisions representing different counseling specialty areas as well as 56 state/international branches and 4 national regions. The divisions were highlighted in Table 2.1. In addition, the association supports a number of professional partners, including the ACA Insurance Trust (ACAIT), the American Counseling Association Foundation (ACAF), the Council for Accreditation of Counseling and Related Educational Programs (CACREP), the Council on Rehabilitation Education (CORE), the National Board of Certified Counselors (NBCC), and Chi Sigma Iota (CSI).

The chapter concluded with a brief description of popular professional associations in fields related to counseling. Here, we briefly discussed the American Art

Therapy Association (AATA), the American Association of Marriage and Family Therapists (AAMFT), the American Association of Pastoral Counselors (AAPC), the American Psychiatric Association (APA), the American Psychiatric Nurses Association (APNA), the American Psychological Association (APA), the National Association of Social Workers (NASW), the National Organization of Human Services, and the National Rehabilitation Counseling Association (NRCA).

KEY TERMS*

ACA Insurance Trust (ACAIT)

Advocacy Competencies

American Art Therapy Association (AATA)

American Association of Marriage and Family Therapy (AAMFT)

American Association of Pastoral Counselors (AAPC)

American Counseling Association (ACA)

American Counseling Association Foundation (ACAF)

American Psychiatric Association (APA)

American Psychiatric Nurses Association (APNA)

American Psychological Association (APA)

Branches and Regions of ACA

Certified Clinical Mental Health Counselor (CCMHC)

Certified Rehabilitation Counselor (CRC)

Chi Sigma Iota (CSI)

Council for Accreditation of Counseling and Related Educational Programs (CACREP)

Council on Rehabilitation Education (CORE)

Counseling Psychology Division (Division 17) of the APA

Counseling Today

COUNSGRADS

Diagnostic and Statistical Manual

Diverse grad-L

Divisions of ACA

Hall, G. Stanley

Journals of ACA Divisions

Journal of Counseling and Development

Master Addictions Counselor (MAC)

Membership Benefits of ACA

Multicultural Counseling Competencies

National Association of School Psychologists (NASP)

National Association of Social Workers (NASW)

National Board for Certified Counselors (NBCC)

National Certified Counselor (NCC)

National Certified School Counselor (NCSC)

National Organization for Human Services (NOHS)

National Rehabilitation Counseling Association (NRCA)

National Vocational Guidance Association (NVGA)

Nationally Certified School Psychologists (NCSP)

Professional associations

Professional partners to ACA

*Information about ACA's divisions, including the names of their journals, can be found in Table 2.1

CHARACTERISTICS OF THE EFFECTIVE COUNSELOR

I've been doing counseling and teaching counseling for over 30 years, and sometimes I think I'm great at what I'm doing, and other times I wonder if I really have the skills necessary to be effective. Because I've taught counseling for so long, I certainly know what I'm supposed to do, but my hunch is that knowing what one is supposed to do and being effective are not always in sync. So, what makes a counselor effective? Is it having a handle on the "proper" skills, is it knowing a variety of skills, or are some other factors needed also? This chapter is going to take a broad look at counselor effectiveness and identify some characteristics of the helper that seem, empirically, to lead to being an effective counselor.

DOES COUNSELING WORK?

In 1952, *Eysenck* examined 24 uncontrolled studies that looked at the effectiveness of counseling and psychotherapy and found that "roughly two-thirds of a group of neurotic patients will recover or improve to a marked extent within about two years of the onset of their illness, *whether they are treated by means of psychotherapy or not*" (p. 322). Although found to have serious methodological flaws, Eysenck's research led to debate concerning the effectiveness of counseling and resulted in hundreds of studies that came to some very different conclusions:

> It is a safe conclusion that as a general class of healing practices, psychotherapy is remarkably effective. In clinical trials, psychotherapy results in benefits for patients that far exceed those for patients who do not get psychotherapy. Indeed, psychotherapy is more effective than many commonly used evidenced-based medical practices....
> (Wampold, 2010a, p. 66)

But what makes counseling effective? First and foremost, some client factors such as readiness for change, psychological resources, and social supports may affect how well a client does in counseling (Asay & Lambert, 1999; Clarkin & Levy, 2004; Wampold, 2010a). However, these factors are intimately related to the counselor's ability to work with the client.

When looking specifically at the counselor, in recent years the importance of the counselor matching treatment methodologies to presenting problems has been emphasized. Called *evidence-based practice* (Norcross, Beutler, & Levant, 2006; Hayes, 2005; Stout & Hayes, 2005), this approach has become commonplace in training clinics. However, it has also become clear that specific counselor qualities, sometimes called *common factors*, seem to be even more important to positive counseling outcomes than matching a treatment approach to a presenting problem (Wampold, 2010a, 2010b, 2010c). For instance, the counselor's ability at creating a strong *working alliance* with the client may be the most significant factor in creating client change (Baldwin, Wampold, & Imel, 2007; Beutler et al., 2004; Marmarosh et al., 2009; Orlinsky, Ronnestad, & Willutzki, 2004). This alliance has been alluded to by almost every counselor and therapist from Freud to the modern-day "new age" counselor. Based on the research, and perhaps some of my own biases, I would contend that this working alliance is composed of the following six components: *empathy*, *acceptance*, *genuineness*, *embracing a wellness perspective*, *cultural competence*, and something that I call the *"it factor."*

In addition to the working alliance, another common factor that seems to be related to positive counseling outcomes is the counselor's ability to deliver his or her theoretical approach (Wampold, 2010a). This factor contains three components: *compatibility with and belief in your theory*, *competence*, and *cognitive complexity*. Let's take a look at all nine essential characteristics for effective counseling that, together, make up these two common factors (see Figure 3.1).

THE NINE CHARACTERISTICS OF THE EFFECTIVE COUNSELOR

EMPATHY

More than any other component, *empathy* has been empirically shown to be related to positive client outcomes and is probably the most important ingredient to building a successful working alliance (Bohart, Elliot, Greenberg, & Watson, 2002; Norcross, 2010). Understanding our clients, or being empathic,

> … means that the therapist senses accurately the feelings and personal meanings that the client is experiencing and communicates this acceptant understanding to the client. When functioning best, the therapist is so much inside the private world of the other that he or she can clarify not only the meanings of which the client is aware but even those just below the level of awareness. Listening, of this very special, active kind, is one of the most potent forces of change that I know. (Rogers, 1989, p. 136)

Whether or not one can truly understand the inner world of another has been discussed for centuries and was spoken of by such philosophers as Plato and Aristotle (Gompertz, 1960). However, *Carl Rogers* (1957) is given credit for bringing this concept to life in the twentieth century. With respect to the counseling relationship, understanding through empathy is seen as a skill that can build rapport, elicit information, and help the client feel accepted (Egan, 2010; Neukrug & Schwitzer, 2006).

FIGURE 3.1 | THE NINE CHARACTERISTICS OF THE EFFECTIVE COUNSELOR

CARL ROGERS IS NOTED FOR DEVELOPING THE MODERN-
DAY DEFINITION OF EMPATHY

Although empathy is an important skill that one learns how to apply, it is also a quality that grows over the years as one increasingly tries to be more understanding to others, be they clients, friends, or significant others. As you move through your counseling program, you will have the opportunity to learn this important skill in what is usually called a "skills" or "methods" class. However, I hope that over the years you also continue to try to increase your ability at being empathic with all people so that you can lead a gentler, more understanding life.

ACCEPTANCE

Acceptance, sometimes called *positive regard*, is another component likely related to building a strong working alliance (Norcross, 2010). Acceptance is an attitude that suggests that regardless of what the client says, within the context of the counseling relationship the client will feel accepted. Just about every counseling approach stresses the importance of acceptance (see Neukrug, 2011). For instance, person-centered counseling suggests that one of the core conditions in the helping relationship is *unconditional positive regard*, or the ability to accept clients "without strings attached." Behavior therapists suggest that issues cannot be discussed and goals cannot be developed if clients do not feel accepted by the therapist or by themselves. Solution-focused behavior therapy stresses the importance of acceptance in helping to quickly develop preferred goals. Reality therapy suggests that the suspension of judgment (acceptance) is one of the critical "tonics" or relationship-building skills. Psychoanalysts talk about the importance of *analytic neutrality* and empathy in building a relationship in which all feelings, thoughts, and behaviors can be discussed. And even *Albert Ellis*, not a person typically known for his relationship-building skills, suggested in his rational emotive behavioral approach that clients be shown unconditional acceptance and not be berated for thinking, feeling, and acting in any particular manner.

A reciprocal relationship exists between empathy and acceptance. If the counselor can be accepting, the client is more likely to reveal deeper parts of him- or herself. Then, if the counselor can be empathic as the client shares these parts, the client will reveal more. Sometimes, these deepest parts are well-held secrets and not liked by the client or condoned by society. It is here that the counselor must show even greater acceptance. This acceptance provides the client with the space to fully understand his or her feelings and actions. Acceptance and empathy are also closely related to genuineness, our next characteristic.

GENUINENESS

Another quality related to positive outcomes in counseling (Beutler et al., 2004; Klein, Kolden, Michels, & Chisholm-Stockard, 2001; Norcross, 2010), *genuineness*, refers to the counselor's ability to be authentic, open, and in touch with his or her feelings and thoughts within the context and parameters of the helping relationship. Thus, one may not have all aspects of one's life "together," but within the counseling relationship, the counselor is real and seen by the client as being in a state of *congruence* (feelings, thoughts, and behaviors are in sync). Carl Rogers (1957) is known for popularizing the word genuineness (or congruence) and for noting that, along with empathy and unconditional positive regard, genuineness was a core condition of the helping relationship.

Genuineness seems to be related to *emotional intelligence*, which is the ability to monitor one's emotions, a quality of which counselors and counseling students seem to have more than others (Martin, Easton, Wilson, Takemoto, & Sullivan, 2004). For instance, monitoring one's emotions may be important when a client shares something that results in the counselor feeling turned off or even angry. "Should I share my feelings about the client at this point?" says the authentic or genuine counselor to himself or herself. Rogers (1957) suggested that it was important to monitor or be aware of those feelings and not always wise to share one's immediate feelings. Sometimes, he suggested that it was best to discuss and understand one's negative feelings with a colleague or supervisor. Other times, he noted, that as the client increasingly shares deeper parts of him- or herself, the counselor gains a greater understanding of those aspects of the client that earlier left the counselor with negative feelings toward the client. This deeper understanding of the client almost always, said Rogers, leads to loving and caring feelings toward the client.

Research by Gelso(Gelso & Carter, 1994; Gelso et al., 2005; Marmarosh et al., 2009) suggests that, regardless of one's theoretical orientation, there exists an ongoing *real relationship* in which the client, to some degree, will see the therapist realistically. This means that at some point in the relationship, the client will sense the "real you" and that the real you will affect the relationship.

EMBRACING A WELLNESS PERSPECTIVE

> The difference in professional quality of life between counselors with high and low Wellness levels in this study was quite strong, suggesting that, overall, greater Wellness translates to dramatically improved professional quality of life. (Lawson & Myers, p. 170. Lawson, 2007; Norcross, 2010; Roach & Young, 2007. Neukrug, 2011, p. 50.)

It is pretty clear that stress, burnout, compassion fatigue, and vicarious traumatization from the work of the counselor, along with unfinished psychological issues, have the potential for preventing the building of a working alliance with clients (Lawson, 2007; Norcross, 2010; Roach & Young, 2007). This is due to the fact that work-related stress and unfinished business are likely to result in empathic blunders, an inability to be accepting, difficulty at building a real relationship, and *countertransference*, "or the unconscious transferring of thoughts, feelings, and attitudes onto the client by the therapist" (Neukrug, 2011, p. 50).

Students of counseling, and counselors in general, need to attend to their own wellness by *embracing a wellness perspective* if they are to be effective counselors. One method of assessing your level of wellness is by examining what Myers and Sweeney (2008) identify as the *Indivisible Self.* This model views wellness as a primary factor composed of five subfactors and also takes into account an individual's context. The factors (*creative self, coping self, social self, essential self*, and *physical self*) and contexts are described in Table 3.1.

You may want to complete an informal assessment on each of the factors and contexts to determine what areas you might want to address in your life. For instance, score yourself from 1 to 5 on each of the subfactors, with 5 indicating the area you most need to work on. Then, find the average for each of the primary five factors (creative self, coping self, etc.). Next, write down the ways you can better yourself in any of the primary or subfactors for which your scores seem problematic (probably scores of 3, 4, or 5).

Table 3.1	Abbreviated Definitions of Components of the Indivisible Self Model

Wellness Factor	Definition
Total Wellness	The sum of all items on the 5F-Wel; a measure of one's general well-being or total wellness
Creative Self	The combination of attributes that each of us forms to make a unique place among others in our social interactions and to positively interpret our world
Thinking	Being mentally active, open-minded; having the ability to be creative and experimental; having a sense of curiosity, a need to know and to learn; the ability to solve problems
Emotions	Being aware of or in touch with one's feelings; being able to experience and express one's feelings appropriately, both positive and negative
Control	Belief that one can usually achieve the goals one sets for oneself; having a sense of planfulness in life; being able to be assertive in expressing one's needs
Work	Being satisfied with one's work; having adequate financial security; feeling that one's skills are used appropriately; the ability to cope with workplace stress
Positive Humor	Being able to laugh at one's own mistakes and the unexpected things that happen; the ability to use humor to accomplish even serious tasks
Coping Self	The combination of elements that regulate one's responses to life events and provide a means to transcend the negative effects of these events
Leisure	Activities done in one's free time; satisfaction with one's leisure activities; having at least one activity in which "I lose myself and time stands still"
Stress Management	General perception of one's own self-management or self-regulation; seeing change as an opportunity for growth; ongoing self-monitoring and assessment of one's coping resource
Self-Worth	Accepting who and what one is, positive qualities along with imperfections; valuing oneself as a unique individual
Realistic Beliefs	Understanding that perfection and being loved by everyone are impossible goals, and having the courage to be imperfect
Social Self	Social support through connections with others in friendships and intimate relationships, including family ties
Friendship	Social relationships that involve a connection with others individually or in community, but that do not have a marital, sexual, or familial commitment; having friends in whom one can trust and who can provide emotional, material, or informational support when needed

(continued)

| TABLE 3.1 | ABBREVIATED DEFINITIONS OF COMPONENTS OF THE INDIVISIBLE SELF MODEL |

Wellness Factor	Definition
Love	The ability to be intimate, trusting, and self-disclosing with another person; having a family or family-like support system characterized by shared spiritual values, the ability to solve conflict in a mutually respectful way, healthy communication styles, and mutual appreciation
Essential Self	Essential meaning-making processes in relation to life, self, and others
Spirituality	Personal beliefs and behaviors that are practiced as part of the recognition that a person is more than the material aspects of mind and body
Gender Identity	Satisfaction with one's gender; feeling supported in one's gender; transcendence of gender identity (i.e., ability to be androgynous)
Cultural Identity	Satisfaction with one's cultural identity; feeling supported in one's cultural identity; transcendence of one's cultural identity
Self-Care	Taking responsibility for one's wellness through self-care and safety habits that are preventive in nature; minimizing the harmful effects of pollution in one's environment
Physical Self	The biological and physiological processes that compose the physical aspects of a person's development and functioning
Exercise	Engaging in sufficient physical activity to keep in good physical condition; maintaining flexibility through stretching
Nutrition	Eating a nutritionally balanced diet, maintaining a normal weight (i.e., within 15% of the ideal), and avoiding overeating
Contexts	
Local context	Systems in which one lives most often—families, neighborhoods, and communities—and one's perceptions of safety in these systems
Institutional context	Social and political systems that affect one's daily functioning and serve to empower or limit development in obvious and subtle ways, including education, religion, government, and the media
Global context	Factors such as politics, culture, global events, and the environment that connect one to others around the world
Chronometrical	Growth, movement, and change in the time dimension that are perpetual, of necessity positive, and purposeful

Note: 5F-Wel = Five Factor Wellness Inventory

Source: Myers, J., & Sweeney, T. J. (2008). Wellness counseling: The evidence base and practice. *Journal of Counseling and Development*, 86, p. 485. Reproduced by permission of John Wiley & Sons, via Copyright Clearance Center.

Finally, although many avenues to wellness exist, one that must be considered for all counselors is attending their own counseling. Counseling for ourselves helps us:

- attend to our own personal issues;
- decrease the likelihood of countertransference;

- examine all aspects of ourselves to increase our overall wellness; and
- understand what it's like to sit in the client's seat.

It appears that counselors and other mental health professionals understand the importance of being in counseling, as 85% of helpers have attended counseling (Bike, Norcross, & Schatz, 2009). However, some counselors resist, perhaps for good reasons (e.g., concerns about confidentiality, feeling as if family and friends offer enough support, or believing they have effective coping strategies) (Norcross, Bike, Evans, & Schatz, 2008). So, have you attended counseling? If not, have you found other ways to work on being healthy and well?

> Counselors are alert to the signs of impairment from their own physical, mental, or emotional problems and refrain from offering or providing professional services when such impairment is likely to harm a client or others. They seek assistance for problems that reach the level of professional impairment, and, if necessary, they limit, suspend, or terminate their professional responsibilities until such time it is determined that they may safely resume their work.... (From the American Counseling Association's 2005 Code of Ethics. Reprinted by permission.)

CULTURAL COMPETENCE

If you were distrustful of counselors, confused about the counseling process, or felt worlds apart from your helper, would you want to go to or continue in counseling? Assuredly not. Unfortunately, this is the state of affairs for many clients from diverse cultural groups. In fact, it is now assumed that clients from nondominant will frequently be misunderstood, often misdiagnosed, and as compared to Whites, find counseling less helpful, attend counseling at lower rates, and terminate counseling more quickly (Davis, 2011; Evans, Delphin, Simmons, Omar, & Tebes, 2005; Sewell, 2009; U.S. Department of Health and Human Services, 2001). Unfortunately, it has become clear that many counselors have not learned how to effectively build a bridge—a working alliance with clients who are different from them.

Clearly, the effective counselor needs to be culturally competent if he or she is going to connect with his or her client (Anderson, Lunnen, & Ogles, 2010). Although some argue that all counseling is cross-cultural, when working with clients who are from a different culture than one's own, the schism is often great. Therefore, all counselors must be cross-culturally competent. One model that can help bridge that gap is D'Andrea and Daniels's (2005) *RESPECTFUL Counseling Model*, which highlights ten factors that counselors should consider addressing with clients:

R – Religious/spiritual identity

E – Economic class background

S – Sexual identity

P – Psychological development

E – Ethnic/racial identity

C – Chronological disposition

T – Trauma and other threats to their personal well-being

F – Family history

U – Unique physical characteristics

L – Language and location of residence, which may affect the helping process. (p. 37)

The RESPECTFUL model can assist you in developing a deeper understanding of all your clients as you develop your skills as a counselor. Chapter 10 will examine cross-cultural issues in more detail and offer some additional models to help you become a culturally competent counselor. In addition, you will have multicultural counseling coursework infused throughout your program and are likely to have a separate course in social and cultural issues to assure your cross-cultural competence.

THE "IT FACTOR"

I worked at a suicide crisis center, and one of the counselors had an uncanny ability to make jokes on the phone that would result in suicidal clients laughing. If I had made those same jokes, it would have driven the caller to commit suicide! "So, is there a bridge nearby?" I would hear him say in a jovial way. This counselor had "it"—a way with words, a special voice intonation, and a way of being that would get the client laughing—the suicidal client. And he knew he had it and he would use *it*. I knew I didn't have *it*—well, I didn't have his *it*, so I knew not to try to make my clients laugh. For me, just listening and being empathic was my way.

I believe all great counselors have their own "*it factors*," or special ways of working with and ultimately building alliances with their clients. And more often than not, these great therapists want us to use their "it factors." So, *Carl Rogers*, who was great at showing empathy, unconditional positive regard, and genuineness, suggested we all use these core conditions with our clients; and *Albert Ellis*, who was a master at challenging his clients' *irrational thinking*, said we all should approach our clients in this manner; and *Michael White*, a *post-modernist* who believed that social injustices fueled mental illness, wanted all counselors to help clients see how oppressed by language they are; and of course *Sigmund Freud*, who believed in the *unconscious*, told us to show analytic neutrality to our clients so that we would allow the unconscious to be projected onto the therapist. But I liked *Salvador Minuchin's* (1974) "it factor" best. A family counselor, Minuchin used the word *joining* in highlighting the importance of each counselor finding his or her unique way of working with clients:

> The therapist's methods of creating a therapeutic system and positioning himself as its leader are known as joining operations. These are the underpinnings of therapy. Unless the therapist can join the family and establish a therapeutic system, restructuring cannot occur, and any attempt to achieve the therapeutic goals will fail. (p. 123)

So, what is your "it factor"? What do you have that's special and will enable you to bond? Is it the way you show empathy, the way you make people laugh, a tone, a look, or a way of being? Do you have it? (see Box 3.1)

| BOX 3.1 | WHAT IS YOUR "IT"? |

Write down the unique personality characteristics that allow you to build a bond with others. Then, the instructor can make a master list on the board. After reviewing the list, discuss which characteristics may be inherent and which may be learned. Can a person acquire new ways of bonding with clients as he or she develops as a counselor?

COMPATIBILITY WITH AND BELIEF IN A THEORY

There are literally hundreds of counseling theories to choose from when working with clients (Gabbard, 1995; O'Leary, 2006; "List of psychotherapies," 2012). However, I find that most of them, for one reason or another, just don't fit me. They don't seem compatible with my way of understanding the world. Maybe it's because they place too much emphasis on genetics, or spirituality, or early child-rearing, or maybe they're just a little too directive, or too nondirective. Perhaps they are too long-term or too brief for my taste. Whatever the reason, they just don't sit well with me. I am not compatible with them, and I choose not to use them. But thankfully, there are enough theories out there with which I am compatible. I drift toward them and those are the ones I use.

Wampold (2010a) suggests that helpers "are attracted to therapies that they find comfortable, interesting, and attractive. Comfort most likely derives from the similarity between the worldview of the theory and the attitudes and values of the therapist" (p. 48). He goes on to say that if you are drawn to a theory, and if you believe that the theory you are drawn to works, then, and only then, you will likely see positive counseling outcomes (Wampold, 2010a, 2010b). So, what theories are you drawn to? If you aren't sure yet, you'll have an opportunity to explore your theoretical orientation in courses in which you will examine your view of human nature and the potential theories it best matches. Want to start the process now? Then go to the survey highlighted in Box 3.2. As you continue to examine your view of human nature and theoretical orientation, over time, you will hopefully feel an increased sense of *compatibility with and belief in a theory* (see Box 3.2).

| BOX 3.2 | WHAT IS YOUR THEORETICAL ORIENTATION? |

Want to take a survey to find the counseling approach to which you are most aligned? Go to the following website: www.odu.edu/sgt and click "book/survey/DVD" to take a 20-minute survey to assess your theoretical orientation.

COMPETENCE

Counselor expertise and mastery (*competence*) has been shown to be a crucial element for client success in counseling (Wampold, 2010a, 2010c; Whiston & Coker, 2000). Competent counselors have a thirst for knowledge. They continually want to improve and expand their expertise at delivering their theories. Such counselors exhibit this thirst through their study habits, their desire to join professional associations, through mentoring and supervision, by reading professional journals, through their belief that education is a lifelong process, and through their ability to view their own approaches to working with clients as always broadening and deepening.

Counselors have both an ethical and legal responsibility to be competent (Corey, Corey, & Callanan, 2011). For instance, Standard C.2 of American Counseling Association's (ACA, 2005) Code of Ethics, "Professional Competence," elaborates on eight areas, including:

(1) practicing within one's boundary of competence;
(2) practicing only in one's specialty areas;
(3) accepting employment only for positions for which one is qualified;
(4) monitoring one's effectiveness;
(5) knowing when to consult with others;
(6) keeping current by attending continuing education activities;
(7) refraining from offering services when physically or emotionally impaired; and
(8) assuring proper transfer of cases when one is incapacitated or leaves a practice.

The legal system reinforces these ethical guidelines because "one function of lawsuits is to encourage competent therapy" (Swenson, 1997, p. 166).

Finally, clients pick up on incompetence. They can see it, smell it, and feel it. And, of course, clients are less likely to improve when a counselor is incompetent. And not surprisingly, incompetent counselors are sued more frequently.

COGNITIVE COMPLEXITY

The best helpers believe in their theories, but are willing to question them. This apparent contradiction makes sense. You have a way of working, but are also willing to constantly examine whether what you're doing is working. Describing this type of person as a critical thinker, Deal (2003) suggests that the cognitively complex person is good at examining problems from multiple perspectives and good at analyzing and evaluating situations. Counselors who view the world with a fair amount of *cognitive complexity* are likely to be more empathic, more open-minded, more self-aware, more effective with individuals from diverse cultures, better able to examine a client's predicament from multiple perspectives, and better able to resolve "ruptures" in the counseling relationship (Deal, 2003; Granello, 2010; McAuliffe & Eriksen, 2010; Norcross, 2010; Wendler, 2009). Such a counselor is willing to integrate new approaches into his or her usual way of doing counseling and is a helper who doesn't believe his or her theory holds the "truth" (Wampold, 2010a).

So, ask yourself, "Am I cognitively complex?" Are you able to self-reflect, question truth, take on multiple perspectives, and evaluate situations in complex ways?

These qualities are often not easily embraced, and most of us work our lifetimes becoming better at them. Hopefully, your counselor training program is one environment where you can examine your ability at exhibiting these qualities and begin your lifelong journey of embracing them more fully (McAuliffe & Eriksen, 2010).

Final Thoughts

Now that we've looked at all nine characteristics, ask yourself, are you empathic, accepting, genuine, wellness oriented, culturally competent, aware of your own "it factor," compatible with and confident in your theory, competent, and cognitively complex? As we start on our journey to help others, let's always think about how we can improve ourselves in all of these areas, as helping ourselves will significantly improve the manner in which we work with others.

SUMMARY

This chapter began by discussing whether or not counseling works. Beginning with Eysenck's controversial and flawed study suggesting counseling was not effective, we moved on to show the overwhelming evidence that counseling is helpful. We then went on to note that there are some client factors that lead to positive counseling outcomes, including the client's readiness for change, psychological resources, and social supports. Then we pointed out that in recent years there has been a move toward counseling methods that are evidence-based, which speaks to the importance of using techniques that fit the client's presenting problem.

Although client factors and evidence-based practice are important, the bulk of the chapter was spent discussing common factors that seem to be particularly important in positive client outcomes. I suggested that that there are nine factors that collectively work toward increasing counseling effectiveness, including six that contribute to the working alliance: empathy, acceptance, genuineness, embracing a wellness perspective, cultural competence, and the "it factor"; and three that contribute to the counselor's ability to deliver his or her theoretical approach: belief in one's theory, competence, and cognitive complexity (see Figure 1.1). Each of these nine factors was discussed, and the chapter concluded by suggesting that embracing all nine of these qualities is a lifelong process.

Key Terms

Acceptance	Countertransference
Analytic neutrality	Creative self
Cognitive complexity	Cultural competence
Common factors	Ellis, Albert
Compatibility with and belief in a theory	Emotional intelligence
Competence	Empathy
Congruence	Essential self
Coping self	Evidence-based practice

Eysenck

Freud, Sigmund

Genuineness

Indivisible Self

It factor

Irrational thinking

Joining

Minuchin, Salvador

Physical self

Positive regard

Post-modernist

RESPECTFUL Counseling Model

Rogers, Carl

Social self

Unconditional positive regard

Unconscious

White, Michael

Wellness (embracing a wellness perspective)

Working alliance

History and Current Trends in the Counseling Profession

Our roots—our history—tell a story about where we have been and who we are today, and suggest in what direction we might be moving. Thus, in this section of the text we discuss antecedents to the counseling profession, the 100-year-old history of the counseling profession, and current trends in the field. We begin by reviewing the early history of mental health treatment. We then explore the roots of social work, psychology, and psychiatry, and describe how these related fields influenced the counseling profession. We then move on to describe, in detail, the history of the counseling profession, which began around the turn of the twentieth century. As we take you through the twentieth century and into the new millennium, you will begin to see that what we are today is intimately related to the kinds of decisions that were made over the past 100 years. This section concludes with a review of some recent trends in the field and some thoughts about likely trends in the future.

PREDECESSORS TO THE COUNSELING PROFESSION: FROM ANTIQUITY TO EARLY SOCIAL WORK, PSYCHOLOGY, AND PSYCHIATRY

Imagine your extended family, siblings, cousins, uncles, and aunts. You all share similar roots, yet you recognize that each family member is distinct and unique— some a bit more unique than others! Our professional family is similar. Our professional cousins—social work, psychology, and psychiatry, are all related to us, yet different in many ways. And if we look back in time, we can see that social work, psychology, psychiatry, and counseling had somewhat different beginnings, with the social work field developing out of the desire to assist the destitute, psychology starting as both a laboratory science and an attempt to understand the nature of the person, psychiatry growing out of modern medicine's effort to alleviate mental illness through medical interventions, and counseling growing out of the early vocational guidance movement of the twentieth century.

This chapter will explore the historical antecedents of the counseling profession. Starting with early antiquity and then briefly reviewing the historical roots of the social work, psychology, and psychiatric professions, we will see how philosophy, religion, and the roots of the early mental health professions impacted counseling in unique and important ways. Chapter 5 will focus solely on the 100-year-old history of the counseling profession.

UNDERSTANDING THE HUMAN CONDITION: FROM EARLY ANTIQUITY TO THE MODERN ERA

> The first counselors were leaders of the community who attempted to provide inspiration for others through their teachings. They were religious leaders such as Moses (1200 B.C.), Mohammed (A.D. 600), and Buddha (500 B.C.). They were also philosophers like Lao-Tzu (600 B.C.), Confucius (500 B.C.), Socrates (450 B.C.), Plato (400 B.C.), and Aristotle (350 B.C.). (Kottler, 2011, p. 30)

Since the dawn of our existence, people have attempted to understand the human condition. Myths, magic, belief in spirits, ritualism, and sacred art have been used by people as means of gaining introspection and understanding the world around us (Ellwood & McGraw, 2009) (see Figure 4.1). Shamans, or individuals who had special status due to their mystical powers, have been considered caretakers of the soul and thought to have knowledge of the future. Later in history, the concept of *soul* often gave way to the concept of *psyche* (see Box 4.1).

Martin Baggarly

| BOX 4.1 | MYTHS AND RITUALS IN YOUR FAMILY OF ORIGIN |

Oftentimes in our own families of origin certain myths and rituals were used to protect us or create a positive sense of mental health. For instance, in my family getting angry was seen as unhealthy, so our myth was to "keep a lid" on our anger. Also, when a person was upset in our family, the individual was invariably asked whether they were hungry—as food seemed a cure for all ills. Other families might pray together, or share "magic artifacts" (stones, stuffed animals). Write down any myths and rituals used in your family and share them in class.

One of the first written treatises of a psychological nature can be traced back to an Egyptian papyrus of 3000 BCE that shows a primitive attempt to understand some basic functions of the brain (Breasted, 1930). Almost 1000 years later, also in ancient Egypt, a wise man who was obviously psychologically minded expounded on the importance of being nonjudgmental, listening, and accurately reflecting a person's inner thoughts within a close, one-on-one relationship:

> If thou searchest the character of a friend, ask no questions, (but) approach him and deal with him when he is alone.... Disclose his heart in conversation. If that which he has seen come forth from him, (or) he do aught that makes thee ashamed for him, ... do not answer. (Breasted, 1934, p. 132)

Such writings show that the "counseling way" clearly preceded modern times. However, it was *Hippocrates* (460–377 BCE), whose treatises reflected on the human condition, who was to greatly change the Western world's view of emotional and physical illnesses. Whereas contemporaries of Hippocrates believed that evil spirits were responsible for such problems, Hippocrates suggested there were environmental, diet related, and other natural causes. In fact, by today's standards, some of his treatment recommendations would be considered right on target; on the other hand, some might seem a bit odd. For instance, for melancholia he recommended sobriety, a regular and tranquil life, exercise short of fatigue, and bleeding, if necessary. For hysteria, he recommended getting married!

With the advent of monotheistic religion, we see abundant examples of humankind's attempt to further understand the self. The Old and New Testaments, the Quran, and other religious writings abound with such examples (Belgium, 1992). For instance, in Buddhism, the Sanskrit term "duhkha" speaks to the pain and suffering that people carry due to what are called *delusive perceptions* (Purton, 1993), and the Old and New Testaments offer us many reflections on the concepts of atonement and guilt—reflections that are closely related to the many painful issues people discuss in counseling:

> The concept of atonement is closely associated to forgiveness, reconciliation, sorrow, remorse, repentance, reparation and guilt. It is a spiritual concept which has been studied since time immemorial in Biblical and Kabbalistic texts. (Williams, p. 83)

With guidance from religious texts, over the years, a number of philosophers and theologians have reflected on the nature of the person, the soul, and the human condition. For example, such philosophers as *Plotinus* (205–270), who believed the soul was separate from the body, had a lasting impact on the dualistic fashion in which the Western world views the mind and body.

The Renaissance in Europe (roughly fourteenth to seventeenth centuries) might be considered the start of the modern era, and with it came the printing press and the writings of modern philosophers. Individuals like *Descartes* (1596–1650), who believed that knowledge and truth was derived through deductive reasoning, and *John Locke* (1632–1704), who believed that the mind is a blank slate, changed our understanding of the human experience. Soon after, *James Mill* (1773–1836) suggested that mental states were a function of associations of ideas that were imprinted or "stamped" onto a passive mind. These individuals and others set the stage for modern psychology, the beginnings of modern-day social work and psychiatry, and the origins of the counseling field.

A BRIEF HISTORY OF SOCIAL WORK

HISTORICAL BACKGROUND

Social work practice can be traced to work with the poor and destitute. For instance, during the 1500s, the *Elizabethan Poor Laws* in England made the Church responsible for overseeing the raising and administering of funds for the destitute (Burger, 2011). Until then, such relief had been provided on a voluntary basis. Modeling that system, during the colonial period in the United States, local governments enacted laws to assist the poor and destitute. Around this same time, organized charities that were usually affiliated with religious groups began to arise.

In the 1800s, the growth of urban populations produced an increasingly large underclass whose needs could not be met by the traditional charitable organizations. Mounting political pressure thus led to the creation of specialized institutions such as reform schools, lunatic asylums, and orphanages. To assist the underprivileged who were not institutionalized, two approaches evolved: the *Charity Organization Society (COS)* and the *settlement movement*. Charity Organization Societies had volunteers, called *friendly visitors*, who would visit the poor, aid in educating children, give economic advice, and assist in alleviating the conditions of poverty. In contrast, the settlement movement had individuals living in the poorer communities.

> In essence it was simply a residence for university men in a city slum.... These critics looked forward to a society that encouraged people's social responsibility, not self-interest, to create a life that was kindly, dignified, and beautiful, as well as progressive and prosperous. Some of these thinkers rejected capitalism in favor of an idealized medieval community. (Leiby, 1978, p. 129)

Idealistic young people in the settlement houses, such as *Jane Addams* (1860–1935) at *Hull House* in Chicago, believed in community action and tried to persuade politicians to provide better services for the poor (Addams, 1910).

Out of involvement with the underprivileged arose articles, books, and eventually social work training programs that focused on *social casework*, *group work*, *advocacy*, and *community organizing*. During the 1940s and 1950s, an increased emphasis on understanding the dynamics of *social systems* and *family systems* emerged. As social workers had already been working with families and social systems, this emphasis became a natural focus for many social work programs. One social worker, *Virginia Satir* (1967), was particularly instrumental in reshaping the practices of the mental health profession to include a greater systems focus.

In 1955, a number of social work organizations combined to form the National Association of Social Work (NASW). In 1960, NASW established the Academy of Certified Social Workers (ACSW), which sets standards of practice for master's level social workers. Today, social workers can be found in a variety of social service settings, from hospitals to mental health centers to agencies that work with the homeless and the poor. Although many social workers today do individual counseling and family therapy, others work in community settings doing advocacy work, and still others administer social service organizations.

SOCIAL WORK'S INFLUENCE ON THE COUNSELING PROFESSION

Social work's emphasis on understanding systems has provided the counseling profession with an understanding of the individual from a family and social system perspective. And, because many of the early family therapists were social workers, counselors have adapted many of these individuals' concepts with clients. Also, social work's emphasis on field experience has rubbed off on counseling, as counselor education programs have increasingly offered more field experience in their training programs. Finally, social work's focus on advocacy is a constant reminder to counselors that their clients are greatly affected by the culture from which they come and the larger dynamics of society. Today, a focus upon *advocacy* and *social justice* has become a major thrust of the counseling profession.

A BRIEF HISTORY OF PSYCHOLOGY

HISTORICAL BACKGROUND

The psychology profession often traces its early beginnings to the great Greek philosophers as far back as the seventh century BCE. These philosophers reflected on the nature of life and the universe. And, as noted earlier, one of the more "modern" Greek philosophers, Hippocrates, offered notions on how to treat mental and physical illness, and *Plato* (427–347 BCE), discussed the idea that introspection and reflection were roads to knowledge, that dreams and fantasies were substitute satisfactions, and that the human condition had physical, moral, and spiritual origins. However, many consider Plato's student *Aristotle* (384–322 BCE) to be the first psychologist in that he used objectivity and reason to study knowledge, and his writings were psychological in nature (Iannone, 2001; Wertheimer, 2000).

Although *Augustine* (354–430) and *Thomas Aquinas* (1225–1274) highlighted the importance of consciousness, self-examination, and inquiry, there was a paucity of writing about "psychological thinking" during the 800-year span between their lives. This was partly due to the rise of Christianity, which at that point downplayed the role of reason and objectivity and highlighted the presence of the supernatural. However, the Renaissance, during the fourteenth to seventeenth centuries, saw a rediscovery of the Greek philosophies and a renewed interest in questions regarding the nature of the human condition. This interest sparked philosophical discussions regarding the nature of the person as well as the development of the scientific method.

Although psychology's beginnings can be traced back to the early philosophers, modern-day psychology began during the nineteenth century and was influenced by the new scientific theories of physics and evolution. For instance, *Wilhelm Wundt* (1832–1920) and Sir Francis Galton (1822–1911), two of the first *experimental psychologists*, developed laboratories to examine how individuals' responses to external stimuli were related to the workings of the mind (Green, 2009). In the United States, *G. Stanley Hall* (1846–1924) and *James Cattell* (1860–1940) opened experimental psychology laboratories in the late 1800s (Capshew, 1992). Also during the nineteenth century, *William James* (1842–1910) published his theory of *philosophical pragmatism*, which suggested that reality is continually constructed as a function of the practical purpose it holds for the individual (Leary, 1992).

Thus we saw the beginning of two important schools of psychology: the philosophical and the scientific.

One natural outgrowth of *laboratory science* was the development of *psychological and educational tests*. For instance, during the early 1900s *Alfred Binet* (1857–1911) developed one of the first intelligence tests, which was used for classroom placement of mentally retarded children in the Paris public schools (Neukrug & Fawcett, 2010). The beginning of the twentieth century saw the first use of school achievement tests, vocational assessment, and some of the first "modern day" personality tests.

The testing movement paralleled the rise of *psychoanalysis*, the first comprehensive psychotherapeutic system. Developed by *Sigmund Freud* (1856–1939), psychoanalysis was influenced by the new emphasis on the scientific method. In fact, *Anton Mesmer* (the term *mesmerize* was derived from his name) (1734–1815) and *Jean-Martin Charcot* (1825–1893) were practicing a new "scientific" technique called *hypnosis*. Freud originally used hypnosis to uncover *repressed memories*, but later stopped in favor of other techniques and subsequently developed his complex theory to understand the origins of human behavior. Freud's views on mental health were revolutionary and continue to profoundly affect the conceptualization of client problems (Appignanesi & Zarate, 2007; Neukrug, 2011). Although he was trained as a physician, Freud's concepts were quickly adopted by the psychology profession.

In addition to traditional psychoanalysis, the end of the nineteenth century saw the beginnings of other schools of psychology. For instance, *Ivan Pavlov* (1849–1936) and others developed behaviorism as they experimented with *classical conditioning*. During this same period, *phenomenological psychology* and *existential psychology* had their beginnings and stressed the nature of existence and the study of reality. Also around this time, *Gestalt psychology* tried to answer questions about how individuals organize experience into reality. The early days of behaviorism, existential psychology, phenomenological psychology, and Gestalt psychology represent the roots of many of today's *cognitive-behavioral* and *humanistically-oriented therapies*.

In 1892, the American Psychological Association (APA) was founded as an association mostly of experimental psychologists (Sokal, 1992). During the mid-1940s APA expanded and embraced many new clinical associations such as Counseling Psychology (Division 17) (Pepinsky, 2001; Routh, 2000; Schmidt, 2000). This division shares a common history with and has goals similar to those of the counseling profession.

Today, we still find experimental psychologists, who work in the laboratory trying to understand the psychophysiological causes of behavior, and clinical and counseling psychologists, who practice counseling and psychotherapy. In addition, we also find other highly trained psychologists doing testing in schools, working within business and industrial organizations, and applying their knowledge in many other areas.

PSYCHOLOGY'S INFLUENCE ON THE COUNSELING PROFESSION

Although psychology was the first profession to use a comprehensive approach to therapy, the counseling field was soon to follow and borrowed many of the theories used by early psychologists. Tests developed by psychologists at the turn of the twentieth century were used by the early *vocational guidance counselors* and later adapted by counselors in many different settings. Research techniques developed by the early experimental psychologists became the precursors to modern-day research tools used by counselors to assess the efficacy of counseling approaches and to evaluate programs they have developed. Finally, many modern-day counseling skills are adaptations from counseling skills developed by psychologists during the early part of the twentieth century. Psychology is truly the first cousin of counseling.

A BRIEF HISTORY OF PSYCHIATRY

HISTORICAL BACKGROUND

Until the late 1700s, mental illness was viewed as something mystical, demonic, and not treatable, but this perspective gradually gave way to new ways of understanding and treating mental illness. In the late 1700s in France, *Philippe Pinel* (1745–1826), known as the *founder of psychiatry*, was one of the first to view insanity from a scientific perspective. Administering two mental hospitals, Pinel removed the chains that bound inmates and made one of the first attempts to treat inmates humanely (Weissmann, 2008).

In the United States, such individuals as *Benjamin Rush* (1743–1813) and *Dorothea Dix* (1802–1887) advocated for more humane treatment of the mentally ill (Baxter, 1994). However, despite their desire to treat the mentally ill more humanely, early treatment was anything but humane (see Box 4.2).

One result of the work of individuals like Rush and Dix, the spread of mental hospitals and the impetus towards more humane treatment of the mentally ill was the founding, in 1844, of the Association of Medical Superintendents of American Institutions for the Insane, the forerunner of the American Psychiatric Association (APA).

In the 1800s, great strides were made in the understanding, diagnosis, and treatment of mental illness. Individuals such as *Emil Kraepelin* (1855–1926) developed

| BOX 4.2 | EARLY MENTAL HOSPITAL IN THE UNITED STATES |

In 1773 the Publick Hospital for Persons of Insane and Disordered Minds admitted its first patient in Williamsburg, Virginia. The hospital, which had 24 cells, took a rather bleak approach to working with the mentally ill. Although many of the employees of these first hospitals had their hearts in the right place, their diagnostic and treatment procedures left a lot to be desired. For instance, some of the leading reasons that patients were admitted included masturbation, womb disease, religious excitement, intemperance, and domestic trouble—hardly reasons for admission to a mental institution. Normal treatment procedures were to administer heavy dosages of drugs, to bleed or blister individuals, to immerse individuals in freezing water for long periods of time, and to confine people to straitjackets or manacles. Bleeding and blistering were thought to remove harmful fluids from the individual's system (Zwelling, 1990).

one of the first *classifications of mental diseases*, and others like *Jean Martin Charcot* (1825–1893) and *Pierre Janet* (1859–1947) saw a relationship between certain psychological states and disorders that were formerly considered only organic in nature (Solomon, 1918).

In the first half of the twentieth century many psychiatrists became entrenched in the *psychoanalytic movement*, others drifted toward *psychobiology*, and still others became involved in *social psychiatry* (Sabshin, 1990). With the spread of psychiatry, perhaps it's not surprising that during the 1950s the American Psychiatric Association developed the first *Diagnostic and Statistical Manual of Mental Disorders* (DSM-I). Now in its fourth edition (DSM-IV-TR), and soon to be in its fifth edition (DSM-5), the purpose of the diagnostic manual is to provide uniform criteria for making clinical diagnoses and enhancing agreement among clinicians (American Psychiatric Association, 2000).

The second half of the twentieth century saw a greater need for psychiatric treatment as the result of the increased use of psychopharmacology, the development of *community-based mental health centers* in the 1960s, and the 1975 Supreme Court ruling of *Donaldson v. O'Connor* (see Box 4.3), which led to the *deinstitutionalization* of hundreds of thousands of hospitalized patients who now needed to be seen in community-based clinics.

Today, with research indicating that some mental illness is predominantly or partially biologically based (Roberts, Kiselica, & Fredrickson, 2002; Schatzberg & Nemeroff, 2009; Neukrug, 2001), psychiatrists have been playing an increasingly important role in the mental health field. In addition, with the advent of new and much improved *psychopharmacological drugs*, psychiatrists have become very important consultants to counselors and other mental health professionals.

BOX 4.3	DONALDSON V. O'CONNOR

Kenneth Donaldson, who had been committed to a state mental hospital in Florida and confined against his will for 15 years, sued the hospital superintendent, Dr. J. B. O'Connor, and his staff for intentionally and maliciously depriving him of his constitutional right to liberty. Donaldson, who had been hospitalized against his will for paranoid schizophrenia, said he was not mentally ill, and he stated that even if he were, the hospital had not provided him adequate treatment.

Over the 15 years of confinement, Donaldson, who was not in danger of harming himself or others, had frequently asked for his release, and had relatives who stated they would attend to him if he were released. Despite this, the hospital refused to release him, stating that he was still mentally ill. The Supreme Court unanimously upheld lower court decisions stating that the hospital could not hold him against his will if he was not in danger of harming himself or others (Swenson, 1997). This decision, along with the increased use and discovery of new psychotropic medications, led to the release of hundreds of thousands of individuals across the country who had been confined to mental hospitals against their will and who were not a danger to themselves or others.

PSYCHIATRY'S INFLUENCE ON THE COUNSELING PROFESSION

Psychiatry's focus on diagnosing mental illness and exploring psychopathology has assisted counselors and other professionals in diagnosis and development of treatment plans for clients, which sometimes includes psychopharmacology. In addition, the awareness that some mental health problems may be organic has helped counselors understand that at times it is critical to make a referral to an expert in psychopharmacology and psychobiology.

CONCLUSION

Despite, or maybe because of their different origins, the fields of social work, psychology, and psychiatry have all impacted the field of counseling. Whether it's the systems or advocacy emphasis of social work; the assessment, research and theoretical underpinnings of psychology; or the diagnosis or psychopharmacology focus of psychiatry; each has provided the counseling field with some important ways to understand mental health and mental illness. As we move into Chapter 5, we will see how the counseling profession both borrowed from these professions and also created its own unique identity as it developed over the past one hundred years. And although all four professions have disparate beginnings, today the fields of social work, psychology, psychiatry, and counseling have all slowly moved toward many of the same theoretical conclusions and can be viewed as having slightly different yet parallel paths (see Figure 4.1).

A LOT OF NAMES AND DATES TO LEARN

Well, there certainly were a fair amount of names to learn about in this chapter, and there will be more in the next. But they are important names and dates because they have influenced our professional identity. To help you remembers some of them, Table 4.1 summarizes most of the important facts in this chapter.

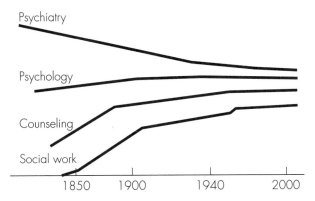

FIGURE 4.1   THE COMING TOGETHER OF THE MAJOR FIELDS OF MENTAL HEALTH

Source: Army Beta Test, found at http://official-asvab.com/armysamples_coun.htm

TABLE 4.1 | SUMMARY OF IMPORTANT HISTORICAL EVENTS

3000 BCE Ancient Egypt	"Psychological" writings found on papyrus
400 BCE Hippocrates	Wrote the first "modern-day" reflections on the human condition
350 BCE Plato	Believed introspection and reflection to be the road to knowledge
350 BCE Aristotle	Considered by many to be "first psychologist"— studied objectivity and reason
250 Plotinus	Believed in dualism—the concept that the soul is separate from the body
400 Augustine	Examined the meaning of consciousness, self-examination, and inquiry
1250 Thomas Aquinas	Examined the meaning of consciousness, self-examination, and inquiry
1500s Elizabethan Poor Laws	Established legislation for the Church to help the destitute in England
1650 Descartes	Believed that knowledge and truth come through deductive reasoning
1700 John Locke	Believed the mind is a blank slate upon which ideas are generated
1800 James Mill	Believed the mind is a blank slate upon which ideas are generated
1800 Philippe Pinel	Founder of the field of psychiatry; viewed insanity from scientific perspective; advocated for humane treatment of the mentally ill
1800 Benjamin Rush	Founder of American psychiatry, advocated for humane treatment of the mentally ill
1800 Anton Mesmer	Discovered the first uses of hypnosis
1800s Charity Organization Societies	Volunteers (friendly visitors) offered assistance to the poor and destitute
1800s Settlement Houses	Individuals lived in communities to help the poor and destitute
1844 Origins of APA	Founding of the Association of Medical Superintendents of American Institutions for the Insane (precursor to the American Psychiatric Association)
1850 Jean Martin Charcot	Used hypnosis to understand disorders, saw the relationship between psychological and organic states
1850 Dorothea Dix	Advocated for humane treatment for the mentally ill, helped establish 41 "modern" mental hospitals
1875 Wilhelm Wundt	First experimental psychologist

(continued)

TABLE 4.1	SUMMARY OF IMPORTANT HISTORICAL EVENTS
1875 Sir Francis Galton	Early experimental psychologist
1890s Sigmund Freud	Developed the theory of psychoanalysis
1890s G. Stanley Hall	Founded the APA; early American experimental psychologist
1890s James Cattell	Early American experimental psychologist
1890s William James	Philosophical Pragmatism: reality is continually constructed as a function of its utility or practical purpose
1889 Jane Addams	Established Hull House in Chicago
Around 1900 Emil Kraepelin	Developed one of the first classifications of mental diseases
Around 1900 Alfred Binet	Developed the first individual intelligence test for the French Ministry of Public Education
Around 1900 Pierre Janet	Saw a relationship between certain psychological states and organic disorders
Around 1900 Ivan Pavlov	Developed one of the first behavioral models of learning
1940s Division 17 of APA	Division 17 formally became part of APA
1950s Virginia Satir	One of first social workers to stress contextual or systems thinking
1950s DSM	First diagnostic manual developed
1955 NASW	National Association of Social Workers founded from a merger of seven associations
1960	NASW establishes Association for Certified Social Workers
1975 Donaldson v. O'Connor	Deinstitutionalization of hundreds of thousands of hospitalized patients

SUMMARY

This chapter examined the history of counseling from its early beginnings to current-day practices. We learned that the human condition has been pondered for thousands of years, and noted that myths, magic, sprits, ritualism, and sacred art are have all been used to understand ourselves and the world around us. We pointed out that shamans, or individuals with special mystical powers, were seen as early caretakers of the soul. We also noted that early treatises that were psychological in nature were found in Egypt and that philosophy, as well as early religious texts, offered us much to ponder from a psychological perspective. Although the Renaissance was void of psychological writings to a large extent, we did note that some individuals like Descartes, John Locke, and James Mill offered us the ingredients for modern psychology.

More specifically, in this chapter we examined the historical roots of the field of social work and saw how social work's emphasis on systems and advocacy has influenced the counseling profession. We also saw how social work's emphasis on "in-the-field" experiences has impacted counselor education training and its recent trends toward increasing practicum and internship hours. In addition to social work, we offered a brief overview of the field of psychology, and noted that many of the philosophical roots of modern-day counseling theories arose from psychology's early beginnings. We examined how laboratory science and research techniques have become important tools for counselors as they research the efficacy of programs they develop and of specific counseling techniques they use. We also examined how tests used by many counselors today had their origins in the early days of testing as originated by psychologists. Finally, we saw how the field of psychiatry has offered us ways of understanding and classifying mental health problems and how crucial it is for counselors to have an understanding of the possible organic nature of some mental health problems.

Key Terms*

Academy of Certified Social Workers (ACSW)

Addams, Jane

Advocacy

American Psychological Association (APA)

Aquinas, Thomas

Aristotle

Augustine

Binet, Alfred

Cattell, James

Charcot, Jean Martin

Charity Organization Society (COS)

Classical conditioning

Classifications of mental diseases

Cognitive-behavioral therapy

Community organizing

Community-based mental health centers

Counseling Psychology (Division 17)

Counseling skills

Deinstitutionalization

Delusive perceptions

Descartes

Diagnostic and Statistical Manual of Mental Disorders

Dix, Dorothea

Donaldson v. O'Connor

Elizabethan Poor Laws

Existential psychology

Experimental psychologists

Family systems

Freud, Sigmund

Friendly visitors

Gestalt psychology

Group work

Hall, G. Stanley

Hippocrates

Hull House

Humanistically oriented therapies

Hypnosis

James, William

Janet, Pierre

Kraepelin, Emil

Laboratory science

Locke, John

Mesmer, Anton

*Please see Table 4.1 for descriptions of individuals and key events.

Mesmerize

Mill, James

National Association of Social Work
(NASW)

Pavlov, Ivan

Phenomenological psychology

Philosophical pragmatism

Pinel, Philippe

Plato

Psyche

Psychoanalysis

Psychoanalytic movement

Psychobiology

Psychological and educational tests

Psychopharmacological drugs

Repressed memories

Rush, Benjamin

Satir, Virginia

Settlement movement

Social casework

Social justice

Social psychiatry

Social systems

Soul

Vocational guidance counselors

Wundt, Wilhelm

HISTORY OF THE COUNSELING PROFESSION

> Counseling represents the fusing of many influences. It brings together the movement toward a more compassionate treatment of mental health problems begun in the mid-nineteenth century France, the psychodynamic insights of Freud and psychoanalysis, the scientific scrutiny and methodology of the behavioral approach, the quantitative science of psychometrics, the humanistic perspective of client-centered therapy, the philosophical base of existentialism, and the practical insights and applications that evolved from the vocational guidance movement. (Belkin, 1988, p. 19)

As you learned from Chapter 4, the counseling profession shares common roots with psychology, social work, and psychiatry. In that chapter we noted how social workers, early on, worked in humane ways with the poor and the destitute, established a systemic perspective to viewing families and communities, and saw the importance of advocacy for their clients. We noted that psychologists focused on testing and research and were the first to embrace a systematic psychotherapeutic approach to working with clients. And we saw that psychiatry's focus on the humane treatment of the mentally ill, the classification of mental illness, and the importance of psychopharmacology changed the way that individuals were treated. All of these events were to profoundly affect the emergence of the counseling profession and impact how counselors were to eventually work. However, our profession has its own unique history, which dates back to the early days of vocational guidance. Let's take a look at the 100-year-old history of counseling.

VOCATIONAL GUIDANCE IN THE 1800s

Although modern-day vocational guidance activities and theory began in the latter part of the 1800s, interest in vocational adjustment far preceded the 1800s. For instance, as far back as the tenth century, writings in an Iraqi text addressed occupational information, while the first job classification system was developed in Spain as early as 1468 by *Sanchez de Arevalo*, who wrote *Mirror of Men's Lives* (Carson & Altai, 1994). At the end of the nineteenth century, dramatic shifts took place in the United States that were partially responsible for the development of the *vocational guidance movement* and ultimately set the stage for the establishment of the counseling profession. At that time in history we saw the rise of social reform movements, the impact of the Industrial Revolution, and an increase in immigration, mostly to large northeastern cities. Jointly, these events led to the large-scale need for vocational guidance. During the early to mid-1800s, prior to the development of *vocational theory*, a number of poorly written, moralistic books on occupational choice were written (Zytowski, 1972). However, by the end of the century, the stage was set for the development of the first comprehensive approaches to *vocational guidance*—approaches that would at least be partially based on the new science of testing (Herr, Cramer, & Niles, 2004).

THE FIRST VOCATIONAL AND GUIDANCE COUNSELORS: EARLY 1900s

> It is difficult even to imagine the difference of conditions now and in the early years of the century.... Think of what life would be without the railroad, only the stage-coach to carry our letters and ourselves across the country. Think of pulling oranges from Florida or California to Boston stores by team. Think of a city without a street-car or a bicycle, a cooking stove or a furnace, a gas jet or electric light, or even a kerosene lamp! Think of a land without photographs or photogravures, Christmas cards or color prints.... (Parsons, cited in Watts, 1994, p. 267)

It was a different world at the beginning of the twentieth century, but the rumblings of a new age were everywhere to be found. Social reformers were caring for the poor and demanding changes in education; psychiatry was changing its methods of treatment for the mentally ill; psychoanalysis and related therapies were in vogue; the modern-day use of tests was beginning; and the impact of the Industrial Revolution could be seen everywhere. In subtle, but important ways, each of these events would affect early vocational guidance and the emergence of the field of counseling.

The first part of the twentieth century saw the beginnings of systematic vocational guidance in America. Although the concepts had been floating around in the latter part of the 1800s, the 1900s brought the first comprehensive approach to vocational guidance. Then in 1907, troubled by the attitudes of youth, *Jesse Davis* (1871–1955) developed one of the first guidance curricula that focused on moral and vocational guidance, which was presented during English composition classes in the Grand Rapids, Michigan, schools. At around the same time *Eli Weaver* (1862–1922), a New York City principal who had written a booklet called *Choosing a Career*, started vocational guidance in New York. Similarly, *Anna Reed* (1871–1946) soon established guidance services in the Seattle school system, and by 1910, 35 cities had plans for the establishment of vocational guidance in their schools (Aubrey, 1977). Although revolutionary in their thinking, many of these early vocational guidance reformers were motivated by moralistic thinking and theories of the time, such as social Darwinism, that suggested individuals should fervently follow their supervisors and "fight their co-workers for advanced status" (survival of the fittest) (Rockwell & Rothney, 1961, p. 352).

The person who undoubtedly had the greatest impact on the development of vocational guidance in America was *Frank Parsons* (1854–1908) (Briddick, 2009a; McDaniels & Watts, 1994). Seen today as the *founder of guidance* in America, Parsons was greatly influenced by the social reform movements of the time, such as the work of *Jane Addams at Hull House* who advocated for better conditions for the poor. Eventually establishing the *Vocational Bureau*, which assisted individuals in "choosing an occupation, preparing themselves for it, finding an opening in it, and building a career of efficiency and success" (Parsons cited in Jones, 1994, p. 288), Parsons hoped that vocational guidance would eventually be established in the public schools—a hope he would not see come to fruition due to his untimely death in 1908. In 1909, his book *Choosing a Vocation* was published post-humously. Soon after his death, perhaps as a tribute to the energy he gave to the vocational guidance movement, his home town of Boston became the site for the first vocational guidance conference. This conference resulted in the founding of the National Vocational Guidance Association (NVGA) in 1913, which is generally considered the distant predecessor of the American Counseling Association (ACA).

Frank Parsons was a man with a vision (Pope & Sveinsdottir, 2005; Briddick, 2009b). He envisioned systematic vocational guidance in the schools, he anticipated a national vocational guidance movement, he foresaw the importance of individual counseling, and he hoped for a society in which cooperation was more important than competition and where concern replaced avarice (Jones, 1994). Clearly, Parsons's principles of vocational guidance greatly affected the broader field of counseling.

Parsons's main thrust toward vocational guidance is usually presented as a three-part process in which an individual would develop:

(1) a clear understanding of yourself, your aptitudes, interests, ambitions, resources, limitations, and their causes;
(2) a knowledge of the requirements and conditions of success, advantages and disadvantages, compensation, opportunities, and prospects in different lines of work; and
(3) true reasoning on the relations of these two groups of facts (Parsons, 1909/1989, p. 5).

However, a deeper examination of Parsons' work shows us that many of his principles eventually became some of the major tenets of the counseling profession (Jones, 1994). For instance, Parsons noted the importance of having an expert guide when making difficult decisions. In addition, he suggested that even an expert guide cannot make a decision *for* a person, as only the individual can decide what's best for him- or herself. He also suggested that the counselor should be frank (genuine) and kind with the client and that it was crucial for the counselor to assist the client in the development of analytic skills. Frank Parsons clearly deserves the title founder of vocational guidance, and in many ways he can also be seen as the *founder of the counseling field*.

Parsons developed the beginnings of a theoretical orientation to counseling and with the founding of NVGA, the vocational guidance movement was established. Although the spread of the movement did not occur as quickly as some might have liked (Aubrey, 1977), a number of acts were eventually passed to strengthen vocational education (Herr, 1985). One such act, the Depression-era *Wagner O'Day Act* of 1932, established the U.S. Employment Services and provided ongoing vocational guidance and placement to all unemployed Americans. *Vocational counseling* as part of the landscape of America was here to stay, and it would soon have an impact on all facets of counseling.

Although vocational guidance in the schools soon became widespread, it was not long before individuals advocated for an approach that attended to a broader spectrum of students' psychological and educational needs. For instance, *John Brewer* (1932) suggested that guidance should be seen in a *total educational context* and that guidance counselors should be involved in a variety of functions in the schools, including adjustment counseling, assistance with curriculum planning, classroom management, and of course, occupational guidance. One tool used by the counselor was the test (Aubrey, 1982).

THE EXPANSION OF THE TESTING MOVEMENT: 1900–1950

> It is doubtful that vocational guidance would have survived without a psychological support base in psychometrics. (Aubrey, 1977, p. 290)

With the advent of the vocational guidance movement, testing was to become commonplace. Parsons, for instance, strongly advocated the use of tests in vocational guidance (Williamson, 1964). During World War I, some of the first crude tests of ability were used on a large-scale basis. For instance, the *Army Alpha* was a test used for "literates" to determine placement of recruits, while the *Army Beta* was used for "illiterates" (see Figure 5.1).

FIGURE 5.1 | PICTURE COMPLETION TEST OF THE ARMY BETA

Source: Army Beta Test, found at http://official-asvab.com/armysamples_coun.htm

The use of tests to assist in vocational counseling was promoted by the development of one of the first major interest inventories, the *Strong Vocational Interest Blank*, in 1927 (Campbell, 1968). This test, which in its revised form is still one of the most widely used instruments of its kind, was to revolutionize vocational counseling. But the use of tests extended beyond vocational assessment. For instance, *Woodworth's Personal Data Sheet* was an early personality instrument used by the military to screen out emotionally disturbed individuals.

The successful large-scale military use of tests led to the development and adoption of similar instruments in the schools, business, and industry (Neukrug & Fawcett, 2010). By the middle of the twentieth century, tests to measure achievement, cognitive ability, interests, intelligence, and personality were commonplace. Although often used in vocational counseling, many of these tests soon found their way into all kinds of counseling practices.

THE SPREAD OF PSYCHOTHERAPY AND ITS IMPACT ON COUNSELING: 1900–1950

> Most sane people think that no insane person can reason logically. But this is not so. Upon reasonable premises I made most reasonable deductions, and that at the time when my mind was in its most disturbed condition. (Beers, C. W. (1948). A mind that found itself (7th ed.). Garden City, NY: Doubleday.)

In 1908, *Clifford Beers* (1876–1943), a Yale graduate who had been hospitalized for years due to schizophrenia, wrote *A Mind That Found Itself*. In 1909, he helped to establish the *National Committee for Mental Hygiene*, which lobbied Congress to pass laws that would improve the deplorable conditions of mental institutions. Soon, this committee began to organize the first *child guidance clinics*, staffed by social workers, psychologists, and psychiatrists. At the same time, *psychoanalysis* was beginning to come out of the elite office of the psychiatrist and work its way into the community. The end of World War I saw a number of psychologists offering their services to returning doughboys who had psychological problems associated with the war (today such problems are often diagnosed as *post-traumatic stress disorder, or PTSD*). Since the long-term treatment approaches of the psychoanalysts were of little use to these clinicians, they soon began to develop new, shorter-term approaches.

As treatment approaches to the individual changed, and as mental health clinics spread, the need for psychological assistants, often with bachelor's or master's degrees, became evident. The master's level assistants often had degrees in social work, but increasingly there were individuals with a relatively new degree—a master's degree in counseling, which had its origins as a degree in vocational guidance. It was a natural transition for individuals with the vocational guidance degree to move into the mental health field, because they were trained both in counseling techniques and in assessment.

The emergence of the counseling field as something other than pure vocational guidance made its greatest leap forward during the 1930s, when, *E. G. Williamson* (1900–1979) developed what is considered the *first comprehensive theory of counseling* (as distinguished from Freud's theory of psychoanalysis). Known as the *Minnesota Point of View* (for the University of Minnesota, where Williamson was a faculty member), or *trait and factor theory*, Williamson's approach initially grew out of the ideas of Frank Parsons. Although originally vocationally oriented, the approach was modified and became a generic approach to counseling and psychotherapy. The trait and factor approach involved a series of five steps, which included:

(1) analysis: examining the problem and obtaining available records and testing on the client;
(2) synthesis: summarizing and organizing the information to understand the problem;
(3) diagnosis: interpreting the problem;
(4) counseling: aiding the individual in finding solutions; and
(5) follow-up: assuring proper support after counseling had ended (Patterson, C. H. (1973). Theories of counseling and psychotherapy (2nd ed.). New York: Harper & Row.)

With the rise of Nazism during the 1930s and 1940s, many humanistic philosophers, psychiatrists, and psychologists fled Europe for the United States and dramatically influenced the field of psychotherapy and education in their new country. One of those influenced by these humanists was *Carl Rogers* (1902–1987). Called one of the most influential psychologists and psychotherapists of the latter part of the twentieth century (The Top 10 …, 2007), Rogers initially worked from a *psychodynamic* perspective at the *Rochester Guidance Center* but later revolutionized the practice of counseling with his *client-centered approach*. His *nondirective approach* to working with individuals was viewed as shorter-term, more humane, more honest, and more viable for most clients than the psychodynamic approaches to counseling. The early 1940s saw the publication of Carl Rogers's book *Counseling and Psychotherapy*, which was to have a major impact on the counseling profession (Rogers, 1942). Rogers and others in the newly established field of *humanistic counseling and education* were responsible for moving the counseling field from a vocational guidance orientation to one with a much broader base. Rogers's approach was ripe for the times, as it reflected the increased focus on personal freedom and autonomy of the post-WWII years (Aubrey, 1977). Although Rogers and other humanists during the 1940s had a great impact on the field of counseling, the second half of the century would witness even more dramatic changes than had already occurred.

EMERGENCE, EXPANSION, AND DIVERSIFICATION: THE 1950s

> If one decade in history had to be singled out for the most profound impact on counselors, it would be the 1950s. (Aubrey, 1977, p. 292)

During the 1950s, the counseling profession shifted increasingly toward a humanistic, nondirective orientation. This decade saw Carl Rogers become an even greater influence on the field as he published his second book, entitled *Client-Centered Therapy: Its Current Practice, Implications and Theory* (Rogers, 1951). In addition, impacted by the push to depathologize individuals, this decade saw the promulgation of *developmental theories* in the areas of *career counseling* (e.g., Ginzberg, Ginsburg, Axelrad, & Herma, 1951; Super, 1953), *child development* (e.g., Piaget, 1954), and *lifespan development* (e.g., Erikson, 1950). These theories stressed the notion that individuals would face predictable tasks as they passed through the inevitable developmental stages of life and that knowledge of such tasks could greatly aid counselors in their work with clients.

Perhaps the most important event that would affect counseling during this time was the 1957 launching of the first satellite in space, Sputnik. The launching of this Russian satellite sent a chill through many Americans and provided the impetus for Congress passing the *National Defense Education Act* (NDEA) in 1958. The NDEA allocated funds for training institutes that would quickly graduate secondary school counselors. These counselors, it was hoped, would identify students gifted in math and science who could be future scientists. The obvious result of this legislation was the significant increase in secondary school counselors in the late 1950s and 1960s. The bill was extended to include the training of elementary school counselors in 1964.

Besides the dramatic increase in school counselors, the 1950s also saw the first full-time college counselors and the beginning of college counseling centers. A natural extension of secondary school counseling, *college counseling centers* often started as vocational guidance centers, but soon morphed into counseling centers (Nugent & Jones, 2009). As with other aspects of the counseling profession, college counseling centers quickly took on the humanistic and developmental approach to working with students and were generally staffed by counselors and psychologists. Other college student services offices (e.g., career centers) that employed counselors also expanded rapidly during this time.

Community agencies also saw an influx of counselors and psychologists during the 1950s. The discovery of antipsychotic, antidepressant, and antianxiety medications, and the controversial yet widespread use of *electroconvulsive therapy* enabled the release of large numbers of people from state hospitals who then found needed services at local community agencies (Kornetsky, 1976; Mehr & Kanwischer, 2008). In addition, this decade saw counselors increasingly staffing *vocational rehabilitation centers*, working to address both the physical and psychological needs of individuals, especially those who had been seriously injured during World War II.

This decade saw the formation of the American Personnel and Guidance Association (APGA, the forerunner of ACA) from a merger of four counseling-related associations, and it was not long before a number of divisions representing the growing diversity of counselors in the field emerged. These included: the American School Counselor Association (ASCA), the Association for Counselor Education and Supervision (ACES), the National Career Development Association (NCDA), the American Rehabilitation Counseling Association (ARCA), and the Counseling Association for Humanistic Education and Development (now the Association for Humanistic Counseling, AHC).

Changes were taking place not only in the counseling profession around this time. In 1945 the American Association of Marriage and Family Counseling (AAMFC, now AAMFT) was formed, and the 1950s saw the formation of the National Association of Social Workers (NASW) and the changing of the name of Division 17 of the APA from the Counseling and Guidance Division to the Division of Counseling Psychology. Whereas Division 17 required a doctorate for full membership, APGA, AAMFT, and NASW were focusing on master's level training.

Differentiation and solidification of the various mental health fields was clearly occurring.

INCREASED DIVERSIFICATION: THE 1960s

During the first half of the twentieth century three approaches to counseling and therapy were particularly popular: *psychodynamic approaches* (e.g., Freud), *directive theories* (e.g., Williamson), and *client-centered theories* (e.g., Rogers) (Gladding, 2013). However, the late 1950s and the 1960s saw a number of new, at the time revolutionary, approaches to counseling to take shape, including the *rational emotive* (cognitive) *approach* of *Albert Ellis* (Ellis & Harper, 1961); *behavioral approaches* of *Albert Bandura* (1969), *Joseph Wolpe* (1958), and *John Krumboltz* (1966a, 1966b); *William Glasser*'s *reality therapy approach* (1961, 1965); the Gestalt approach of *Fritz Perls* (1969); the communication approach of *transactional analysis* (Berne, 1964); and the *existential approaches* of *Viktor Frankl* (1963), *Rollo May* (1950), and others. These counseling approaches were at least partially developed due to the increased demand for therapists. Can you imagine being a young mental health professional during this time? The sheer number of new theories and new thought-provoking approaches to working with clients would have been incredibly stimulating!

The need for counselors and other mental health professionals expanded as a direct result of the passage of many legislative actions related to President Johnson's *Great Society* initiatives (Kaplan & Cuciti, 1986). One such legislative act, the *Community Mental Health Centers Act* of 1963, funded the nationwide establishment of mental health centers to provide short-term inpatient care, outpatient care, partial hospitalization, emergency services, and consultation and education services. These centers made it possible for individuals with adjustment problems, as well as those with severe emotional disorders, to obtain free or low-cost mental health services. Approximately 600 community-based mental health centers were established as a result of this act (Burger, 2011).

Many other acts were also passed during this decade. For instance, amendments to the 1964 NDEA expanded the training of counselors to include counselors from elementary school through junior college (Lambie & Williamson, 2004). In fact, by 1967 nearly 20,000 school counselors had been trained as a result of this act. In addition, a number of other acts provided job opportunities for counselors, such as the *Manpower Development and Training Act, Job Corps, Elementary and Secondary Education Act, Head Start*, and the *Work Incentive Program*. Other key legislative initiatives such as the *Civil Rights Act, Economic Opportunity Act*, and *Voting Rights Act* helped to reshape attitudes toward social problems and community service, with one result being a more accepting attitude toward the counseling profession. Clearly, the 1960s was a decade of expansion, acceptance of counselors, and diversification of the counseling profession largely as the result of legislative actions.

With expansion and diversification came an increased need for professionalism in the field. Thus, it was at this time that we saw the emergence of *ethical standards of practice*, such as APGA's first ethical code in 1961. The 1960s also saw a flurry of activity around the need for accreditation standards of counseling programs.

Meetings were held throughout the country that would be the precursors to the development, in 1981, of the Council for Accreditation of Counseling and Related Educational Programs (CACREP). Finally, the 1960s saw the continued expansion of APGA with increased membership, the formation of what would become the Association for Assessment in Counseling and Education (AACE) and the National Employment Counseling Association (NECA), and the recommendation in 1964 by APGA to have state branches (ACA, 1995a).

CONTINUED PROLIFERATION OF THE COUNSELING FIELD: THE 1970s

The 1970s produced a number of events that increased the need for counselors. For instance, the 1975 Supreme Court decision in *Donaldson v. O'Connor* led to the deinstitutionalization of tens of thousands of state mental hospital patients who had been hospitalized against their will (see Box 4.3). This case concluded that individuals who were not in danger of harming themselves or others could not be held against their will. With the release of individuals from the hospitals came an increased need for community mental health counselors. Thus, in 1975 Congress passed an expansion of the original *Community Mental Health Centers Act* and extended from five to twelve the categories of services that mental health centers were required to provide. They included:

1. Short-term inpatient services
2. Outpatient services
3. Partial hospitalization (day treatment)
4. Emergency services
5. Consultation and education
6. Special services for children
7. Special services for the elderly
8. Preinstitutional court screening
9. Alcoholism services
10. Follow-up care for mental hospitals
11. Transitional care from mental hospitals
12. Drug abuse services

The 1970s also saw the passage of legislation for individuals with disabilities. These laws increased the demand for highly trained rehabilitation counselors and expanded the role of school counselors. For instance, the *Rehabilitation Act* of 1973 ensured vocational rehabilitation services and counseling for employable adults who had severe physical or mental disabilities that interfered with their ability to obtain and/or maintain a job. The *Education for All Handicapped Children Act* of 1975 (PL94-142) ensured the right to an education within the least restrictive environment for all children identified as having disabilities that interfered with learning. PL94-142 resulted in school counselors increasingly becoming an integral part of the team that would determine the disposition of students with disabilities.

This decade also saw a major shift in the training of counseling students. The influence of the humanistic movement had fully taken hold by the 1970s, and a number of individuals began to develop what became known as *microcounseling skills training* (Carkhuff, 1969; Egan, 1975; Ivey & Gluckstein, 1974). The teaching of microcounseling skills was based on many of the skills deemed critical by Carl Rogers and other humanistic counselors and psychologists. These packaged ways of training counselors showed that basic counseling skills, such as attending behaviors, listening, and empathic understanding, could be learned in a relatively short amount of time and that the practice of such skills would have a positive impact on counseling outcomes (Neukrug, 1980). It was also during this decade that we began to see the blossoming of publications in the area of *cross-cultural counseling*. Seminal works by *Derald Sue, Paul Pedersen, William Cross, Donald Atkinson*, and others began to make their way into the counselor education curriculum.

The 1970s was also the decade of increased professionalization in the field. For instance, the early 1970s saw the Association for Counselor Education and Supervision (ACES) provide drafts of standards for master's level counseling programs. National *credentialing* became a reality when *certification* was offered for the first time by the Council on Rehabilitation Education (CORE) in 1973 and by the National Academy for Certified Mental Health Counselors (NACMHC) in 1979 (Sweeney, 1991). Finally, state *licensure* had its beginnings when, in 1976, Virginia became the first state to offer licensing for counselors.

The legislative actions of the 1970s led to increased diversification of the counseling field, resulting in large numbers of counselors settling into the mental health, rehabilitation, higher education, and school counseling specialty areas. One result of this diversification was the burgeoning membership in APGA, which reached 40,000, and the founding of a number of divisions of ACA (then called APGA), including the Association for Multicultural Counseling and Development (AMCD, in 1972), the Association for Spiritual, Ethical, and Religious Values in Counseling (ASERVIC, in 1974), the Association for Specialists in Group Work (ASGW, in 1973), the International Association of Addictions and Offender Counselors (IAAOC, in 1972), and the American Mental Health Counselors Association (AMHCA, in 1978) (ACA, 1995a; Goodyear, 1984).

RECENT CHANGES IN THE FIELD: 1980–2000

The 1980s and 1990s saw continued expansion and diversification as well as a settling-in phase marked by an increased focus on professionalism. Counselors could now be found in almost any mental health setting, while expanded services were offered in colleges and schools. Counselors also began to practice in areas where minimal mental health services had been provided, including substance abuse agencies, agencies that worked with older persons, and business and industry. With the profession clearly having come of age, it became evident that there was an urgent need for the standardization of training and the credentialing of counselors. Therefore, in 1981 the Council for Accreditation of Counseling and Related Educational Programs (CACREP) was formed to further delineate standards for the profession. Today, CACREP accredits master's programs in school counseling; clinical mental health counseling; marriage, couple, and family counseling; addictions counseling; career counseling; student affairs and college counseling; and doctoral programs in counselor education and supervision (see Chapter 7 for a detailed discussion of CACREP).

The 1980s and 1990s saw a phenomenal increase in the types of credentials being offered and the numbers of individuals becoming certified or licensed. In 1982, APGA (now ACA) established the National Board for Certified Counselors

(NBCC) and began to administer the first national generic certification exam for counselors (NBCC, 2011b). In addition, in 1994 the International Association of Marriage and Family Counselors (IAMFC, n.d.a), a division of ACA, began to offer a credential as a Certified Family Therapist (CFT). It was also during this decade that an increasing number of states began offering licensure for counselors (Neukrug, Milliken, & Walden, 2001). Probably one of the greatest changes in the field of counseling during the 1980s and 1990s was the increased focus on *multi-cultural counseling* (Claiborn, 1991). This new emphasis was partly due to CACREP's requirement that multicultural counseling be infused into the curricula of all accredited graduate programs, the ever-increasing volumes of work being published in the field of multicultural counseling, and the 1991 adoption by AMCD of *Multicultural Counseling Competencies*, which counseling training programs were encouraged to follow (Arredondo et al., 1996; Evans & Larrabee, 2002).

The 1990s also saw an increased emphasis on the importance of ethical issues in counseling. Whereas prior to 1980 few counseling texts discussed ethical issues to any great extent, this decade saw research and publications on *ethics* greatly expanded with particular focus on ethical decision-making, ethics in supervision, ethics in teaching, and even the ethics of online counseling (ACA, 1995b; Attridge, 2000, 2004). Not surprisingly, the 1990s brought a revision of the *ACA Code of Ethics* as well as the development of separate ethical guidelines for online counseling by ACA and by NBCC.

In 1992 the American College Personnel Association (ACPA), one of ACA's founding divisions, disaffiliated from the association. Also, in the latter part of the 1990s the boards of the two largest ACA divisions, AMHCA and ASCA, both threatened disaffiliation from ACA. This movement toward independent functioning of the divisions was a precursor to the divisional autonomy that was to occur in the twenty-first century.

There is little doubt that the changes that took place during the 1980s and 1990s were reflected in changes in the professional associations. In 1983 APGA changed its name to the American Association for Counseling and Development (AACD), and in 1992 the association underwent another name change to the more streamlined American Counseling Association (ACA). This name change seemed here to stay.

NVGA ⟹ APGA ⟹ AACD ⟹ ACA

The 1980s and 1990s saw the founding of a number of new divisions, including the Association for Counselors and Educators in Government (ACEG, in 1994), the Association for Adult Development and Aging (AADA, in 1986), the International Association of Marriage and Family Counselors (IAMFC, in 1989), the American College Counseling Association (ACCA, in 1991), the Association for Gay, Lesbian and Bisexual Issues in Counseling (AGLBIC, in 1997; now ALGBTIC). Around the same time, an affiliate organization was founded: Counselors for Social Justice (CSJ, 1999). Membership in ACA soared and by 2000 had surpassed 55,000, with AMHCA and ASCA representing the two largest divisions. At that point, ACA had 17 divisions and 1 affiliate, representing the differing specialty areas in counseling, with close to 500 counselor training programs in the United States (Hollis & Dodson, 2000).

THE NEW MILLENNIUM: 2000 AND ON

The first decade of the new millennium brought cutting edge issues to the forefront. Some of these, which will be expanded on in Chapter 6: Current Issues and Future Trends in the Counseling Profession, stand out:

1. *Credentialing*: All 50 states now offer licensing of professional counselors (California was the last state in 2010), and there has been a great expansion of the number and types of credentialed counselors.
2. *Licensure Portability*: With all 50 states now having licensure laws, in 2012 ACA began to push for license portability, sometimes called reciprocity, of one's license from state to state.
3. *Division Expansion and Autonomy*: Some of ACA's 19 divisions, such as ASCA and AMHCA, have become increasingly autonomous and have expanded their membership.
4. *Evidence-based Practice and Common Factors in Counseling*: The new millennium has seen a push toward using methods in counseling that match the client's presenting problem as well as the common factors of all counseling approaches that lead to positive client outcomes.
5. *Multicultural Counseling*: Although this movement started over twenty years ago, it continues to pick up speed and expand: ACA endorsed the Multicultural Counseling Competencies in 2002 and more research and training continues to be conducted.
6. *Social Justice Focus*: With the adoption of the *Advocacy Competencies* in 2003, ACA fully embraced a new social justice focus.
7. *ASCA's National Model*: With the adoption of the ASCA National Model in 2003, ASCA began its push toward a new model of school counseling.
8. *New Ethics Code*: In 2005, ACA adopted a new ethics code, which addresses changing times and a changing counseling profession.
9. *New CACREP Standards*: In 2009, CACPREP revised its standards and increased the number of credits needed in some specialty areas. Although many of the former standards remained, new focuses on social justice, leadership, crisis counseling, disaster, trauma counseling, and more were added.
10. *Crisis, Disaster, and Trauma Counseling*: With CACREP's 2009 standards requiring a focus on crisis, disaster, and trauma counseling, it became clear that this area would be important in the years to come.
11. *20/20: A Vision for the Future of Counseling*: Thirty-one counseling associations have come together to develop a common vision for counseling as well as a new definition of counseling (see Box 5.1).

BOX 5.1	YOUR VISION FOR THE FUTURE

On your own, develop a list of important skills, knowledge, and tools that might be needed for the future of counseling and that were not discussed in this chapter. Then create and discuss a combined list in class.

A LOT OF NAMES AND DATES TO LEARN

The names and events highlighted in this chapter are important because they are the backbone of our professional identity. We have become what we are because of our history, and the present will shape what we will be in the future. So, let's embrace our history. And, to help you do so, Table 5.1 summarizes most of the important facts in this chapter.

TABLE 5.1	SUMMARY OF IMPORTANT HISTORICAL EVENTS (CONT'D FROM CHAPTER 4)
1906 Eli Weaver	Developed vocational guidance in New York City schools
1907 Jesse Davis	Developed one of the first guidance curriculums in Grand Rapids, Michigan, schools
1908 Anna Reed	Established vocational guidance in the Seattle school system
1908 Frank Parsons	Founder of vocational guidance; developed the first comprehensive approach to vocational guidance
1908 Clifford Beers	Institutionalized for schizophrenia; wrote *A Mind That Found Itself*; advocated for humane treatment of the mentally ill
1913 NVGA	National Vocational Guidance Association formed: distant forerunner of ACA
1917 Army Alpha Test	First large-scale use of tests of ability
1917 Woodworth Personal Data Sheet	One of the first structured personality tests
1927 Strong Interest Inventory	One of the first interest inventories to assist in career counseling process
1930 E. G. Williamson	Developed the first comprehensive theory of counseling, called the Minnesota Point of View, or trait and factor approach
1932 John Brewer	Suggested that guidance be seen in a total educational context
1932 *Wagner O'Day Act*	Established the U. S. Employment Service
1940s Carl Rogers	Developed a nondirective approach to counseling, advocate of humanistic counseling and education
1940s Division 17 of APA	Division 17 formally became part of APA
1945 AAMFT	AAMFT officially formed
1952 APGA	American Personnel and Guidance Association formed out of four associations: forerunner of ACA
1955 NASW	National Association of Social Workers founded from a merger of seven associations
1958 NDEA	*National Defense Education Act*: training for and expansion of school counselors
1961 Ethical Codes	Development of first APGA guidelines for ethical behavior

(*continued*)

TABLE 5.1 | SUMMARY OF IMPORTANT HISTORICAL EVENTS

1960s Great Society Initiatives	Numerous laws passed under President Johnson: development of social service agencies nationally
1963 *Community Mental Health Centers Act*	Federal law provided for the establishment of community mental health centers nationally
1970s	Development of microcounseling skills training (e.g., Carkhuff, Ivey, Egan)
1970s Cross-cultural Issues	Seminal works published in the area of cross-cultural counseling by such individuals as Donald Atkinson, William Cross, Paul Pedersen, Derald Sue
1973 *Rehabilitation Act*	Ensured access to vocational rehabilitation services for adults; increased need for trained rehabilitation counselors
1973 CORE	Council for Rehabilitation Education offered the first credentialing for counselors
1975 PL94-142	*Education of All Handicapped Children Act* provided access to education within least restrictive environments: passage of this act extended the need for school counselors
1975 *Donaldson v. O'Connor*	Supreme Court decision leading to deinstitutionalization of mental hospital patients
1979 NACMHC	National Academy for Certified Mental Health Counselors offered national certification
1981 CACREP	Council for Accreditation of Counseling and Related Educational Programs was founded: established accreditation standards for counseling programs
1982 NBCC	National Board for Certified Counselors offered generic certification for counselors
1983 AACD	APGA became the American Association for Counseling and Development (AACD)
1990s Increased Emphasis	Increased focus on ethical issues, accreditation, professionalism, and multicultural issues
1990s	Many new divisions of ACA founded
1992 ACA	AACD becomes the American Counseling Association
1991 Multicultural Competencies	Proposed and adopted by AMCD: competencies suggest how to address multicultural training
1994 CFT	IAMFC offers national certification as a Certified Family Therapist (CFT)
2000–present	Division expansion and autonomy
2000–present	Evidence-based practice
2000–present	Credentialing: all 50 states have licensure; expansion of certification processes
2002–present	Multicultural Counseling Competencies are adopted by ACA

(continued)

TABLE 5.1	SUMMARY OF IMPORTANT HISTORICAL EVENTS
2003–present	Social Justice Focus/Advocacy Competencies are adopted by ACA
2003–present	ASCA's National Model is approved
2005–present	New ethical code adopted
2009–present	New CACREP standards
2009–present	Crisis, Disaster, and Trauma Training is infused into curriculum
2010–present	20/20 Standards: A new vision for counseling
2012–present	Push for licensure portability

© Cengage Learning 2014

SUMMARY

This chapter examined the unique history of the counseling profession. With its early focus on vocational counseling, we saw how, over the years, the counseling profession has moved from the somewhat moralistic, directive approach of vocational guidance to the humanistic approach it adopted starting in the 1940s. We examined how the profession expanded and diversified in the latter part of the twentieth century and how a number of legislative actions during that part of the century greatly influenced the direction and expansion of the profession. We explored how the development of ACA paralleled the expansion and diversification of the profession during the twentieth century. We also saw how the professionalism of the counseling field increased over the years, as evidenced by the expansion of ACA, the creation of ethical standards, the increase in the types and numbers of individuals becoming credentialed, and the establishment of accreditation standards for counseling programs.

As we shifted our focus to the current century, we highlighted a number of issues that will continue to be important to the counseling profession. These included a continued increase in the numbers and types of credentialed counselors; new ACA divisions and the assertion by other divisions of their autonomy from ACA; a focus on evidence-based practice; ACA's endorsement of the Multicultural Counseling Competencies and an expanded focus on multicultural counseling research and training; endorsement by ACA of the Advocacy Competencies and a new social justice focus; adoption of ASCA's National Model and a push for a new training paradigm in school counseling; adoption of a new ethics code; adoption of new CACPREP standards; a new focus on crisis, disaster, and trauma training; and the recent adoption of "20/20: A vision for the future of counseling."

KEY TERMS*

A Mind That Found Itself	Advocacy Competencies
ACA Code of Ethics	Association for Humanistic Counseling (AHC)
Addams, Jane	

*Please see Table 5.1 for descriptions of individuals and key events.

American Association for Counseling and Development (AACD)

American Association of Marriage and Family Counseling (AAMFC, now AAMFT)

American College Counseling Association (ACCA)

American College Personnel Association (ACPA)

American Counseling Association (ACA)

American Mental Health Counselors Association (AMHCA)

American Personnel and Guidance Association (APGA)

American School Counselor Association (ASCA)

Army Alpha

Army Beta

ASCA's National Model

Association for Adult Development and Aging (AADA)

Association for Assessment in Counseling and Education (AACE)

Association for Counselor Education and Supervision (ACES)

Association for Counselors and Educators in Government (ACEG)

Association for Gay, Lesbian and Bisexual Issues in Counseling (AGLBIC)

Association for Multicultural Counseling and Development (AMCD)

Association for Specialists in Group Work (ASGW)

Association for Spiritual, Ethical, and Religious Values in Counseling (ASERVIC)

Atkinson, Donald

Bandura, Albert

Beers, Clifford

Behavioral approaches

Brewer, John

Career counseling

Certified Family Therapist (CFT)

Certification

Child development

Child guidance clinics

Choosing a Career

Choosing a Vocation

Civil Rights Act

Client-centered theories

Client-Centered Therapy: Its Current Practice, Implications and Theory

College counseling centers

Common Factors

Community Mental Health Centers Act

Council for Accreditation of Counseling and Related Educational Programs (CACREP)

Council on Rehabilitation Education (CORE)

Counseling Association for Humanistic Education and Development

Counseling and Psychotherapy

Counselors for Social Justice (CSJ)

Credentialing

Crisis, Disaster, and Trauma Counseling

Cross, William

Cross-cultural counseling

Davis, Jesse

Developmental theories

Directive theories

Division 17 of the APA (Counseling Psychology)

Division Expansion and Autonomy

Donaldson v. O'Connor

Economic Opportunity Act

Education for All Handicapped Children Act (PL94-142)

Electroconvulsive therapy

Elementary and Secondary Education Act

Ellis, Albert

Ethical standards of practice

Ethics

Evidence-based practice

Existential approaches

First comprehensive theory of counseling

Founder of guidance

Founder of the counseling field

Frankl, Viktor

Glasser, William

Great Society

Head Start

Hull House

Humanistic counseling and education

International Association of Addictions and Offender Counselors (IAAOC)

International Association of Marriage and Family Counselors (IAMFC)

Job Corps

Krumboltz, John

Licensure

Licensure portability

Lifespan development

Manpower Development and Training Act

May, Rollo

Microcounseling skills training

Minnesota Point of View

Mirror of Men's Lives

Multicultural counseling

Multicultural Counseling Competencies

National Academy for Certified Mental Health Counselors (NACMHC)

National Association of Social Workers (NASW)

National Board for Certified Counselors (NBCC)

National Career Development Association (NCDA)

National Committee for Mental Hygiene

National Defense Education Act (NDEA)

National Employment Counseling Association (NECA)

National Vocational Guidance Association (NVGA)

Nondirective approach

Parsons, Frank

Pedersen, Paul

Perls, Fritz

Post-traumatic stress disorder, or PTSD

Psychoanalysis

Psychodynamic

Psychodynamic approaches

Rational emotive approach

Reality therapy approach

Reed, Anna

Rehabilitation Act

Rochester Guidance Center

Rogers, Carl

Sanchez de Arevalo

Social Justice Focus

Strong Vocational Interest Blank

Sue, Derald

Total educational context

Trait and factor theory

Transactional analysis

20/20: A Vision for the Future of Counseling

Vocational Bureau

Vocational counseling

Vocational guidance

Vocational guidance movement

Vocational rehabilitation centers

Vocational theory

Voting Rights Act

Wagner O'Day Act

Weaver, Eli

Williamson, E. G.

Wolpe, Joseph

Woodworth's Personal Data Sheet

Work Incentive Program

CURRENT ISSUES AND FUTURE TRENDS IN THE COUNSELING PROFESSION

> From the astrologer came the astronomer, from the alchemist came the chemist, from the mesmerist came the mental specialist. The quack of yesterday is the professor of tomorrow. (Sir Arthur Conan Doyle, 1922, p. 15)

What seems archaic from our past was cutting edge then. And, what seems cutting edge today will seem antiquated in years to come. Yet, as humans, we seem driven to create and progress. Sometimes, what initially is developed for the good of humanity becomes dreaded and feared. For instance, those who discovered the lobotomy and those who created new counseling approaches later shown to be harmful believed that what they were discovering was humane. As we create and invent new things, we are constantly called to monitor their worth. We must be careful to not be swept up by the newness of what we are inventing, and must always take into account moral and ethical implications. Otherwise, we may create something we will later regret:

> When you see something that is technically sweet, you go ahead and do it and you argue about what to do about it only after you have had your technical success. That is the way it was with the atomic bomb. (Oppenheimer, J. R. (1954). In the matter of J. Robert Oppenheimer. Washington, DC: United States Atomic Energy Commission, Personnel Security Board.)

This chapter is about change and progress as our profession develops and integrates new ideas, new technologies, new standards, and new ways of being a counselor. First, the chapter will examine five trends in how we are likely to do counseling: increased training in crisis, disaster, and trauma counseling; life-coaching; genetic counseling; adaptations to classic counseling approaches; and the use of radical new counseling approaches. The chapter will then explore the impact of technology on counselors, with a particular focus on computers and related technologies, counseling online, and guidelines for Internet counseling and other technologies. Next, we will look at trends in health management, including the impact of managed care on counselors, how psychopharmacology affects our work with clients,

---

BOX 6.1 | YOUR VIEW OF THE FUTURE

As a new counselor, make a list of the issues you think are cutting edge and important to the counseling profession. After you read the chapter, your instructor will give you an opportunity to share your list with others in the class.

© Cengage Learning 2014

and changes in the *Diagnostic and Statistical Manual* (DSM). Next we will look at recent and predicted changes in our professional standards, such as our ethical codes, credentialing, accreditation, standards in international counseling, and multicultural and advocacy competencies. We will conclude by focusing on two recent professional issues that will influence our professional identity as counselors: division expansion and division autonomy, and the 20/20 vision statement. But before we start, let's do a quick check-in and see what you think might be some important issues in the near future (see Box 6.1).

COUNSELING

In this section of the chapter we will examine the potential impact of a number of new approaches to counseling, including crisis, disaster, and trauma counseling; life-coaching; genetic counseling; extensions and adaptations to the classic counseling approaches; and radical new approaches.

CRISIS, DISASTER, AND TRAUMA COUNSELING

The shock of hurricane Katrina and the horror of the attack on the twin towers taught us that, as a country, our readiness to react to a disaster was not adequate and that many counselors were unprepared to address *crisis, disasters, and trauma*. Thus, in recent years there has been a push to have counselors trained to work with individuals in crisis, people who have lived through disasters, and those who have experienced traumatic incidents. With this in mind, the 2009 standards of the Council for the Accreditation of Counseling and Related Programs (CACREP, 2009) have included crisis, disaster, and trauma counseling as an area that should be included in the curriculum. Today, programs cannot become accredited without showing they require a separate course in crisis, disaster, or trauma counseling *or* have competencies in these areas infused in already existing courses (Graham, 2010).

LIFE-COACHING

Although it has been seen as a service that was provided by non-counselors, *life-coaching* has slowly and steadily moved into the counseling realm. In contrast to counseling, coaching spends little time examining the past, focuses on solutions and goals, is viewed as a partnership rather than as a therapeutic relationship, is strength-based, does not require diagnosis or third-part payments, and is often conducted in a less-structured environment than is counseling (Patterson, 2008;

Shallcross, 2011). Life coaches will not necessarily replace counselors, but rather, coaching may be a new hat counselors can wear as part of a treatment modality or helping strategy.

Counselors may find coaching an attractive alternative to counseling because of the increased freedom and reduced paperwork. Additionally, the coaching relationship is less clinical, and clients may experience less stigma seeing a coach as compared to a counselor. Drawbacks to coaching include the fact that it may not be conducive to digging up underlying, core issues, and the fact that few, if any, health insurance companies cover coaching services (Shallcross, 2011). In addition, because coaching sacrifices depth in favor of efficiency, it probably has limited efficacy in treating more serious mental health issues. In the coming years, we will see whether life coaches become more prevalent, and whether coaching slowly moves into the mainstream of counseling services.

GENETIC COUNSELING

As the genetic causes of various physical and mental health problems are discovered, *genetic counseling* promises to be an important aspect of what the counselor does. In fact, the U.S. Bureau of Labor Statistics (2008) reports there are over 59,000 genetic counselors. Genetic counselors hold graduate degrees in any number of areas including law, medicine, and counseling, and it is projected that growth in this profession will be "faster than average." The American Board of Genetic Counseling (ABGC, 2010) accredits genetic counseling programs and offers a certification in genetic counseling.

In many cases, the identification of the gene that causes a disorder or carries a predisposition to a disorder will precede the actual treatment of the disease. For instance, as a result of genetic research, individuals now have the ability to know whether or not they have the gene for Huntington's Disease (HD), a debilitating, progressive, neurological disease which has no cure and leads to a horrible death within five years (Pence, 2004; 2010). HD is one of many genetic diseases. For instance, some forms of diabetes, cancer, dementia, heart disorders, bipolar disorders, and schizophrenia, as well as tendencies toward depression, anxiety disorders, and a host of other physical and mental health problems will likely be found to have genetic links.

The ability to identify whether or not one carries a gene for a disorder raises a number of issues, including whether or not one should be tested for a disease, how a person should live his or her life knowing that a gene for a disease is present, whether one should have children if not tested or if one discovers the gene is present, and whether to share the knowledge that one carries a gene for a particular disease with family and friends (McDaniel, 2005; Pence, 2010). These are difficult personal decisions with which a well-trained counselor might assist (Brown, 2008; Douthit, 2006).

ADAPTATIONS TO THE CLASSIC COUNSELING APPROACHES

The twentieth century saw the development of a number of classic approaches to counseling. As we moved toward the end of the century, adaptations to those approaches began to arise. Today, these changes continue. For instance, many of the *post-psychoanalytic models* have moved significantly away from stressing the role *instincts* play in the formation of the *ego* and toward the importance of relationships in ego formation. Some of the more popular approaches include *Eriksen's psychosocial theory, object relations theory, self-psychology,* and *relational-intersubjectivity approaches* (Neukrug, 2011). Also, many adaptations of *cognitive-behavioral therapy* have been developed and have drastically moved away from the more traditional approaches practiced by the early theorists. Some of these include *multimodal therapy,* which assesses a wide range of client domains; *dialectical behavior therapy* (DBT), which uses a mixture of mindfulness, behavioral analysis, and cognitive techniques; *acceptance and commitment therapy* (ACT), which views behaviors and cognitions as a complex web of relational associations and uses a mixture of cognitive therapy, behavioral techniques and Eastern philosophy; and *constructivist therapy,* which views therapy as a mechanism to help clients understand their meaning-making systems through cognitive schemas. As these approaches gain in popularity, we will increasingly find counselors using them.

RADICAL NEW APPROACHES

In addition to adaptations of the classic approaches, in recent years more radical approaches have been developed and have found a niche in the practice of counseling. For instance, *eye movement desensitization response* (EMDR) therapy focuses on how rhythmic stimulation (e.g., rapid eye movements, tapping) can lessen symptoms associated with traumatic events; *motivational interviewing* uses empathy, "change talk," collaboration, and gentle nudging to induce change in clients; *gender aware therapy (feminist therapy* and therapy that emphasizes men's issues when *counseling men*) focuses on the way that men and women are impacted by cultural stereotypes and how men and women can develop new, more adaptive roles; *positive psychology* helps clients (and nonclients) focus on their strengths and helps them develop a positive framework so they can live more fulfilling lives (see Box 6.2); and *complementary, alternative, and integrative therapies* use a holistic approach that focuses on all aspects of a person's wellness, such as wellness instruments (see Chapter 3), body awareness therapy, and scented oils to help people heal and become whole (Neukrug, 2011).

TECHNOLOGY

COMPUTERS AND RELATED TECHNOLOGIES

As of 2009, 77% of homes in the United States had computers and 68% of these used the Internet (U.S. Department of Commerce, 2011). These are amazing statistics,

BOX 6.2	WHAT IS YOUR POSITIVITY RATIO?

Want to determine your positivity ratio? Go to http://www.positivityratio.com/ and take the quiz.

especially in light of the fact that only 20% of households had a computer in 1992, only 19% had Internet access in 1998, and the first PCs were sold about 30 years ago (U.S. Department of Commerce, 2000).

Counselors and other mental health professionals have quickly adapted to the use of computers (Layne & Hohenshil, 2005). For instance, counselors now use computers and other technologies (e.g., interactive videos, CDs, DVDs) in case management, record keeping, diagnosis, case conceptualization, testing and assessment, career counseling, record keeping, billing, marketing, and assisting clients in the learning of new skills (e.g., parenting skills, assertiveness training, vocational skills training) (Goss & Anthony, 2009).

Computers and the use of the Internet have also been shown to be successful in training counselors and other helping professionals (Conn, Roberts, & Powell, 2009; Hayes, 2008; Trepal, Haberssroh, Duffey, & Evans, 2007; Vaccaro & Lambie, 2007). But perhaps the greatest change in the use of technology has been the expansion of the Internet. The Internet has brought us home pages for our professional associations, e-mails to colleagues and supervisors, distribution lists and electronic mailing lists of professionals who have common interests, video streaming for professional conferencing, Web-based courses, Web-based portfolios, search engines for research, downloadable files on just about any counseling-related subject you might think of, interactive websites where you can learn more about the counseling field, online supervision (Goss & Anthony, 2009) (see Box 6.3), and the controversial topic of counseling online (see next section).

Today, journals like the *Journal of Computing in Higher Education* and the *Journal of Technology in Counseling* address cutting-edge technological issues. As we move into the future, technology will continue to change the delivery of counseling services and the ways in which counselors learn.

COUNSELING ONLINE

When I first learned about counseling on the Internet I thought it was a joke. "How could one develop the depth of the relationship online?" "How could one read another person's nonverbal behaviors?" And "How could one soothe a person in his or her deepest moments of pain?" I pondered. But recently something has changed. I think it was the counselor avatar I saw one of my students show in class. Suddenly, I realized the potential of counseling over the Internet. I am slowly becoming a convert. So given that it's here to stay, let's look at some of the

BOX 6.3	MERGING THE PAST WITH THE FUTURE

As I write this book, I am in the process of developing two websites entitled "Stories of the Great Therapists" and "Great Therapists of the Twentieth Century (GTTC)." These sites enable individuals to hear oral stories about famous therapists and interact with animations of famous therapists to learn more about them. If you get a chance, go to: www.odu.edu/sgt and look for these websites.

TABLE 6.1 | DRAWBACKS AND BENEFITS OF INTERNET COUNSELING

Drawbacks	Benefits
• It can allow clients to hide behind the anonymity of the Internet (especially if a video camera is not used).	• Because Internet counseling can sometimes seem more anonymous, clients might be able to reveal issues they would be embarrassed or afraid to reveal in person.
• It raises concerns about how to respond if a client is suicidal or homicidal.	• It provides counseling services for those individuals who live in areas where there are few mental health professionals.
• It can raise concerns about security and confidentiality if other individuals can hack into a counseling session.	
• It may lower the ability of the counselor to appropriately read the client.	• It provides additional options for the supervision of the counselor through the use of professional discussion boards and online supervision.
• It prevents the kind of here-and-now relationship that is present when people are face-to-face.	• It has the potential to offer lower cost services because rented office space is not needed.
• It raises credentialing issues for individuals conducting counseling, as interstate commerce laws may not apply on the Internet.	• It can allow clients to seek out counseling services at times at which traditional counseling services may not be available (e.g., 6 a.m., 10 p.m.).
• It may not be covered by insurance companies.	
• Technological difficulties could be problematic.	• It allows clients concerned about leaving their homes (e.g., those with agoraphobia or disabilities or those who live in high crime areas) to feel safe.
• Counseling online typically moves more slowly than face-to-face counseling.	
• For clients counseled through a typing method (e.g., e-mail), the amount communicated is typically less than when speaking and counselor response time can be slower.	• It allows counselors to potentially counsel multiple clients at one time, as counseling online typically moves more slowly than face-to-face counseling.

© Cengage Learning 2014

positives and negatives of *counseling online* (Haberstroh, Parr, Bradley, Morgan-Fleming, & Gee, 2008) (see Table 6.1).

Today, there is even a professional association that has arisen that supports online counseling. Requirements for joining the American Distance Counseling Association (ADCA) (see http://adca-online.org) include a state license in a mental health profession and one year of online counseling experience. Given that counseling online is certainly different than face-to-face counseling, a number of guidelines have been developed to ensure that clients are afforded the best and most ethical services possible. The next section examines some of these.

GUIDELINES FOR INTERNET COUNSELING AND OTHER TECHNOLOGIES

Knowing that online counseling was inevitably going to gain popularity, ACA developed *Ethical Standards for Internet Counseling* in 1999 (Kocet, 2006). More recently, ACA incorporated ethical guidelines for a wide range of technological applications into its 2005 ethics code (ACA, 2005). You are encouraged to read the many specific items in *"Section A.12: Technology Applications."* Briefly summarizing some of the highlights of this aspect of the code, we find it is important to do the following:

1. Inform clients of the benefits and limitations of technology.
2. Ensure that clients are physically, emotionally, and intellectually able to use the technology, and if not, find a way to deliver services face-to-face if possible.
3. Ensure that technology doesn't violate the law.
4. Seek "business, legal, and technical assistance"—especially if services cross state or national borders.
5. Ensure that clients give informed consent (see code for a wide range of informed consent particulars).
6. Ensure that any websites are properly maintained (see code for a wide range of activities related to this item).

TRENDS IN HEALTH MANAGEMENT

Recent changes in health management have dramatically affected how counselors work. Some of these will likely continue as we move further into this century. This section of the chapter will explore the effects of managed care, psychopharmacology, and the use of the *Diagnostic and Statistical Manual* (DSM).

MANAGED CARE

Health Maintenance Organizations (HMOs), *Preferred Provider Organizations* (PPOs), and *Employee Assistance Programs* (EAPs) have arisen to monitor the kinds of services afforded to the consumers they serve. Usually, they do this by overseeing medical and mental health services: for example, ensuring that consumers have adequate, but not limitless, services. Whether they have done this successfully has certainly been debated (Braun & Cox, 2005; Wilcoxon, Magnuson, & Norem, 2008). One thing is clear, however—*managed care* has cut into the ability of private practitioners to make a living by limiting counseling sessions.

Ironically, managed care has provided another possible place of employment for counselors (Clawson, Henderson, Schweiger, & Collins, 2008; Ritter, Vakalahi, & Kiernan-Stern, 2009). For instance, some managed care organizations have designated clinicians for whom they provide office space, and subscribers must see one of these clinicians unless they receive special authorization to see someone else. Organizations such as these will often hire master's-level counselors. Other managed care organizations select specific private practices to which they will refer, and counselors are often included as designated providers. Finally, due to the overseeing of clinicians' work by managed care, some HMOs, PPOs, and EPAs will hire counselors to review the casework of other clinicians.

PSYCHOPHARMACOLOGY

Remember when advertising a drug was unheard of? Well, maybe you're too young— but I do. And trust me: it was not that long ago. Now, drugs are everywhere, and despite the fact that the modern-day use of *psychotropic medications* started about 50 years ago, recent advances in brain research and the subsequent development of new medications have had a dramatic effect on treatment strategies (Preston, O'Neal, & Talaga, 2010).

Today, there are promising new medications that can be beneficial in the treatment of psychoses, depression, anxiety, attention deficit disorder, dementia, and other mental disorders and emotional disturbances (Kalat, 2009; Schatzberg & Nemeroff, 2009). With 13% of Americans taking *antidepressants*, 6% taking *antianxiety drugs*, and others taking additional psychotropic medications, literally millions of Americans now take medication as a partial or full treatment for psychological problems (U.S. Department of Health and Human Services, 2010). In today's world, to treat an individual without knowledge of the effectiveness of these medications would be incompetent practice, as noted in the ACA ethical code:

> Counselors recognize the need for continuing education to acquire and maintain a reasonable level of awareness of current scientific and professional information in their fields of activity. They take steps to maintain competence in the skills they use, are open to new procedures, and keep current with the diverse populations and specific populations with whom they work. (ACA, 2005 Code of Ethics. Reprinted by permission.)

DSM AND DIAGNOSIS

Developed by the American Psychiatric Association, the first *Diagnostic and Statistical Manual* (DSM-I) was published in 1952 and, over the years, has become the system by which almost all mental health clinicians make diagnoses. Although there are benefits and drawbacks to the current DSM (*DSM-IV-TR*) (see Table 6.2), all counselors today need a working knowledge of this classification system. Whereas counseling programs had traditionally played down the importance of *diagnosis* (Jones, 2010; Patureau-Hatchett, 2009), this attitude has changed as counselors have realized that sometimes a diagnosis helps in treatment planning, that a diagnosis is typically needed by insurance companies and managed care organizations if treatment is to be authorized, and that knowledge of diagnosis is necessary if we are to talk intelligently with our related mental health professionals.

DSM-IV-TR is a big book, and takes time to learn. And now that counselors have become adept at using it, it's going to change. In 2013 we will have a new DSM—the *Diagnostic and Statistical Manual-5 (DSM-5)*. And, some of the changes will be radical, such as a new definition of a *mental disorder* and the proposed collapsing of three of the five current axes. Axis I and Axis II (the Mental Disorders) will be collapsed with Axis III—Medical Conditions. (American Psychiatric

TABLE 6.2	DRAWBACKS AND BENEFITS OF DSM-IV-TR DIAGNOSIS

Drawbacks	Benefits
• Objectifies and depersonalizes the person, as we view him or her in a dispassionate manner, much like watching a rat in a maze.	• Offers us a way of understanding the person more deeply, as we are challenged to make a thorough assessment of the client.
• Labeling can lead to a self-fulfilling prophecy whereby the individual is seen as the diagnosis, is treated in a manner consistent with that diagnosis, and therefore is reinforced for that diagnostic label.	• By understanding the diagnostic label and by knowing the research in the field, we can better match treatment plans and use of medication with the diagnosis, thus leading to better therapeutic outcomes.
• Provides clinicians with a common language that enables them to discuss clients as if they were not real people with real concerns.	• Offers clinicians a common language by which they can consult with one another and jointly come up with more effective treatment decisions.
• Creates artificial categories that we buy into, and thus we believe such diagnoses exist. In fact, such diagnoses are a social construction and are thus a function of the values of society.	• Provides clear-cut diagnostic categories from which research designs can be generated and new treatments found.

© Cengage Learning 2014

Association, 2010). Many other changes are proposed. No doubt, older counselors and new counseling students will soon be learning a new diagnostic classification system.

CHANGING STANDARDS

ETHICAL CODE

The 2005 *ethics code of ACA* includes a number of revisions that challenge counselors to work in new ways. For instance, the code replaces the term *clear and imminent danger* with *serious and foreseeable harm*, increases the *restrictions on romantic and sexual relationships*, softens the admissibility of *dual relationships* (now, often called *multiple relationships*), includes a statement on counseling for *end-of-life care* for terminally ill clients, increases *attention to social and cultural issues*, allows counselors to *refrain from making a diagnosis*, highlights the importance of having a *scientific basis for treatment modalities*, requires counselors to have a *transfer plan* for clients, adds *guidelines for how and when to use technology*, and includes a statement about the *right to confidentiality for deceased clients* (ACA, 2005; Kaplan et al., 2009). This new code will affect the manner in which many counselors work in the 21st century.

Ethics codes change periodically, and that is positive, for such change generally means they better match the needs of consumers and the roles of counselors.

However, change is also not easy. Learning about the intricacies of a new code and how to apply the changes can take time, and some counselors who do not spend this time will be lagging behind in their ability to offer ethical services. Perhaps this is why many credentialing boards today require a certain number of their continuing education requirements to be in ethics.

CREDENTIALING

Counselor *credentialing* has continued to expand, and today, there are about 80,000 National Certified Counselors (NCCs) and 120,000 Licensed Professional Counselors (LPCs) (ACA, 2011a; National Board for Certified Counselors [NBCC], 2011a). With NBCC now offering subspecialty certifications in clinical mental health counseling, school counseling, and addictions counseling and with every state in the country as well as Puerto Rico and the District of Columbia having licensure laws, credentialing has and will continue to become increasingly important for job attainment, third-party reimbursement, and professional recognition.

Finally, now that counselors have obtained licensure in all 50 states, portability of licenses between states has become a pressing issue. Currently, ACA is pushing for states to allow for portability and the American Association of State Counseling Boards (AASCB) has designed a system that would allow counselors to register their credentials, which state licensure boards could access and make decisions about whether individuals could be licensed within their states (AASCB, 2012; ACA, 2012c). This is an important first step to having *national portability*, sometimes called *reciprocity*, between states (AASCB, 2012).

COUNCIL FOR ACCREDITATION OF COUNSELING AND RELATED EDUCATIONAL PROGRAMS (CACREP)

Today, well over half of the counseling programs in the country are *accredited*, and this number will undoubtedly increase quickly in the years to come. These new programs will be following the recent 2009 CACREP standards, which have made some important changes that will affect the counseling profession. A few of these changes included the following (CACREP, 2009):

1. The requirement of training in crisis, disaster, and trauma counseling.
2. An increased focus on leadership training, advocacy, and social justice.
3. A requirement that, after 2013, new full-time faculty hired into a CACREP-accredited program must have graduated from a doctoral program in counselor education and supervision.
4. Movement toward assessment of what students have learned in contrast to only looking at what they are taught.
5. The removal of the community counseling and gerontological counseling specialty areas.
6. The addition of a specialty area in addiction counseling, and the merging of the student affairs specialty area with the college counseling specialty area into student affairs and college counseling.

7. The requirement of 60 semester credits for clinical mental health counseling (starting in 2013); marital, couple, and family counseling; and addiction counseling. (The requirement of 48 semester credits for career counseling, student affairs and college counseling, and school counseling is the same as in previous years).

Such changes will undoubtedly impact how counselor education is taught and the ways in which new students implement counseling practice.

INTERNATIONAL REGISTRY OF COUNSELLOR EDUCATION PROGRAMS (IRCEP)

The International Registry of Counsellor Education Programs (IRCEP) is an organization that was created by the Council for Accreditation of Counseling and Related Educational Programs (CACREP) in 2009 (CACREP, 2012a). A subsidiary of CACREP, IRCEP's vision is to "promote the ongoing development and recognition of the counselling profession worldwide through the creation of a registry of approved counsellor education programs that use common professional requirements essential to the education and training of counsellors regardless of culture, country, region, work setting, or educational system" (CACREP, 2012b, Vision of IRCEP section) (note that the British spelling of "counselling" is used). IRCEP's mission focuses on: creating standards, approving programs, maintaining a registry of approved programs, and networking counselors, students, and professionals in the field in an effort to foster excellence (CACREP, 2012b).

CACREP accredited programs can apply for IRCEP approval, and today, about 30 universities are IRCEP approved (CACREP, 2012c). The benefits of IRCEP approval include a review from an international group of counselors, the prestige of international recognition, and more.

MULTICULTURAL COUNSELING AND ADVOCACY COMPETENCIES

Developed in 1991 by the Association for Multicultural Counseling and Development (AMCD), the *Multicultural Counseling Competencies* were officially adopted by ACA in 2002. These competencies delineate *attitudes and beliefs, knowledge, and skills* in three areas: the counselor's awareness of the client's worldview, the counselor's awareness of his or her own cultural values and biases, and the counselor's ability to use culturally appropriate intervention strategies (Arredondo, 1999; Arredondo et al., 1996). Then, in 2003, ACA endorsed the *Advocacy Competencies*, which encompass three areas (client/student, school/community, public arena), each of which are divided into two levels: whether the counselor is *acting on behalf of the competency area* or *acting with the competency area* (Toporek, Lewis, & Crethar, 2009). The purpose of the competencies is to ensure that counselors are actively taking steps toward helping clients overcome some of the external and oppressive barriers they face in their lives.

Although both sets of competencies are described in Chapter 10, they are highlighted here because they have greatly impacted, and will continue to affect, counselors' work with clients from nondominant groups. To be an effective counselor today means you must be a culturally competent counselor who fights against social injustices.

PROFESSIONAL ISSUES

Division Expansion and Division Autonomy

Since 2000, we have seen the addition of two new divisions of ACA: the Association for Creativity in Counseling (ACC) and Counselors for Social Justice (CSJ). With nineteen divisions covering a vast array of counseling interests, ACA is a diverse group. After nearly a century of pulling together the divisions into one unified force under ACA, some divisions are asserting that their differences are too great to continue to justify this unification. Some initiatives, such as the development, in 2003, of the American School Counselor Association's National Model (*ASCA National Model*; ASCA, 2005) which increases the focus of the school counselor toward student learning, and the American Mental Health Counselors Association's (AMHCA) push towards a greater clinical focus has made these divisions deeper. Today, one can join some divisions without the being a member of ACA. In fact, whereas a large proportion of ACA use to be school counselors, today, they represent only 10 percent of its membership (ACA, 2009).

Although we are all counselors, we have many different strengths and areas of expertise, which is reflected in our individual professional identities and the professional associations to which we belong. What will happen to ACA and its divisions? At this point, it's anybody's guess, but wherever we go, we'll end up stronger.

A Push Toward Unity: The 20/20 Vision Statement

There are many contrasts in life. Just as I write a section on the split between ACA and some divisions, I switch gears and focus on unity. In sharp contrast to the problems between some divisions and ACA is the development of the *20/20 vision statement*. In 2009, ACA, along with the 30 counseling organizations, decided it was time for the counseling profession to develop a shared vision—an understanding that would unite all counselors toward the future. Then, at the ACA national conference in 2010 these counseling associations came together to develop "20/20: A Vision of the Future of Counseling." This shared vision includes the following:

- Sharing a common professional identity is critical for counselors.
- Presenting ourselves as a unified profession has multiple benefits.
- Working together to improve the public perception of counseling and to advocate for professional issues will strengthen the profession.
- Creating a portability system for licensure will benefit counselors and strengthen the counseling profession.
- Expanding and promoting our research base is essential to the efficacy of professional counselors and to the public perception of the profession.
- Focusing on students and prospective students is necessary to ensure the ongoing health of the counseling profession.
- Promoting client welfare and advocating for the populations we serve is a primary focus of the counseling profession. (ACA, 2010b, "Principles section")

BOX 6.4	THE CLASSES VIEW OF THE FUTURE

Remember the list of "cutting edge" issues you wrote down when you began this chapter. Perhaps you and the rest of the class can share lists. What similarities did you find to the list in the chapter? What differences? What items did you include that seem critical and which I should probably add to in this chapter? Discuss, and then let me know.

Today, the 20/20 delegates continue to work, and as noted in Chapter 1, they recently came up with a shared definition of counseling. It is hoped that their work will result in increased unity through shared missions and that goals will coalesce (see Box 6.4).

SUMMARY

This chapter examined current issues and future trends in the counseling profession. Beginning with how we provide counseling, we noted that counselors had not been adequately trained in crisis, disaster, and trauma counseling and that training in these areas is now required in counseling programs. We pointed out the differences between life-coaching and counseling and noted that for some counselors, life-coaching may be a viable alternative or addition to doing counseling. Noting that research on the genome has made it easier for individuals to discover whether they may have the gene for a disease, we pointed out the importance of genetic counseling. We also noted a number of extensions and adoptions to the classic approaches to counseling and then identified some new, radical approaches to counseling—all of which we may see more of in the years to come.

Moving on to the area of technology, we identified a whole range of activities that may be changed due to technological innovations in the field of counseling. However, of all the changes, we noted that counseling online is probably the most interesting and the most controversial. We thus delineated a number of drawbacks and benefits to counseling online. Partly due to the ethical concerns raised with counseling individuals online, ethical guidelines were developed to monitor the use of this technology. These guidelines are currently embedded in ACA ethics code. We identified aspects related to the ethical use of technology and encouraged readers to examine "Section A.12: Technology Applications" of the code in detail.

Relative to trends in health management, we pointed out that managed care has led to the limiting of the number of counseling sessions as oversight and cost cutting has become important. However, we also noted that some counselors find jobs at managed care organizations. We next stressed that a large percentage of Americans today use psychotropic medications and that knowledge of such medications was becoming increasingly important if counselors are to practice ethically and competently. The last part of this section involved a discussion of the *Diagnostic and Statistical Manual*. Here we identified a number of drawbacks and benefits of the DSM and also noted that the new DSM-5, which will include many changes, will likely be published in 2013.

As the chapter continued we noted that in the area of standards we will see continued numbers of individuals becoming credentialed and discussed recent push toward licensure portability. We pointed out that more programs will become CACREP accredited and identified some of the changes in the 2009 standards. We also noted that CACPREP has developed IRCEP, which is an international registry of counselor education programs whose purpose is to promote the development of counseling and counselor education worldwide. This part of the chapter concluded with a brief discussion of ACA's endorsement of the Multicultural Counseling Competencies and of the Advocacy Competencies. These two important standards have had, and will continue to have, a great impact on how counselors work and will be discussed further in Chapter 10: Multicultural Counseling and Social Justice: The Fourth and Fifth Forces.

The chapter concluded with a brief discussion of recent division expansion and division autonomy and the fact that this has changed the face of the counseling profession today. However, it ended by highlighting the fact that 30 organizations have endorsed the recent 20/20 vision statement which delineates a shared vision of counseling.

KEY TERMS

Acceptance and commitment therapy (ACT)

Accredited

Acting on behalf of the competency area or acting with the competency area

Adaptations to the classic counseling approaches

Advocacy Competencies

American Association of State Counseling Boards (AASCB)

American Board of Genetic Counseling (ABGC)

American Distance Counseling Association (ADCA)

American Mental Health Counselors Association (AMHCA)

American School Counselor Association (ASCA)

Antianxiety drugs

Antidepressants

ASCA National Model

Association for Multicultural Counseling and Development (AMCD)

Association for Creativity in Counseling (ACC)

Attention to social and cultural issues

Attitudes and beliefs, knowledge, and skills

Clear and imminent danger

Cognitive-behavioral therapy

Complementary, alternative, and integrative therapies

Computers and related technologies

Constructivist therapy

Council for Accreditation of Counseling and Related Programs (CACREP)

Counseling men

Counseling online

Counselors for Social Justice (CSJ)

Credentialing

Crisis, disasters, and trauma

Diagnosis

Diagnostic and Statistical Manual DSM-IV-TR

Diagnostic and Statistical Manual-5 (DSM-5)

Dialectical behavior therapy (DBT)

Dual relationships

Ego

Employee Assistance Programs (EAPs)

End-of-life care

Eriksen's psychosocial theory

Ethical Standards for Internet Counseling

Ethics code of ACA

Eye movement desensitization response (EMDR)

Feminist therapy

Gender aware therapy

Genetic counseling

Guidelines for how and when to use technology

Guidelines for Internet Counseling and Other Technologies

Health Maintenance Organizations (HMOs)

International Registry of Counsellor Education Programs (IRCEP)

Journal of Computing in Higher Education

Journal of Technology in Counseling

Licensed Professional Counselors (LPCs)

Life-coaching

Managed care

Mental disorder

Motivational interviewing

Multicultural Counseling Competencies

Multimodal therapy

Multiple relationships

National Certified Counselors (NCCs)

National portability

Object relations theory

Positive psychology

Post-psychoanalytic models

Preferred Provider Organizations (PPOs)

Psychotropic medications

Radical new approaches

Reciprocity

Refrain from making a diagnosis

Relational-intersubjectivity approaches

Restrictions on romantic and sexual relationships

Right to confidentiality for deceased clients

Scientific basis for treatment modalities

"Section A.12: Technology Applications"

Self-psychology

Serious and foreseeable harm

Transfer plan

Trends in health management

20/20 vision statement

STANDARDS IN THE COUNSELING PROFESSION

This last section identifies important standards in the counseling profession and helps us further delineate who we are and how we distinguish ourselves from related mental health professionals. We begin by focusing on the CACREP accreditation process, the accrediting body for most counseling programs, although we also list accrediting bodies in related mental health fields. Next, we define credentialing and highlight the many credentials in the counseling profession. We contrast these with related credentials in non-counseling mental health professions. The next standard we discuss is ethics, and we distinguish ethics from values and morality and examine the relationship between ethics and the law. We explore the importance of an ethical code and spend a fair amount of time discussing ACA's ethical code, although we list other, related codes. We point out ethical "hot spots," models of ethical decision-making, how to report ethical violations and legal issues related to ethical violations, and the importance of malpractice insurance and of knowing our "best practices" so we can best serve clients and avoid lawsuits. Finally, the last chapter of this section focuses on multicultural counseling and suggests that social justice work is a sub-section of this important area. We highlight reasons why counseling is not working for many clients from nondominant groups and go on to define a number of important words and terms associated with multicultural counseling. We offer models to help us understand ourselves and clients from diverse cultures and describe two relatively recent standards: the Multicultural Counseling Competencies and the Advocacy Standards.

Accreditation in Counseling and Related Fields

> Unfortunately, the United States is cluttered with bogus "institutions of higher learning" that issue master's and doctor's "degrees" that are not worth the paper they are printed on and that can even get you into legal trouble if you attempt to proffer them as legitimate credentials.... Avoid these rip-offs as you would the plague. (Keith-Spiegel, P., & Wiederman, M. W. (2000). *The complete guide to graduate school admission: Psychology, counseling and related professions* (2nd ed.). Mahwah, NJ: Erlbaum.)

When I graduated from my doctoral program there were no accredited programs in counseling. The professional identity of the counselor and counselor educator were still forming, and it was not unusual to find others with related degrees in fields like psychology, teaching alongside those who had degrees in counselor education. It's now 30 years later and we have come far. In fact, today, the Counsel for Accreditation of Counseling and Related Educational Programs (CACREP) requires that full-time faculty who are hired to teach in accredited programs must have doctoral degrees in counselor education, preferably from a CACREP-accredited program. Accreditation has pushed us toward a unified professional identity, one in which all faculty in counselor education will have degrees in counselor education, one in which all students will eventually graduate from accredited programs, and one in which all programs will be following the same curriculum guidelines. This chapter explores accreditation. We will look at the many benefits of accreditation as well as a few of its drawbacks. We will identify the accreditation process in related mental health fields. But mostly, we will look at CACREP—explore its history, how it currently accredits programs, and we will discuss the future of accreditation in the counseling profession. Let's start with the *history of CACREP*.

A BRIEF HISTORY OF CACREP

> The acronym CACREP is a mouthful to say.... In fact, without the Council for Accreditation of Counseling and Related Educational Programs, counseling would be far less credible as a profession compared to other human service fields that

have such an agency. (Sweeney, T. J. (1992). CACREP: Precursors, promises, and prospects. *Journal of Counseling and Development*, 70(6), 667–672.)

Professionals in mental health fields often have responsibilities that heavily impact the lives of others, many of whom are exceptionally vulnerable. Shoddy or inept training can result in a helper harming his or her clients, oftentimes inadvertently. Accreditation has been one way of assuring that programs are meeting minimum standards while promoting excellence in training professionals. Some of the first programs to offer training standards were in social work during the early part of the twentieth century—soon to be followed by psychology programs in the mid-1940s (Morales, Sheafor, & Scott, 2007; Sheridan, Matarazzo, & Nelson, 1995). Although starting a little later than these closely related professions, the counseling field has made great strides in its efforts toward accreditation.

The idea of having standards for counselor education programs can actually be traced back to the 1940s (Sweeney, 1992); however, it was not until the 1960s that such standards began to take form with the adoption of training standards for elementary school counselors, secondary school counselors, and student personnel workers in higher education (Altekruse & Wittmer, 1991). Soon, the Association for Counselor Education and Supervision (ACES) began to examine the possibility of merging these various standards into one document entitled the *Standards for the Preparation of Counselors and Other Personnel Service Specialists* (Altekruse & Wittmer, 1991; Sweeney, 1995). Although the standards were being unofficially used as early as 1973, it was not until 1979 that the American Personnel and Guidance Association (APGA), now the American Counseling Association (ACA), officially adopted them, and in 1981 APGA created the Council for the Accreditation of Counseling and Related Educational Programs (CACREP), a freestanding incorporated legal body that would oversee the accrediting process (Brooks & Gerstein, 1990). Adoption of the CACREP standards started slowly, and they have gone through a number of revisions prior to taking on their most recent form, which went into effect in January of 2009. Today, these standards are the benchmark to which most counseling programs try to conform (see CACREP, 2012d).

Considering the vast number of changes that most programs have to make and the amount of time it takes to implement such changes, it is a tribute to CACREP that about two-thirds of the close to 450 counseling programs are accredited (CACREP, 2012e; National Board for Certified Counselors [NBCC], 2012; Ritchie & Bobby, 2011). Of these, over 50 programs offer doctoral degrees in counselor education (CACREP, 2012e). With New York and California fairly recently obtaining licensure for counselors, it is likely that there will be a push in those states to accredit additional counseling programs. As you might guess, all evidence seems to indicate that there will be continued expansion of the number of CACREP-accredited programs.

BENEFITS OF ACCREDITATION

One of the reasons that CACREP accreditation has spread so rapidly is the many *benefits of accreditation* (D'Andrea & Liu, 2009; McGlothlin & Davis, 2004; O'Brien, 2009). Some of these include the following:

- Accreditation is the impetus for setting high standards and almost always results in improved programs and a stronger sense of professional identity.

| BOX 7.1 | Developing Accreditation Standards |

In small groups, or as a class, consider what you would require of a counseling program if you were an accreditation body charged with developing accreditation standards.
  Specifically, speak to each of the following:

1. Admissions requirements
2. Curriculum
3. Number of credits
4. Faculty/student ratio
5. Minimum number of full-time faculty
6. Minimum full-time to adjunct faculty ratio
7. Degrees and experience of faculty
8. Comprehensive exam and/or thesis
9. Acceptability of online or distance learning courses
10. Number of total hours for field placement (e.g., practicum and internship)
11. How you might assess the program
12. Other?

© Cengage Learning 2014

- Accredited programs often attract better students and better faculty.
- Students in accredited programs study from a common curriculum, are generally more knowledgeable about core counseling issues, and usually participate in more intensive and longer fieldwork experiences.
- CACREP accreditation is often the standard used by credentialing bodies to determine who is eligible to become certified or licensed.
- Students in accredited programs can take the national counselor exam to become nationally certified counselors (NCC) far earlier than students from non-accredited programs.
- Some third-party payers are beginning to reimburse only students who graduate from CACREP-accredited programs.
- It is often easier to be admitted to a doctoral program if you have graduated from a CACREP-accredited program.
- Those who graduate from accredited programs generally have better job opportunities.

Although you can see why CACREP-accredited programs may have an edge over non-accredited programs, a non-accredited program may still be a strong program. In fact, some have argued that accreditation limits the focus of the curriculum and the kinds of faculty who can teach, and does not allow small programs to thrive (see Box 7.1).

A QUICK OVERVIEW OF CACREP STANDARDS

Today, CACREP (2009) offers standards for master's degrees in *clinical mental health counseling* (54 semester credits until 2013, thereafter 60 credits), *school counseling* (48 credits), *student affairs and college counseling* (48 credits), *career counseling*

(48 credits), *addiction counseling* (60 credits), and *marriage, couple, and family counseling* (60 credits). It also offers standards for the *doctoral degree in counselor education and supervision*. Please note, however, that you will find CACREP-accredited master's degree programs in counseling with different names from the ones just noted (e.g., community counseling). These programs were accredited under previous standards. As their accreditation periods run out, they will either become re-accredited under one of the new names or less likely, give up their accreditation.

MASTER'S-LEVEL STANDARDS

For all master's programs seeking CACREP accreditation, the *master's-level standards* delineate a variety of requirements within three primary areas: The *learning environment, professional identity,* and *professional practice.* In addition, each specialty area has a wide range of additional curriculum requirements that need to be covered if that specialty area is to be accredited. The following offers brief descriptions of these areas.

THE LEARNING ENVIRONMENT This aspect of the accreditation process sets minimal standards for structure and evaluation of the institution, the academic unit (the counseling program), faculty and staff, and evaluation. For instance, institutions are expected to support the counseling program financially, have adequate research and scholarly resources available, provide personal counseling for students, provide support for faculty to participate in professional organizations, provide an adequate instructional environment, and much more.

The academic unit should require the minimum number of credits as noted earlier; make attempts at attracting and retaining diverse students; provide a mission statement; have an orientation for students; have a 10:1 faculty student ratio; provide a student handbook; show evidence that students are covered by professional liability insurance; for practicum or internship, have no more than 12 students in group supervision with one supervisor; have an admissions process that considers cultural context, aptitude, and career goals; and more.

In relation to faculty and staff, CACREP recommends specific teaching loads, requires a minimum of three full-time faculty, mandates that faculty have relevant experience and earned doctorates in counselor education, requires faculty to be involved with counseling professional organizations and engaged in scholarship and service activities, requires programs to have a faculty member who directs the program and one who oversees field placements, and more.

The last area of the learning environment is evaluation. Here CACREP requires that programs have a process of systematic evaluation of the program, that students evaluate faculty, and that field placements and graduates from programs are evaluated.

PROFESSIONAL IDENTITY The second primary area that CACREP reviews, professional identity, focuses on the foundation of the program (e.g., mission statement and objectives) and knowledge that should be learned in the program. The focus on the foundations of programs includes ensuring that each program has a mission statement, specifies program objectives, and promotes student participation in professional organizations. Knowledge of the program includes having appropriate syllabi, ensuring that technology is infused throughout the program, ensuring that research on counseling is infused throughout the coursework, and demonstrating that eight "common-core curricular experiences" are covered in the program (see Table 7.1).

PROFESSIONAL PRACTICE The last primary area that CACREP examines, professional practice, specifies a broad range of qualifications needed to supervise students in their field placements (practicum and internship). In addition, it identifies the minimum number of hours for practicum and for internship. For practicum, students must complete a minimum of 100 hours of field work with at least 40 of them being direct service hours (working with clients). One hour of individual or triadic

TABLE 7.1 | CACREP'S EIGHT COMMON-CORE CURRICULAR EXPERIENCES

Common-Core Curriculum Area	Brief Description*
1. Professional Orientation and Ethical Practice	"… studies that provide an understanding of all of the following aspects of professional functioning …" (p. 10)
2. Social and Cultural Diversity	"… studies that provide an understanding of the cultural context of relationships, issues, and trends in a multicultural society …" (p. 10)
3. Human Growth and Development	"… studies that provide an understanding of the nature and needs of persons at all developmental levels and in multicultural contexts …" (p. 11)
4. Career Development	"… studies that provide an understanding of career development and related life factors …" (p. 12)
5. Helping Relationships	"… studies that provide an understanding of the counseling process in a multicultural society …" (p. 12)
6. Group Work	"… studies that provide both theoretical and experiential understandings of group purpose, development, dynamics, theories, methods, skills, and other group approaches in a multicultural society …" (p. 13)
7. Assessment	"… studies that provide an understanding of individual and group approaches to assessment and evaluation in a multicultural society …" (p. 13)
8. Research and Program Evaluation	"… studies that provide an understanding of research methods, statistical analysis, needs assessment, and program evaluation …" (p. 14)

*Each common-core curriculum has numerous objectives, which are not listed above. For a full description of the common-core curricula, go to www.cacrep.org, click on "download a copy of the 2009 CACREP Standards," and review pages 10 through 14.

Source: Council for Accreditation of Counseling and Related Programs (CACREP). CACREP 2009 standards.

supervision (two supervisees with one supervisor), per week, and 1.5 hours of group supervision, per week, are also required. For internship, students must complete a minimum of 600 hours of fieldwork with at least 240 of them being direct service hours. Also required for internship is 1 hour per week of individual and/or triadic supervision and 1.5 hours, per week, of group supervision.

SPECIALTY AREA DOMAINS It has been said that an individual who obtains a degree in counseling is first a counselor, and secondarily a school counselor, clinical mental health counselor, college and student affairs counselor, and so forth. Thus, all students who graduate from CACREP-accredited programs have coursework in the *common-core curriculum* areas noted in Table 7.1 and must complete the same number of field placement hours. However, there certainly are differences among specialty areas, so CACREP also delineates the knowledge, skills, and practices that students must learn based on their *specialty areas*. For instance, clinical mental health counseling requires student learning in the following knowledge, skills, and practice areas: foundations; counseling, prevention, and intervention; diversity and advocacy; assessment; research and evaluation; and diagnosis. The specialty areas of student affairs and college counseling and of marriage, couple, and family counseling require the same knowledge, skills, and practice areas with the exception of diagnosis. School counseling also requires the same areas with the exception of diagnosis and with the addition of academic development, collaboration and consultation, and leadership. However, specific content within these areas can vary greatly. Since this information would take too long to describe in this text, if you would like further information about these domains see pp. 30–51 of the 2009 CACREP standards (click on the 2009 CACREP standards at www.cacrep.org).

DOCTORAL-LEVEL STANDARDS

CACREP-accredited doctoral programs in counselor education and supervision must conform to *doctoral-level standards*. First, they must show that students they accept have addressed all of the master's level standards as noted above. Thus, if a student enters a doctoral program from a non-CACREP-accredited university, the program must show how this student would meet equivalence with a student who had graduated from a CACREP-accredited program. For instance, sometimes students from non-CACREP-accredited programs will have to take additional courses to show equivalency. In addition, doctoral programs require a minimum of 96 semester hours of graduate level credits. Also, as with master's programs, guidelines for learning environment, professional identity, and professional practice are offered for doctoral programs as well as specific learning outcomes for supervision, teaching, research and scholarship, counseling, and leadership and advocacy.

FINAL THOUGHTS ON CACREP ACCREDITATION

To meet the accreditation standards, most programs find that they need to undertake at least moderate changes. Following the changes, and often while they are being made, a *self-study report* is written that spells out how the program meets each of the sections of the program standards. This report is then sent, with an

BOX 7.2	ASSESSING YOUR PROGRAM

Your instructor will make available the CACREP accreditation standards or tell you how to access them. The instructor will then assign various aspects of the standards to individuals or small groups (e.g., a group might be assigned the core-curricular standards). After reviewing the standards:

1. Summarize the aspect of the standards you examined.
2. Using those aspects of the standards you reviewed, critically evaluate your counseling program.
3. Make suggestions for change in your counseling program as a result of your critical review in part b.
4. Critically review the standards. What makes sense? What could be changed?

application, to the CACREP office, which has independent readers review the report. If the report is accepted, then a CACREP team is appointed to visit and review the program and make a final recommendation for or against accreditation (see Box 7.2). Ultimately, the CACREP board decides on whether or not to accept this recommendation. Finally, CACREP recently created the International Registry of Counselor Education Programs (IRCEP) whose focus is to foster excellence in training programs internationally. A new organization, IRCEP is discussed in Chapter 6: Current Issues and Future Trends in the Counseling Profession (see www.ircep.org).

OTHER ACCREDITING BODIES

A number of other accreditation bodies set standards in related fields. For instance, the Council on Rehabilitation Education (CORE, 2011) accredits rehabilitation counseling programs. Although CORE and CACREP discussed the possibility of a merger, such talks fell through and are currently on hold (The CACREP Connection, 2007). In another related field, we find training centers being approved by the American Association of Pastoral Counselors (AAPC, 2005–2012d). These centers do not offer degrees, but do offer training in pastoral counseling. Usually, a pastoral counselor already has obtained his or her degree in counseling or a related field prior to going to one of these training centers.

In the field of psychology, the Commission on Accreditation (CoA) of the American Psychological Association currently sets standards for doctoral-level programs in counseling and clinical psychology (APA, 2012b). The Council on Social Work Education (CSWE, 2012) is responsible for the accreditation of both undergraduate and graduate social work programs, while the American Association for Marriage and Family Therapy's, Commission on Accreditation for Marital and Family Therapy Education (COAMFTE) is an accrediting body for marriage and family therapy programs (AAMFT, 2002–2011b). Although somewhat in conflict with CACREP's accreditation of marriage and family therapy counseling programs, this commission has accredited about 115 marriage and family therapy programs in the United States and Canada (AAMFT, 2002–2011c). Finally, the

Council for Standards in Human Service Education (CSHSE) sets standards for undergraduate human services programs (CSHSE, 2010).

SUMMARY

This chapter examined accreditation in counseling and related fields and began with a brief history of the Council for the Accreditation of Counseling and Related Educational Programs (CACREP). It was first noted that in the counseling profession, the idea of standards dates back to the 1940s, although the official CACREP standards were not adopted until 1981. Making quick progress, today CACREP accredits about two-thirds of institutions that offer counseling programs and currently accredits 50 doctoral programs.

The next part of the chapter highlighted some of the benefits of accreditation, including better programs, better faculty, better students, a stronger professional identity, more field experiences, an easier time becoming credentialed, the maintenance of high standards, the possibility of having an easier time getting third-party reimbursements, and an easier time getting a job or getting into a doctoral program. On the other hand, we noted that accreditation may limit the kinds of faculty and courses taught and makes it difficult for small programs to thrive. Offering a quick overview of the CACREP standards, we pointed out that the 2009 standards is for the accreditation of programs in clinical mental health counseling, school counseling, student affairs and college counseling, career counseling, addiction counseling, and marriage, couple, and family counseling. CACREP also accredits doctoral programs in counselor education and supervision. It was pointed out that the CACREP standards delineate requirements within three primary areas: the learning environment, professional identity, and professional practice. Each of these areas was briefly described. In addition, it was noted that on the master's level, specialty area domains of knowledge, skills, and practice are described and on the doctoral level, specific learning outcomes are delineated. It was stressed that an individual who obtains a degree in counseling is first a counselor, and secondarily a school counselor, clinical mental health counselor, college and student affairs counselor, and so forth. Finally, the accreditation process was described briefly.

In addition to CACREP, other accreditation or approval processes exist and those were listed in this chapter. Some of the more common ones in the mental health fields include the Council on Rehabilitation Education (CORE), the approval process of the American Association of Pastoral Counselors (AAPC), the American Psychological Association's Commission on Accreditation (CoA), the Council on Social Work Education (CSWE), the American Association of Marriage and Family Therapists' (AAMFT), Commission on Accreditation for Marital and Family Therapy Education (COAMFTE), and the Council for Standards in Human Service Education (CSHSE).

KEY TERMS

Addiction counseling

American Association for Marriage and Family Therapy (AAMFT)

American Association of Pastoral Counselors (AAPC)

American Counseling Association (ACA)

CREDENTIALING IN COUNSELING AND RELATED FIELDS

> It is the year 1224 in the city of Sicily, and a young physician gathers his credentials to file for a medical license. He collects proof that he has studied for over eight years in physick, surgery and logic. He proudly adds a letter from his master physician mentor extolling his extraordinary skill in leech placement and uncanny facility in astrology. The young physician nervously heads off, credentials in hand, to be examined in public by a committee of master physicians. If he passes, the emperor himself will issue a medical license. If he fails, he will be jailed if he attempts to practice medicine again. (Scoville, E., & Newman, J. S. (2009, May). A very brief history of credentialing. *ACP Hospitalist*. Retrieved from http://www.acphospitalist.org/archives/2009/05/ newman.htm. Reprinted by permission of the American College of Physicians.)

As you can see from the above quote, credentialing in the allied health professions can be traced back to the 13th century when the Holy Roman Empire set requirements for the practice of medicine (Hosie, 1991). Interestingly, today, the process of obtaining a credential is not dissimilar to the process in 1224 Sicily. First, you study for a number of years. Then you demonstrate that a mentor (e.g., supervisor) deems you ready, and finally, you take a credentialing exam. However, unlike the young physician in the quote above, *you* won't get jailed if you fail your credentialing exam.

This chapter will explore the credentialing process. First, we will offer a brief overview of the history of credentialing in the mental health professions. Then, we will describe benefits of credentialing. The difference between registration, certification, and licensure will next be explained. This will be followed up by a description of the different kinds of credentials in the counseling profession and then in related mental health professions.

A BRIEF HISTORY OF CREDENTIALING

Despite the fact that the credentialing of professionals started hundreds of years ago, in the mental health professions, credentialing is a modern-day phenomenon. Although Puerto Rico enacted a law regulating the practice of social work in 1934, and California did the same in 1945, credentialing of social workers was slow to pick up speed (Biggerstaff, 1995; Dyeson, 2004). In fact, it wasn't until the 1980s, when 25 states passed regulation of social worker credentials (generally called *licenses*), that this process really took off, and by 1993 all states and the District of Columbia obtained regulation of social workers. Today, the Association of Social Work Boards (ASWB) helps states with their licensing process (see www.aswb.org/). Paralleling the licensing of social workers, in 1960 the Academy of Certified Social Workers (ACSW) was established and represented the first national credential (the "ACSW") for those who had the qualifications to join (National Association of Social Workers [NASW], 2012b).

In the field of psychology, the American Board of Professional Psychology was formed in 1947 and, in 1949, first offered *board certifications* of psychologists in three specialty areas (Bent, Packard, & Goldberg, 2009). Today, the purpose of this certification is to show excellence in a specialty area, and the board now offers certification in 14 specialty areas. Meanwhile, during the 1950s California and New York became two of the first states to license psychologists (Cummings, 1990), and by 1977, all 50 states had enacted a process for the licensure of psychologists.

Although the first credentialing of counselors can be traced back to the certification of school counselors in the 1940s (Bradley, 1995), other forms of counselor credentialing did not begin until the 1970s. In 1974, rehabilitation counseling set the stage by establishing the Certified Rehabilitation Counselor (CRC) credential through the Commission on Rehabilitation Counselor Certification (CRCC) (Livingston, 1979). Then, in 1982 the National Board for Certified Counselors (NBCC) was established to "monitor a national certification system, to identify those counselors who have voluntarily sought and obtained certification, and to maintain a register of those counselors" (NBCC, 2011b, Our History section, para. 1). Over the years, NBCC has expanded and has certified over 80,000 counselors as National Certified Counselors (NCC), National Certified School Counselors (NCSC), Certified Clinical Mental Health Counselors (CCMHC), and Master Addictions Counselors (MAC) (NBCC, 2011a, 2011b).

Spurred on by psychologists trying to prevent counselors the right to independent practice, in 1974 the American Personnel and Guidance Association (APGA) (now the American Counseling Association [ACA]) created the *Licensure Committee* to assist in the development and passage of credentialing bills for counselors (Bloom et al., 1990; Brooks & Gerstein, 1990). In 1976, Virginia became the first state to pass a licensing law for counselors (the *first counselor licensure*) and other states soon followed suit. By 2010, all 50 states, Puerto Rico, and the District of Columbia offered licensing and today there are approximately 120,000 licensed counselors nationally (see ACA, 2011a).

During the latter part of the twentieth century, many states passed licensing laws for marriage and family counselors. Today, every state licenses marriage or family counselors, usually called Licensed Marriage and Family Therapist (LMFT). Requirements for licensing can vary dramatically from state to state as a function of whether the state follows the curriculum guidelines set by the Council for the Accreditation of Counseling and Related Educational Professions (CACREP), the

guidelines set forth by the American Association of Marriage and Family Therapists' (AAMFT) Commission on Accreditation of Marriage and Family Therapy
(COAMFTE), or other guidelines. The American Association for Marital and Family
Therapy Regulatory Boards (AAMFTB) helps states regulate the licensing process. In
addition to licensure, in 1994 the International Association of Marriage and Family
Counselors (IAMFC), a division of ACA, developed a certification process through
the National Credentialing Academy (NCA) that enables a marriage and family counselor to become a Certified Family Therapist (CFT) (NCA, n.d.a).

BENEFITS OF CREDENTIALING

Credentialing offers many benefits to the counselor, the counseling profession, and
the consumer of counseling services (Bloom, 1996; Corey, Corey, & Callanan,
2011). Some of the benefits of credentialing include the following:

1. *Increased professional identity.* A credential is a method of delimiting a
   professional group by establishing certain criteria that all credentialed members
   must meet. This helps identify who belongs to the profession and highlights
   areas of expertise of the professional group.
2. *Increased sense of professionalism.* Credentialing increases the status of
   members of a profession because it assures minimum levels of competency
   have been met by those who practice.
3. *Demonstrating expertise within a profession.* Credentialing shows that some
   individuals within a profession may have more expertise in a specialized area
   than others within that same professional group (e.g., a counselor with a
   certification as a Master Addictions Counselor versus one who does not
   have this credential), thus making it easier for the consumer to choose which
   professionals they may wish to see.
4. *Gaining parity.* Credentialing helps counselors achieve parity with closely
   related mental health professions in the areas of status, salary, and insurance
   reimbursement.
5. *Protecting the public.* Credentials help the public identify those individuals
   who have the appropriate training and skills versus those who do not.

TYPES OF CREDENTIALING

Although credentialing takes many forms, the three most common include registration, certification, and licensure.

REGISTRATION

Registration is the simplest form of credentialing and involves a listing of the
members of a particular professional group (Sweeney, 1991). Registration, which
is generally regulated by each state, implies that each registered individual has
acquired minimal competence, such as a college degree and/or apprenticeship in
his or her particular professional area. Registration of professional groups usually

implies that there is little or no regulation of that group. Generally registration involves a modest fee. Today, few states provide registration for professionals, instead opting for the more rigid credentialing standards of certification and/or licensure.

CERTIFICATION

Certification involves the formal recognition that individuals within a professional group have met certain predetermined standards of professionalism (ACA, 2012d). Although more rigorous than registration, certification is less demanding than licensure. Generally, certification is seen as a *protection of a title* (Remley & Herlihy, 2010); that is, it attests to a person's attainment of a certain level of competence but does not define the *scope and practice* of a professional (what a person can do and where he or she can do it). A yearly fee must usually be paid to maintain certification.

Certification is often overseen by national boards, such as the National Board for Certified Counselors (NBCC, 2011a, 2011b). Although national certification suggests that a certain level of competence in a professional field has been achieved, unless a state legislates that the specific national certification will be used at the state level, such certification carries little or no legal clout. Many individuals will nevertheless obtain certification because it is an indication that they have mastered a body of knowledge, which can sometimes be important for hiring and promotion. Certification often requires ongoing continuing education for an individual to maintain his or her credential.

Finally, some certifications are offered by states in specialized areas (e.g., substance abuse, child abuse), and professionals should contact their appropriate state regulatory office to inquire what certifications a state offers and the rules and competencies needed to become certified in their states.

LICENSURE

The most rigorous form of credentialing is *licensure*. Generally regulated by states, licensure denotes that the licensed individual has met rigorous standards and that individuals without licenses cannot practice in that particular professional arena (ACA, 2011b, 2012d). Whereas certification protects the title only, licensure generally defines the scope of what an individual can and cannot do. For instance, in Virginia the counselor licensing law not only defines the requirements one must meet to become licensed, but also defines what is meant by counseling, who can do it, the limits of *confidentiality and privileged communication*, legal regulations related to suspected violations of the law (e.g., child abuse), and other various restrictions and regulations (Virginia Board of Counseling, 2011).

In terms of day-to-day professional functioning, the most important aspect of counselor licensure has become the fact that in most states licensure carries with it legislation that mandates *third-party reimbursement* privileges. Such legislation requires insurance companies to reimburse licensed individuals for counseling and psychotherapy. As with certification, licensure generally involves a yearly fee, and often continuing education requirements are mandated (see Box 8.1).

BOX 8.1	THE TOPSY-TURVY WORLD OF CREDENTIALING

Professional school counselors are required by law and/or regulation in every state, the District of Columbia, Guam, Puerto Rico, and the Virgin Islands to obtain a state-issued credential in order to be employed in public schools. In some states, this credential is called "certification"; others term it "licensure" or "endorsement." (Lum, 2010, p. 2)

As is evidenced by this quote, there are many caveats to the definitions of registration, certification, and licensing. For instance, although I was a licensed psychologist in Massachusetts and New Hampshire, when I moved to Virginia, the psychology licensing board would not license me. I was, however, quite content to obtain my license as a professional counselor (LPC). You see, state licenses are often not reciprocal.

Also, whereas some state boards of education use the word *certification* for school personnel (e.g., teachers, school counselors, school psychologists), others use the word *licensure*. In both cases, it usually means the same—that the individual has successfully graduated from a state-approved program in his or her respective area. However, there is no rhyme or reason why one state will use the words *certified school counselor* while another will use *licensed school counselor*. And, in these cases, the words do not carry the same meaning as the national certifications or state licenses described earlier.

Finally, you will find other idiosyncratic usages of the words *certification* and *licensure* depending on the state in which you live. So check your state regulations to be sure you know how credentialing operates where you live.

© Cengage Learning 2014

CREDENTIALING FOR COUNSELORS

Within the past 30 years great strides have been made in the credentialing of counselors. From the credentialing of rehabilitation counselors, to the expansion of counselor certification and licensure, to the recent certification of family counselors, the credentialing process in counseling has now taken firm hold. The following describes some of the more prominent counselor credentials.

COUNSELOR LICENSURE

As noted earlier, the movement toward all states providing professional counselor licensure began in 1976 when Virginia became the first state to pass a counselor licensing law. Today there are about 120,000 licensed counselors nationally (see Bradley, 1995; ACA, 2011a). Although usually called Licensed Professional Counselors (LPCs), some states use alternative names (e.g., Licensed Counselor). As some densely populated states like New York and California have just recently approved counselor licensure, the current number of LPCs will surely rise quickly. Although the National Counselor Exam (NCE, see next section) is used by many states for the licensure exam, licensure is almost always more involved than certification. For instance, in addition to an exam, licensure generally includes a minimum of two years of post-master's-degree supervision, sometimes additional coursework, and other requirements depending on the state.

Finally, now that all 50 states have counselor licensure, ACA and the American Association of State Counseling Boards (AASCB) has designed a system in which counselors can register their credentials with AASCB and state licensure boards can access them and determine whether a counselor can be licensed within their state (AASCB, 2012; ACA, 2012c; Kaplan, 2012). This *portability* or *reciprocity* of license would make it easier for counselors to move between states.

NATIONAL COUNSELOR CERTIFICATION

Established in 1982 to maintain and monitor a National Counselor Certification process, the National Board for Certified Counselors (NBCC) has credentialed over 80,000 counselors as National Certified Counselors (NCCs) (NBCC, 2011a). Students who have graduated from a CACREP-approved program may take the National Counselor Exam (NCE) prior to their graduation and, assuming they pass, are certified upon graduation. Those who have not graduated from a CACREP-approved program may take the NCE immediately following graduation; however, they become an NCC only after they have successfully completed a minimum of two years of post-master's experience with 100 hours of supervision and 3,000 hours of work experience (NBCC, 2011c). Finally, many states use the NCE or the National Clinical Mental Health Counselor Exam (NCMHCE; see next section) as part of their licensing process (NBCC, 2011d).

SPECIALTY CERTIFICATIONS IN COUNSELING

As noted earlier, in 1974 the Commission on Rehabilitation Counselor Certification (CRCC, 2011; Livingston, 1979) was one of the first organizations to offer credentialing in counseling, and since its inception, CRCC has credentialed over 35,000 Certified Rehabilitation Counselors (CRCs). CRCC's purpose is to promote quality services for individuals with disabilities and provide leadership and advocacy in rehabilitation counseling.

To highlight expertise in particular counseling specialty areas, NBCC offers three *specialty certifications* in addition to the NCC described in the last section: Certified Clinical Mental Health Counselor (CCMHC), National Certified School Counselor (NCSC), and Master Addictions Counselor (MAC). The NCC is a pre- or co-requisite to these specialties (NBCC, 2011a, 2011b).

Have expertise in couples and family counseling? Then you might be interested in becoming a Certified Family Therapist (CFT). As noted earlier, this certification was developed by the International Association of Marriage and Family Counselors (IAMFC) through the National Credentialing Academy (NCA). Its primary purpose has been to provide a national certification process to ensure professional growth (NCA, n.d.b). The certification is open to individuals who hold a wide-range of graduate degrees in the helping professions and can show verification of graduate training in marriage and family work, post-graduate supervision, and letters of recommendations or endorsement (NCA, n.d.c).

Finally, each state may have its own unique certifications for master level counselors (e.g., substance abuse, child abuse) and you should check with the regulatory office of your state to see if there may be some other counselor certification for which you might be eligible.

CREDENTIALED SCHOOL COUNSELORS

State boards of education credential school counselors but vary on whether they call the credentials a *license, certification*, or simply an *endorsement*. In any case, the requirements are the same: to have graduated from a *state-approved school counseling program*. Some states credential K–12 school counselors while others credential school counselors at the elementary, middle, and high school levels. Not all states currently require school counselors at all grade levels (American School Counselor Association, 2006–2012).

COUNSELOR CREDENTIALING: A UNIFYING FORCE

In the past 25 years, the credentialing process has done much for the professionalization of the counseling field. Signifying competence in our field, counselor licensure or certification has become a unifying force that suggests a high level of professionalism. Similar to the medical field, in which one is first a physician and secondarily a cardiologist, pediatrician, psychiatrist, and so forth, a counselor is first a counselor and secondarily a Licensed Professional Counselor, National Certified Counselor, Certified Rehabilitation Counselor, Master Addictions Counselor, National Certified School Counselor, Certified Clinical Mental Health Counselor, Certified Family Therapist, or Credentialed School Counselor (see Box 8.2).

CREDENTIALING IN RELATED GRADUATE-LEVEL HELPING PROFESSIONS

> It is recognized that there is competition for clients among professionals providing mental health services and that there is also concern about the degree of preparation and expertise of a number of professions to deliver those services. (Garcia, 1990, p. 495)

Although written over 20 years ago, this quote is still relevant today. Competition between credentialed mental health professionals is real, and whether or not a professional is credentialed will make a huge difference in one's ability to obtain

---

BOX 8.2	CREDENTIALS OBTAINED, CREDENTIALS DESIRED

In your class, have each person write down all the credentials he or she holds—even if they are not in the helping professions. Have your instructor place them on the board, and discuss what it took to obtain each credential. Then, write all the credentials that each person in the class wants to obtain. Have your instructor place them on the board and discuss what is needed to obtain each credential.

---

clients. Let's take a look at some of the different credentials available to our professional cousins.

SOCIAL WORK CREDENTIALING

On the national level, a number of credentials exist for the many master's-level social workers. For instance, master's-level social workers can be members of the Academy of Certified Social Workers (ACSW), become Licensed Clinical Social Workers (LCSWs), be Qualified Clinical Social Workers (QCSW), be Diplomates in Clinical Social Work (DCSW), or hold a number of specialty certifications (NASW, 2012b).

ACADEMY OF CERTIFIED SOCIAL WORKERS (ACSW) To be a member of ACSW, an individual needs to be a member of NASW, have two years of postgraduate social work employment and supervision, be professionally validated by a supervisor and two work colleagues, and have 20 hours of continuing education.

LICENSED CLINICAL SOCIAL WORKER (LCSW) Like counselor licensure, becoming an LCSW is state-driven, and requirements can vary from state to state. However, most states require a 60-credit master's degree in social work, supervision beyond the master's degree, and a licensing exam in order to obtain one's LCSW.

QUALIFIED CLINICAL SOCIAL WORKER (QCSW) These social workers need to be members of NASW, document 3,000 hours of postgraduate supervised clinical experience, and hold state social work licenses or certifications based on an exam (e.g., LCSW) or be members of ACSW.

DIPLOMATE IN CLINICAL SOCIAL WORK (DCSW) Diplomates in clinical social work need to be members of NASW, document five years of postgraduate clinical experience, complete 20 hours of clinical course work, provide professional evaluations of their work and show evidence of knowledge of ethics, and hold state clinical licenses or be members of ACSW.

SPECIALTY CERTIFICATIONS There are *eight specialty certifications in social work*, each with different qualifications. They include certifications in clinical work, gerontology, hospice and palliative work; youth and family; health care; addictions; case management; and education (NASW, 2012c).

PSYCHOLOGY CREDENTIALING

The most frequent kinds of credentials in psychology include licensed psychologist, credentialed school psychologist, and certified school psychologist.

LICENSED PSYCHOLOGIST Generally, those who hold doctorates in clinical psychology, counseling psychology, or a Psy.D. can become *licensed psychologists*. The requirements for licensure as a psychologist are fairly consistent from state to state and require two years of post-doctoral clinical supervision and the passing of a national licensing exam, although each state sets its own cut-off scores for passing. Licensure as a psychologist ensures access to third-party reimbursement and allows one to practice independently.

PSYCHOLOGY CERTIFICATIONS Established in 1947, the American Board of Professional Psychology (ABPP) is the major national credentialing body for psychologists and offers *board certifications in 14 areas*: Clinical child and adolescent psychology, clinical health psychology, clinical neuropsychology, clinical psychology, cognitive and behavioral psychology, counseling psychology, couple and family psychology, forensic psychology, group psychology, organizational and business consulting psychology, psychoanalysis in psychology, rehabilitation psychology, and school psychology. The certification process includes a review of credentials, an examination of peer-reviewed case examples, an oral exam, and sometimes a written exam (APBB, 2012).

CREDENTIALED SCHOOL PSYCHOLOGIST State boards of education certify *credentialed school psychologists*, with most states requiring a master's degree or more (e.g., Ed.S.) in school psychology. States vary on whether they call the credential a license or a certification, but in either case, the requirements are the same: to have graduated from a state-approved school psychology program.

NATIONAL CERTIFIED SCHOOL PSYCHOLOGIST Sponsored by the National Association of School Psychologists (NASP), certification as a National Certified School Psychologist (NCSP) requires 60 graduate semester hours of coursework, a 1,200-hour internship, and passing of a national exam (NASP, n.d.b). Currently, there are approximately 12,000 National Certified School Psychologists (E. Rossen, personal communication, March 9, 2011).

COUPLE, MARRIAGE, AND FAMILY THERAPY CREDENTIALING

Today, each state has enacted a credentialing law for couple, marriage, and family counseling, with credentialed professionals being called Licensed Marriage and Family Therapists (LMFT). In some cases, state licensure boards have followed the guidelines set forth by the American Association of Marriage and Family Therapists (AAMFT). In other cases, licensure has been subsumed under the counseling board and tends to follow CACREP guidelines. Still other boards have set their own guidelines for *couple, marriage, and family therapy credentialing*.

PSYCHIATRY CREDENTIALING

Because licensure as a physician is not specialty-specific, individuals are licensed as medical doctors, not pediatricians, psychiatrists, surgeons, and so forth. Therefore, a physician who obtains a license within a state can theoretically practice in any area of medicine. However, because hospital accreditation standards generally require the hiring of *board-certified physicians*, almost all physicians today are board-certified in a specialty area. Board certification means that the physician has had additional experience in the specialty area and has taken and passed a rigorous exam in that area. Thus, most psychiatrists are not only licensed physicians within the state where they practice, but are generally *board-certified in psychiatry* (American Board of Medical Specialties, 2006–2012).

PSYCHIATRIC-MENTAL HEALTH NURSE CREDENTIALING

There are two levels of psychiatric-mental health nurses—the basic and the advanced. Basic Psychiatric Mental Health Nurses (PMHN) generally do not have advanced degrees and can work with clients and families doing entry-level psychiatric nursing. In contrast, Psychiatric-Mental Health—Advanced Practice Registered Nurses (PMH—APRN) can do a wide-range of mental health services, can prescribe medication, and can receive third-party reimbursement in many states (American Psychiatric Nurses Association, n.d.).

ART THERAPY, PASTORAL COUNSELING, AND OTHER CERTIFICATIONS

Credentialing of mental health professionals is not limited to the credentials listed above. For instance, certification exists for some kinds of expressive therapies (e.g., Registered Art Therapist [ATR], see Art Therapy Credentials Board, 2007). Similarly, the American Association for Pastoral Counselors (AAPC, 2005–2009b) offers a certification process for those who are interested in becoming Certified Pastoral Counselors (CPCs). Generally, these individuals cannot become licensed unless they hold degrees in areas in which the state offers licensure (e.g., counseling, social work, psychology). However, some states will allow them to apply for licensure if they take additional coursework that matches the curriculum requirements of the existing state licenses (Wadeson, 2004). No doubt, other credentials in related mental health professions exist.

OVERVIEW

Table 8.1 lists the various credentials identified in this chapter along with their acronyms and where you can find additional information about them.

TABLE 8.1 | VARIOUS CREDENTIALS, ACRONYMS, AND WEB ADDRESSES

Counselor Credentialing	Acronym	Website for Additional Information
Licensed Professional Counselor	LPC	www.aascb.org/
National Certified Counselor	NCC	www.nbcc.org/OurCertifications
Certified Rehabilitation Counselor	CRC	www.crccertification.com/
Certified Clinical Mental Health Counselor	CCMHC	www.nbcc.org/OurCertifications
National Certified School Counselor	NCSC	www.nbcc.org/OurCertifications

(continued)

TABLE 8.1	VARIOUS CREDENTIALS, ACRONYMS, AND WEB ADDRESSES	

Counselor Credentialing	Acronym	Website for Additional Information
Master Addictions Counselor	MAC	www.nbcc.org/OurCertifications
Certified Family Therapist	CFT	http://nationalcredentialingacademy.com/
Credentialed School Counselor	—	www.schoolcounselor.org/content.asp?contentid=242
Social Work Credentialing		
Licensed Clinical Social Worker	LCSW	www.aswb.org/ (click "find a licensing board")
Academy of Certified Social Workers	ACSW	www.naswdc.org/credentials/
Diplomate in Clinical Social Work	DCSW	www.naswdc.org/credentials/
Eight Specialty Certifications	—	www.naswdc.org/credentials/
Psychology Credentialing		
Licensed Psychologist	—	www.asppb.net/
Fourteen Specialty Certifications	—	www.abpp.org (click "Member Specialty Boards")
Credentialed School Psychologist	—	www.nasponline.org/certification/state_info_list.aspx
National Certified School Psychologist	NCSP	www.nasponline.org/certification/index.aspx
Couple, Marriage, and Family Therapy Credentialing		
Licensed Marriage and Family Therapist	LMFT	aamft.org (click "directories" then "MFT Licensing Boards")
Psychiatry Credentialing		
Licensed Physician	—	www.fsmb.org/
Board Certification	—	www.abms.org/About_Board_Certification/
Psychiatric-Mental Health Nurse Credentialing		
Basic Psychiatric Mental Health Nurse	PMHN	
Psychiatric Mental Health—Advanced Practice Registered Nurse	PMH—APRN	www.apna.org (click "About Psychiatric Health Nurses")
Other Certifications		
Registered Art Therapist	ATR	www.atcb.org/registration_atr/
Certified Pastoral Counselor	CPC	aapc.org (click "Member" then "Certifications")

LOBBYING FOR CREDENTIALING AND COUNSELING-RELATED ISSUES

Political action committees, lobbyists, and offering free lunches to legislators—certainly these are not within the realm of counselors, or are they? In point of fact, *lobbying* and grassroots efforts that counseling associations take to introduce and/or defeat legislation have become crucial to the survival of the counseling profession (see ACA, 2012e). For instance, if counselors hadn't lobbied for the establishment of elementary and middle school counselors, they would not be in existence today. Similarly, counselors had to continually push to obtain licensure of professional counselors in all 50 states. And, in a circular manner, once we obtain our credentials, we have more credibility to lobby for our profession.

Today, we must continue to lobby to ensure that we are included as providers for various health insurance plans, to lower counselor to student ratios in the schools, and to ensure that state and federal funding sources are aware of counselors in all specialty areas. Who pays for our lobbying efforts? We do! A portion of our professional association membership fees goes to pay for lobbyists and legislative initiatives that will support our own interests. When you do *not* join your professional association, you reap the benefits for which others are paying!

SUMMARY

This chapter presented an overview of credentialing in the mental health professions with a particular focus on counselor credentialing. We began by noting that credentialing in the allied health professions is hundreds of years old, but highlighted the fact that credentialing in the mental health professions is relatively new, starting in the twentieth century.

We pointed out that early credentialing started with regulation of social workers in Puerto Rico and California, and noted that by 1993 all 50 states had licensure of social workers, which is overseen by the Association of Social Work Boards (ASWB). We noted that psychology offered certifications in the 1940s and today offers 14 certification specialty areas. We also pointed out that by 1977 all 50 states had psychology licensure.

In counseling, we noted that certification of school counselors started in the 1940s, that in 1974 the first rehabilitation counselor was certified, and in 1976 Virginia was the first state to license counselors. In 2010, all 50 states, Puerto Rico, and the District of Columbia had counselor licensure. We also noted that today, the National Board for Certified Counselors (NBCC) offers certification as a National Certified Counselor (NCC), and subspecialties as a National Certified School Counselor (NCSC), Certified Clinical Mental Health Counselor (CCMHC), and Master Addictions Counselors (MAC). We also noted that every state licenses marriage and family counselors and that there is a national certification as a family therapist (CFT).

Some of the many benefits of credentialing that we highlighted included increased professional identity, increased sense of professionalism, identifying expertise within a profession, gaining parity with other mental health professionals, and protection of the public.

Next in the chapter, we described the difference between registration, certification, and licensure, with licensure being the most rigorous, as it defines the requirements to become credentialed and defines the scope of what a person can do.

The next part of the chapter identified the various types of credentialed counselors as well as related credentialed mental health professionals. For counselors, we identified Licensed Professional Counselors (LPCs), National Certified Counselors (NCCs), Certified Rehabilitation Counselors (CRCs), Certified Clinical Mental Health Counselors (CCMHCs), National Certified School Counselors (NCSCs), Master Addictions Counselors (MACs), Certified Family Therapists, and credentialed school counselors. We noted a new system for licensure portability developed by ACA and AASCB.

Some of the credentialed professionals we noted in social work included Licensed Clinical Social Workers (LCSWs), members of the Academy of Certified Social Workers (ACSW), Qualified Clinical Social Workers (QCSWs), Diplomates in Clinical Social Work (DCSWs), and those with specialty certifications in one or more of eight areas. In psychology, we distinguished between licensed psychologists (counseling, clinical, and Psy.D.) and school psychologists (state-credentialed and National Certified School Psychologists [NCSPs]). We also noted that the American Board of Professional Psychology (ABPP) offers board certifications in 14 areas.

Other credentialed professionals we noted were Licensed Marriage and Family Therapists (LMFTs), board certified psychiatrists, basic Psychiatric Mental Health Nurses (PMHN), Psychiatric-Mental Health—Advanced Practice Registered Nurses (PMH—APRN), Registered Art Therapists (ATR), and Certified Pastoral Counselors (CPCs). Table 8.1 identified most of these credentials and gave websites where you can find more information about them. The chapter concluded with a quick note about the importance of lobbying for credentialing and counseling-related issues.

KEY TERMS*

Academy of Certified Social Workers (ACSW)

American Association for Marital and Family Therapy Regulatory Boards (AAMFTB)

American Association for Pastoral Counselors (AAPC)

American Association of Marriage and Family Therapists (AAMFT)

American Association of State Counseling Boards (AASCB)

American Board of Professional Psychology (ABPP)

American Counseling Association (ACA)

American Personnel and Guidance Association (APGA)

Art Therapy Credentials Board

Association of Social Work Boards (ASWB)

Basic Psychiatric-Mental Health Nurses (PMHN)

Benefits of credentialing

Board certification

Board certifications in psychology in 14 areas

Board-certified in psychiatry

Board-certified physicians

Certification

---

*Please see Table 8.1 for the names and websites for most of the credentials covered in this chapter.

Certified Clinical Mental Health Counselor (CCMHC)

Certified Family Therapist (CFT)

Certified Pastoral Counselors (CPCs)

Certified Rehabilitation Counselor (CRC)

Commission on Rehabilitation Counselor Certification (CRCC)

Commission on the Accreditation of Marriage and Family Therapy (COAMFTE)

Confidentiality and privileged communication

Council for the Accreditation of Counseling and Related Professions (CACREP)

Couple, Marriage, and Family Therapy Credentialing

Credentialed School Counselor

Credentialed School Psychologist

Diplomates in Clinical Social Work (DCSW)

Eight specialty certifications in social work

Endorsement

First counselor licensure

History of credentialing

International Association of Marriage and Family Counselors (IAMFC)

License

Licensed Clinical Social Workers (LCSWs)

Licensed Counselor

Licensed Marriage and Family Therapist (LMFT)

Licensed Professional Counselors (LPCs)

Licensed Psychologists

Licensure

Licensure committee

Lobbying

Master Addictions Counselors (MAC)

National Association of School Psychologists (NASP)

National Board for Certified Counselors (NBCC)

National Certified Counselors (NCC)

National Certified School Counselors (NCSC)

National Certified School Psychologist (NCSP)

National Clinical Mental Health Counselor Exam (NCMHCE)

National Counselor Certification

National Counselor Exam (NCE)

National Credentialing Academy (NCA)

Portability

Psychiatric-Mental Health—Advanced Practice Registered Nurses (PMH—APRN)

Protection of a title

Psychiatric-Mental Health Nurse Credentialing

Psychiatry Credentialing

Psychology Certification

Psychology Credentialing

Reciprocity

Registered Art Therapist (ATR)

Registration

Scope and practice

Specialty certifications

Specialty certifications in counseling

State boards of education

State-approved school counseling program

Third-party reimbursement

Types of credentialing

ETHICS IN COUNSELING | CHAPTER 9

One time, I had a suicidal client leave her session saying she was going to kill herself. Upon hearing what happened, my supervisor looked at me and said, "Get in my car." We chased her down, stopped her, and had her involuntarily committed. Another time, a 14-year-old client told me he was having an incestuous relationship with his sister. I had to break confidentiality, tell his parents, and have child protective services get involved. Another time, I was testing a high school girl. Based on her responses to some questions, I thought she had been molested. When I asked her, she began to sob. I then had to break confidentiality and tell school officials. Another time, I was working with a colleague who was misrepresenting his credentials. I had to sit down and talk with him and let him know that what I thought he was doing was unethical, and that if he did not change, I would report him. These are some of the difficult ethical dilemmas we face as counselors, and I'm sure, if you have not yet faced some difficult dilemmas in your career, you will. This chapter discusses values, morality, ethics, best practices, and the law. Let's take a look.

DEFINING VALUES, ETHICS, MORALITY, AND THEIR RELATIONSHIP TO THE LAW

Although we are not constantly faced with situations such as the ones just described, in our work as counselors we are periodically confronted with complicated and sometimes delicate situations. In these moments, we need to respond in the best manner possible, and it helps if we know the difference between our moral, ethical, and legal obligations.

Morality is generally concerned with individual conduct and often reflects the values from an individual's family, religious sect, culture, or nationality. In contrast, *ethics* generally describes the collectively agreed-upon correct behaviors within the context of a professional group (Remley & Herlihy, 2010). Therefore, what might be immoral behavior for a minister might be ethical behavior for a counselor. For instance, relying on his or her sect's religious writings, a minister might oppose abortion. On the other hand, relying on ethical guidelines that assert a client's

| BOX 9.1 | Discussing Controversial Ethical Behaviors |

Review the counselor behaviors in Table 9.1 and identify four or five you think are particularly controversial. In class, make a list of the items seen as most controversial by a large portion of the class. Then discuss. When you are finished, what consensus, if any, have you come to? Is it difficult to come to consensus on potential ethical dilemmas? Do you think it would be difficult to come to consensus on the development of an ethical code? Finally, if time allows, cross-reference the controversial behaviors discussed in class with aspects of ACA's ethical code (see ACA, 2005).

© Cengage Learning 2014

right to self-determination, a counselor might support a client's decision to have an abortion. Sometimes an individual's moral beliefs will conflict with his or her professional ethics (e.g., when a clinician's religious beliefs concerning abortion are in conflict with ethical obligations to preserve the client's right to self-determination). Clearly, trying to make sense of one's values—what is personally right or wrong—while trying to stay ethically on-target can be quite an undertaking at times! And to make things even more confounding, sometimes the law will contradict one's values, sense of morality, and even professional ethics:

> When legislatures pass laws requiring conduct incompatible with ethical codes, professional associations first try to change the laws. If that fails, they modify the ethical codes to fit the new laws. (Swenson, L. C. (1997). *Psychology and law for the helping professions* (2nd ed.). Belmont, CA: Brooks/Cole.)

Finally, despite the fact that ethical codes guide our professional behaviors, perceptions of what is or is not ethical can vary greatly. For instance, when 535 members of the American Counseling Association were asked to rate whether or not 77 potential counselor situations were ethical, Neukrug and Milliken (2011) found a great deal of disparity on a number of items (see Box 9.1 and Table 9.1).

THE DEVELOPMENT OF AND NEED FOR ETHICAL CODES

Ethical codes are a relatively recent development in the mental health professions. For instance, in 1953, the American Psychological Association (APA) published its first code of ethics, and in 1960, the National Association of Social Workers (NASW) adopted its code. Soon after, in 1961, the American Counseling Association (ACA) developed its ethical code. Codes are always undergoing revisions (see ACA, 2005; APA, 2010; NASW, 2008) and serve multiple purposes (Corey, Corey, & Callanan, 2011; Dolgoff, Loewenberg, & Harrington, 2009). For instance, they:

- protect consumers and further the professional standing of an organization;
- are statements about the maturity and professional identity of a profession;
- guide professionals toward certain types of behaviors that reflect the underlying values considered desirable in the profession;
- offer a framework for the sometimes difficult ethical decision-making process; and
- can be offered as one measure of defense if a professional is sued for malpractice.

TABLE 9.1 | WHAT IS ETHICALLY CORRECT BEHAVIOR?

Counselor Behavior	% Ethical	Counselor Behavior	% Ethical
1. Being an advocate for clients	99	22. Refraining from making a diagnosis to protect a client from a thirdparty (e.g., an employer who might demote a client)	55
2. Encouraging a client's autonomy and self-determination	98		
3. Breaking confidentiality if the client is threatening harm to self	96		
4. Referring a client due to interpersonal conflicts	95	23. Bartering (accepting goods or services) for counseling services	53
5. Having clients address you by your first name	95	24. While completing a dissertation, using the title *Ph.D. Candidate* in clinical practice	48
6. Making a diagnosis based on DSM-IV-TR	93	25. Withholding information about a minor despite parents' request	48
7. Using an interpreter to understand your client	89	26. Selling clients counseling products (e.g., books, videos, etc.)	47
8. Self-disclosing to a client	87	27. Using techniques that are not theory- or research-based	43
9. Counseling an undocumented worker (illegal immigrant)	87	28. Pressuring a client to receive needed services	43
10. Consoling your client through touch (e.g., hand on shoulder)	84	29. Becoming sexually involved with a former client (at least 5 years after the counseling relationship ended)	43
11. Publicly advocating for a controversial cause	84		
12. Keeping client records on your office computer	74	30. Not allowing clients to view your case notes about them	43
13. Attending a client's formal ceremony (e.g., wedding)	72	31. Referring a client, unhappy with his or her homosexuality, for reparative therapy	38
14. Counseling a terminally ill client on end-of-life decisions including suicide	69	32. Accepting only clients who are male or clients who are female	37
		33. Guaranteeing confidentiality for group members	37
15. Providing counseling over the Internet	68	34. Charging for individual counseling although seeing a family	35
16. Hugging a client	67	35. Accepting clients only from specific cultural groups	32
17. Not being a member of a professional association	66	36. Breaking the law to protect your client's rights	32
18. Counseling a pregnant teenager without parental consent	62	37. Reporting a colleague's unethical conduct without first consulting the colleague	30
19. Telling your client you are angry at him or her	62		
20. Sharing confidential information with an administrative supervisor	59	38. Sharing confidential client information with a colleague	29
21. Guaranteeing confidentiality for couples and families	58	39. Not reporting suspected spousal abuse	29

(*continued*)

TABLE 9.1 | WHAT IS ETHICALLY CORRECT BEHAVIOR?

Counselor Behavior	% Ethical	Counselor Behavior	% Ethical
40. Not having malpractice coverage	28	60. Making grandiose statements about your expertise	6
41. Counseling a client engaged in another helping relationship	27	61. Giving a gift worth more than $25 to a client	5
42. Seeing a minor client without parental consent	25	62. Keeping client records in an unlocked file cabinet	5
43. Viewing a client's web page (e.g., Facebook) without consent	23	63. Not participating in continuing education	5
44. Counseling diverse clients with little cross-cultural training	22	64. Engaging in a counseling relationship with a friend	5
45. Having sex with a person your client knows well	22	65. Terminating the counseling relationship without warning	5
46. Setting your fee higher for clients with insurance	22	66. Not offering a professional disclosure statement	3
47. Counseling without training in the presenting problem	20	67. Referring a client satisfied with his/her homosexuality for reparative therapy	3
48. Not allowing clients to view their records	17	68. Lending money to your client	3
49. Trying to change your client's values	13	69. Sharing confidential information with a significant other	3
50. Kissing a client as a friendly gesture (e.g., greeting)	13	70. Not reporting suspected abuse of an older client	1
51. Accepting a client's decision to commit suicide	12	71. Not informing clients of legal rights (e.g., HIPAA, FERPA, confidentiality)	1
52. Accepting a gift from a client that's worth more than $25	12	72. Stating you are licensed when you are in the process of obtaining a license	1
53. Revealing confidential information if a client is deceased	11	73. Revealing a client's record to his or her spouse without permission	<1
54. Counseling a colleague with whom you work	11	74. Not reporting suspected abuse of a child	<1
55. Having dual relationship (e.g., client is your child's teacher)	10	75. Attempting to persuade a client to adopt a religious belief	<1
56. Telling your client you are attracted to him or her	10	76. Implying that a certification is the same as a license	<1
57. Not having a transfer plan should you become incapacitated	9	77. Not revealing the limits of confidentiality to your client	<1
58. Trying to persuade a client to not have an abortion	8		
59. Treating homosexuality as a pathology	6		

Source: Neukrug, E., & Milliken, T. (2011). Counselors' perceptions of ethical behaviors. *Journal of Counseling and Development, 89,* 206–216.

However, there are limitations to ethical codes (Corey et al., 2011; Dolgoff et al., 2009; Remley & Herlihy, 2010). In fact, ethical codes:

- do not address some issues and offer no clear way of responding to other issues;
- sometimes have conflicts within the same codes, between the codes and the law, and between the codes and counselors' value systems;
- are sometimes difficult to enforce;
- do not always involve the public in the code construction process or take into account the public's interests; and
- do not always address cutting-edge issues.

CODES OF ETHICS IN THE HELPING PROFESSIONS

ACA's Ethics Code: A Brief Overview

To keep up with the changing values of society and in the counseling profession, *ACA's ethical code* changes every ten years or so (Kaplan et al., 2009; Kocet, 2006; Ponton & Duba, 2009). The following summarizes the current eight sections of ACA's ethical code (ACA, 2005). You are strongly encouraged to read the whole code in detail, which can be found at http://www.counseling.org/Resources/ (then click "Ethics").

Section A: The Counseling Relationship Highlighting important issues within the counseling relationship, this section stresses the importance of respecting the client and looking out for the client's welfare by (1) keeping good records and having a plan for counseling; (2) obtaining informed consent prior to and during treatment; (3) consulting with others who are working with your client; (4) avoiding harm and not imposing your own values; (5) knowing role limitations when working with a client, such as not engaging in sexual relationships with clients and those close to them; (6) knowing how to advocate for clients at various levels (e.g., institutional, societal); (7) understanding the importance of identifying roles when working with multiple clients (e.g., group and family counseling); (8) knowing how to screen and protect clients participating in groups; (9) knowing how to provide effective care for terminally ill clients; (10) knowing rules related to fees and bartering; (11) knowing how to effectively terminate and refer clients; and (12) being able to navigate the intricacies of technology when working with clients.

Section B: Confidentiality, Privileged Communication, and Privacy Section B examines the importance of (1) respecting clients' rights to confidentiality and privacy; (2) knowing exceptions to client confidentiality (e.g., when a client is in danger of harming him- or herself or another); (3) knowing when and how to share confidential information; (4) understanding the nature of confidentiality relative to group and family work; (5) understanding the nature of confidentiality when working with clients who lack the capacity to give informed consent (e.g., children, incapacitated adults); (6) preserving the confidentiality of records; (7) protecting confidentiality in research; and (8) maintaining confidentiality when serving in a consultative role.

Section C: Professional Responsibility This section discusses the importance of (1) knowing the ethical code; (2) practicing within one's professional competence and knowing what to do when one is professionally or psychologically impaired; (3) accurately advertising and promoting oneself; (4) accurately representing one's credentials and qualifications; (5) not discriminating against clients; (6) knowing one's public responsibilities, including not engaging in sexual harassment, accurately reporting information to third parties (e.g., insurance companies, courts), being accurate when using the media (e.g., radio talk shows), and not making unjustifiable treatment claims; and (7) assuring that the public can distinguish personal from professional statements.

Section D: Relationships with Other Professionals   Section D highlights the importance of (1) maintaining mutually respectful relationships with colleagues, employers, and employees despite differing counseling approaches; forming strong, interdisciplinary relationships with others; and addressing unethical situations and negative working conditions when they might arise and (2) when acting as a consultant, assuring that one is competent, understands the needs of the consultee, and obtains informed consent from the consultee.

Section E: Evaluation, Assessment, and Interpretation   This section highlights the importance of (1) using reliable and valid assessment instruments and assuring client welfare when assessing; (2) being competent in the use of assessment instruments and using the information gained appropriately; (3) obtaining informed consent from clients; (4) releasing data only to those identified by clients; (5) making accurate diagnoses and taking into account cross-cultural issues; (6) choosing instruments based on good reliability, validity, and cross-cultural fairness; (7) assuring proper testing conditions; (8) assuring non-discrimination; (9) knowing proper ways to score and interpret instruments; (10) assuring test security; (11) assuring test information is up to date and not obsolete; (12) assuring that sound, scientific knowledge is used in the construction of assessment instruments; and (13) assuring objective results when conducting forensic evaluations.

Section F: Supervision, Training, and Teaching   Section F examines the importance of (1) supervisors being responsible for the welfare of supervisees' clients; (2) supervisors obtaining ongoing training; (3) supervisors maintaining ethical relationships with supervisees, including respect for nonsexual boundaries; (4) supervisors obtaining informed consent, assuring access to consultation when they are not available, and assuring that supervisees know standards and are familiar with proper procedures for termination; (5) supervisors evaluating and offering feedback to supervisees; (6) counselor educators being competent, infusing multicultural issues, integrating theory and practice, assuring the rights of students, being careful when presenting "innovative" techniques, assuring adequate field placements, and assuring that students and supervisees present professional disclosure statements to clients; (7) counselor educators assuring student welfare by offering orientations and providing self-help experiences; (8) students knowing their ethical codes regarding what to do if impaired; (9) counselor educators offering ongoing feedback to students and remedial help if needed; (10) counselor educators knowing they are prohibited from having sexual relationships with current students or otherwise misusing the power they hold over students; and (11) counselor educators actively work to have students gain awareness, knowledge, and skills about other cultures and how they affect the counseling relationship.

Section G: Research and Publication   A wide range of ethical areas are discussed in this section, including (1) research responsibilities, such as the appropriate use of human research participants; (2) the rights of research participants, such as offering informed consent, assuring confidentiality, and understanding the use of deception in research; (3) standards for maintaining appropriate relationships with research participants; (4) methods for accurately reporting results; and (5) guidelines for accurately publishing results.

SECTION H: RESOLVING ETHICAL ISSUES This final section of the ethical code explains the proper steps to take in the reporting and resolution of suspected ethical violations. It addresses (1) possible conflicts between ethical codes and the law; (2) how to deal with suspected violations, such as first addressing the individual informally, and if no resolution is forthcoming, or if the violation is of such a nature to have caused harm to another, how to approach the appropriate ethics committee; and (3) the importance of working with ethics committees.

RELATED ETHICAL CODES AND STANDARDS

Some of ACA's divisions and affiliated groups have established ethical codes in lieu of ACA's, or standards of best practices that supplement ACA's code (see Table 9.2). Sometimes, one must choose the code to which one will adhere. For instance, if one is a member of American School Counseling Association (ASCA) and ACA and is also a Nationally Certified Counselor (NCC), which of the three codes does one follow? Although all three are fairly similar, there are some differences, and bouncing among codes to decide which one to follow when faced with a difficult ethical dilemma is not the best way to make a decision. However, if time permits, reflecting on the different codes and debating the knowledge held in each might be smart when faced with a difficult situation.

Although, as a counselor you should adhere to the code of the counseling organization listed in Table 9.2 which best fits your work situation, it's always

TABLE 9.2	WEBSITES FOR THE ETHICAL CODES OR BEST PRACTICE STATEMENTS OF SELECT COUNSELING ORGANIZATIONS
Association	**Website**
(AMHCA, 2010) American Mental Health Counselors Association	www.amhca.org/ (click "About AMHCA" and then "Code of Ethics")
(ASCA, 2010) American School Counselor Association	www.schoolcounselor.org (click "School Counselors & Members" then "Legal and Ethical")
(IAMFC, n.d.b) International Association of Marriage and Family Counselors	www.iamfconline.com (click "Professional Development" and then "Ethical Codes")
(ASGW, 2007) Association for Specialists in Group Work	www.asgw.org (then click "Standards and Practices" and then "Best Practices")
(NBCC, 2005) National Board for Certified Counselors	www.nbcc.org/ethics (then click "NBCC Code of Ethics")
(CRCC, 2010) Commission on Rehabilitation Counselor Certification	www.crccertification.com (then click "CRC/CCRC Code of Ethics")

interesting to explore ethical codes in related mental health professions. In addition to the codes listed in Table 9.2, ethical codes in related mental health professions that you might be interested in examining include those of the American Psychological Association (APA, 2010), the National Association of Social Workers (NASW, 2008), the American Association for Marriage and Family Therapy (AAMFT, 2001), the American Psychiatric Association (APA, 2009), and the National Organization of Human Services (NOHS, 1996).

ETHICAL HOT SPOTS FOR COUNSELORS

By examining complaints filed against counselors, inquiries made by helpers regarding ethical problem areas, and research that examines ethical concerns with which counselors most struggle (Birky & Collins, 2011; Bradley, Hendricks, & Kabell, 2011; Glosoff & Freeman, 2007; Neukrug & Milliken, 2011), a number of ethical hot spots can be identified. Table 9.3 groups some of these issues into logical categories. After reviewing Table 9.3, read Box 9.2.

TABLE 9.3	ETHICAL HOT SPOTS GROUPED INTO LOGICAL CATEGORIES

The Counseling Relationship

- Counseling a terminally ill client about end-of-life decisions
- Using techniques that are not theory or research based (evidence-based)
- Pressuring a client to receive needed services
- Trying to have a client adopt the counselor's values

Legal Issues

- Refraining from making a diagnosis to protect a client from a third party (e.g., an employer who might demote a client)
- Breaking the law to protect a client's rights
- Reporting or not reporting child abuse, spousal abuse, or elder abuse

Social and Cultural Issues

- Referring a gay or lesbian client for reparative therapy
- Based on personal preference, only accepting clients who are male, female, or from specific cultural groups
- Not having expert knowledge on social and cultural concerns, including advocacy work, when working with clients

Relationships and Boundary Issues

- Attending a client's wedding, graduation ceremony, or other formal ceremony
- Hugging a client
- Bartering (accepting goods or services) for counseling services
- Selling a product to your client that is related to the counseling relationship (e.g., book, audiotape, etc.)
- Having sex with a current client
- Having sex with a former client

(continued)

TABLE 9.3	ETHICAL HOT SPOTS GROUPED INTO LOGICAL CATEGORIES

Confidentiality

- Guaranteeing confidentiality for couples and families or for group members
- Withholding information about a minor client despite a parent's request for information
- Not allowing clients to view case notes about them
- Sharing confidential client information with a colleague who is not your clinical supervisor
- Guaranteeing confidentiality for a deceased client

Informed Consent

- Seeing a minor client without parental consent
- Not obtaining informed consent
- Counseling a pregnant teenager without parental consent

Professional/Practice Issues

- Not being a member of a professional association in counseling
- Misrepresentation of credentials
- Inappropriate fee assessment
- Reporting a colleague's unethical conduct without first consulting with the colleague
- Not having malpractice coverage (on your own or through your agency/setting)
- Engaging in a helping relationship with a client while the client is in another helping relationship

Technology

- Keeping client records on your office computer
- Providing counseling over the internet
- Looking at your client's social network page (e.g., Facebook) without his or her permission or knowledge
- Using online tools, such as a cam or Skype, to conduct supervision

BOX 9.2	DISCUSSING CONTROVERSIAL ETHICAL BEHAVIORS

As you did earlier when you reviewed controversial ethical behaviors, review the ethical hot spots in Table 9.3 and identify four or five you think are particularly controversial. In class, make a list of the items seen as most controversial by a large portion of the class. Add others not on the list, if you wish. Then discuss. When you are finished, to what consensus, if any, have you come? Is it difficult to come to consensus on potential ethical dilemmas? Do you think it would be difficult to come to consensus on the development of an ethical code? Finally, if time allows, cross-reference the controversial behaviors discussed in class with aspects of ACA's (2005) ethical code (go to: http://www.counseling.org/Resources/and then click "Ethics").

RESOLVING ETHICAL DILEMMAS: MODELS OF ETHICAL DECISION-MAKING

Since making difficult ethical decisions can be a complex task for any counselor, in addition to ethics codes, *models of ethical decision-making* have been developed to assist you in this process (Cottone & Claus, 2000; Welfel, 2010). The following examines four types of models: problem-solving, moral, social constructionist, and developmental.

PROBLEM-SOLVING MODELS

Problem-solving models provide a step-by-step approach to making ethical decisions. Hands-on and practical, they are particularly useful for the beginning counselor. One such approach, developed by Corey et al. (2011), includes eight steps: (1) identifying the problem or dilemma, (2) identifying the potential issues involved, (3) reviewing the relevant ethical guidelines, (4) knowing the applicable laws and regulations, (5) obtaining consultation, (6) considering possible and probable courses of action, (7) enumerating the consequences of various decisions, and (8) deciding on the best course of action.

MORAL MODELS (PRINCIPLE AND VIRTUE ETHICS)

Two *moral models* that have taken on prominence in recent years are called *principle ethics* and *virtue ethics*. Stressing inherent principles to which the counselor should subscribe, Kitchener's (1984, 1986; Urofsky, Engels, & Engebretson, 2008) principle ethics model is often described as foundational to ethical codes. Her model describes the role of six principles to consider in ethical decision-making: *autonomy* has to do with protecting the independence, self-determination, and freedom of choice of clients; *nonmaleficence* is the concept of "do no harm" when working with clients; *beneficence* is related to promoting the good of society, which can be at least partially accomplished by promoting the client's well-being; *justice* refers to providing equal and fair treatment to all clients; *fidelity* is related to maintaining trust (e.g., keeping conversations confidential) in the counseling relationship and being committed to the client within that relationship; and *veracity* has to do with being truthful and genuine with the client, within the context of the counseling relationship. The clinician who employs this model will use these principles to guide his or her decision-making process.

Whereas principle ethics focuses on *foundational rules* when making ethical decisions (e.g., protect the autonomy of the client; promote the good of society) virtue ethics focuses on the moral character of the counselor making the ethical decision (Kleist & Bitter, 2009). In other words, principle ethics is focused on duties, or how one should act when faced with ethical dilemmas; virtue ethics suggests ideals of behavior that counselors should strive for throughout their careers (Wilczenski & Cook, 2011). In this context, Meara, Schmidt, and Day (1996) suggest that virtuous helpers are *prudent*, or careful and tentative in their decision-making; maintain *integrity*; are *respectful*; and are *benevolent*. In addition, virtuous counselors strive to make ideal decisions based on their understanding of their profession and the community. They do this by being self-aware, being compassionate, understanding cultural differences, being motivated to do good, and having vision concerning decisions that are made.

SOCIAL CONSTRUCTIONIST PERSPECTIVE

The *social constructionist* perspective to ethical decision-making sees knowledge (e.g., knowledge in codes) as intersubjective, changeable, and open to interpretation (Guterman & Rudes, 2008). This approach suggests that reality is socially constructed, constituted through language, and organized and maintained through narrative (stories), and that there are no essential truths (Freedman & Combs, 1996). Taking a *post-modernist* perspective, this approach views traditional ways of understanding ethical dilemmas to be problematic at times and the result of the language used and embedded in one's culture and in society. Those who adhere to a social constructionist approach view language as subtly, and sometimes not so subtly, oppressing others, particularly those from nondominant groups. These individuals question what is often taken for granted (e.g., diagnosis, theoretical assumptions) and look for dialogue with others to develop new ways of understanding situations.

Those who embrace a social constructionist perspective don't expect answers to come from a code, from within themselves, or from within other people. Instead, they view solutions to problems as coming out of dialogue between clients, counselors, and others (e.g., supervisors and others in the client's world) (Cottone, 2001, 2004). These individuals approach clients with humility and wonder, as equals, and as collaborators with whom solutions to ethical problems can be jointly worked out.

DEVELOPMENTAL MODELS

Developmental models, created by individuals like *William Perry* (1970) and *Robert Kegan* (1982, 1994), suggest that individuals at lower levels of development have less of some qualities that are considered positive for counselors than those who are at higher levels (Lambie, Hagedorn, & Ieva, 2010; Linstrum, 2005). Although not specifically developed for ethical decision-making, these models suggest that counselors at lower levels of development tend to believe there are correct and specific answers to the complex ethical dilemmas they may face. These counselors often adhere to rigid views of the truth and expect and hope that formal documents, such as ethical codes, hold the answers to complex ethical dilemmas. They are also likely to look at those in positions of authority and power (e.g., supervisors) as being able to quickly tell them the correct answers when faced with thorny ethical dilemmas. These counselors can be said to be making meaning from what Perry calls a *dualistic* perspective, in that they view the world in terms of black-and-white thinking, concreteness, rigidity, oversimplification, stereotyping, self-protectiveness, and authoritarianism. In contrast, higher-level counselors, sometimes called individuals *committed in relativism*, are more complex thinkers, flexible, empathic, sensitive to the contexts of ethical dilemmas, and nondogmatic, and have viewpoints but are open to differing opinions (Cottone, 2001; Neukrug, Lovell, & Parker, 1996; McAuliffe & Eriksen, 2010). Although few adults (or counselors) reach the highest levels of this development (Lovell, 1999), these models suggest that, if afforded the right opportunities, most adults can.

You can see that individuals who are at lower levels would make ethical decisions in very different ways from individuals at higher levels. Counselor education programs often offer opportunities to support and challenge students to move toward these higher levels of development.

SUMMARIZING AND INTEGRATING THE MODELS

Often, the models just presented are not used in isolation. After reviewing the different models in Table 9.4, read the ethical dilemma presented in Box 9.3. First, consider separately how the problem-solving, moral, and social constructionist models would approach the ethical dilemma faced in the vignette. Then, using a developmental model, consider how a person of higher development could integrate all the models in responding to the dilemma.

TABLE 9.4 | SUMMARY OF ETHICAL DECISION-MAKING MODELS

	Theoretical Assumptions	Principles/Key Points	Role of Counselor
Problem-Solving Model	Step-by-step, practical, pragmatic hands-on approach	Eight steps (see p. 133)	Go through the steps, one by one.
Moral Models			
Principle Ethics	Moral principles, sometimes called rules, play a major role in ethical decision-making. Six principles are the foundation of ethical codes. Decisions are based on these principles and on what should be done.	One example: Kitchener's six principles of autonomy, nonmaleficence, beneficence, justice, fidelity, and veracity	Consider principles or rules in making an ethical decision.
Virtue Ethics	Moral character plays a major role in ethical decision-making. Throughout his or her professional career, the counselor strives to make ideal decisions based his or her moral character.	One example: Meara, Schmidt, and Day's four virtues of being prudent, integrity, respectfulness, and benevolence	A counselor has a sense of moral character throughout his or her work life and tries to follow the values that reflect that character. Some values might be: self-awareness, compassion, cultural astuteness, consideration of doing good, having a vision, and embracing the making of ethical decisions.

(continued)

TABLE 9.4	SUMMARY OF ETHICAL DECISION-MAKING MODELS		
	Theoretical Assumptions	Principles/Key Points	Role of Counselor
Social Constructionist Model	Knowledge in codes is intersubjective, changeable, and open to interpretation. Realities are socially constructed, constituted through language, and organized and maintained through narrative (stories). There are no essential truths. Ethical dilemmas may be the results of inequities in society subtly supported through language.	Solutions to ethical dilemmas come out of dialogue between a counselor, his or her clients, his or her supervisor, and others.	Approach clients with humility and wonder, as equals, and as collaborators with whom solutions to ethical problems can be jointly worked out. Use dialogue with clients, colleagues, and supervisors to jointly work through ethical dilemmas.
Developmental Model	Counselors at lower levels of development have less of some qualities effective in ethical decision-making than do those who are at higher levels. All individuals can increase their levels of development.	*Dualistic counselors:* Black-and-white thinking, concrete-ness, stereotyping, oversimplification, self-protectiveness, and authoritarianism. *Relativistic counselors:* Complex thinking, openness to differing opinions, flexibility, empathy, sensitivity to the context of the ethical dilemma, and nondogmaticness.	Embody the qualities of a relativist in an effort to work through ethical dilemmas.

REPORTING ETHICAL VIOLATIONS

Section H of ACA's (2005) *Code of Ethics* provides guidelines on how to proceed if one suspects a counselor is violating an ethical guideline. It states that if a counselor believes that another counselor is in violation of the ethics code, the counselor should try to resolve the issue informally by discussing the situation directly with the counselor suspected of violating the guideline. If no resolution is found, or if substantial harm is suspected, then counselors are asked to take further action, which could include "referral to state or national committees on professional ethics,

| BOX 9.3 | USING THE ETHICAL DECISION-MAKING MODELS |

Angela, an 84-year-old great grand-mother, has four children and thirteen grand-children and is dying of pancreatic cancer. Her disease is debilitating and she is in quite a bit of pain. Therefore, as her counselor, you have agreed to see her periodically in her home. You know that she only has a few precious months to live. At one point, during a counseling session, she tells you that her pain is getting the best of her and that the morphine that is given to her barely takes the pain away. She is a proud woman and does not want her children or her grandchildren to see her suffer. She asks you whether you could expedite her death by giving her a dose of morphine that she knows will kill her. Although you refuse, she tells you that if you don't help her out, she'll do it on her own. She tells you that she wants her children and grandchildren to remember her as a healthy strong woman, not sickly. You leave thinking she is likely going to kill herself. What should you do?

© Cengage Learning 2014

voluntary national certification bodies, state licensing boards, or to the appropriate institutional authorities" (ACA, 2005, Standard H.2.c.).

When a complaint is received, ethics committees examine whether they have the jurisdiction to address the complaint. For instance, if a complaint concerning a licensed counselor is brought to the ACA ethics committee and the counselor is not an ACA member, then the committee would likely refer the complainant to the ethics committee of the state in which the counselor is licensed. One study that examined complaints made against Licensed Professional Counselors (LPCs) found that only about 10% of complaints were seen as justified and/or within the jurisdiction of the licensing board. Of those that were adjudicated, over one-third had their licenses revoked, about one-fifth had their licenses suspended, and smaller numbers were asked to undergo supervision, received letters of reprimand, were fined, or had some other action taken against them (Neukrug, Milliken, & Walden, 2001).

LEGAL ISSUES RELATED TO ETHICAL VIOLATIONS

CIVIL AND CRIMINAL LIABILITY

In instances of alleged malpractice, complainants most often initiate *civil suits* against counselors, although counselors can also be charged with *criminal violations* in the criminal courts. For example, if a counselor is alleged to have had sex with a client, and if sex with a client is in violation of a state statute, a prosecuting attorney (e.g., District Attorney) could bring criminal charges against the counselor in criminal court while the client (the alleged victim) pursues a civil court action against the counselor seeking monetary damages. Anyone can bring a civil lawsuit alleging virtually anything; however, outlandish cases are generally dismissed in a timely manner and some states have even set up procedures to penalize individuals for arbitrary and capricious acts of malicious prosecution and abuse of process in filing unwarranted lawsuits. Finally, because ethical guidelines are not legal documents, they tend to hold more weight in civil courts than in criminal courts, because the burden of proof is less demanding in civil cases.

THE ROLE OF ETHICAL CODES IN LAWSUITS

Although ethical codes are not legal documents, they can be powerful pieces of evidence in a court of law. For instance, a counselor would have difficulty defending having had sex with a client, as the ethical code asserts that sex with a client is inappropriate. However, cases are often not clear-cut. For example: a counselor has sex with a former client whom she had seen as a client six years earlier. Feeling abused, the former client seeks out a prosecutor who determines that the statute is unclear about when a client stops being a client and files criminal charges against the counselor. The counselor brings the ACA ethical code to court, which states that "Sexual or romantic counselor–client interactions or relationships with former clients, their romantic partners, or their family members are prohibited for a period of 5 years following the last professional contact" (ACA, 2005, Standard A.5.b.). However, the prosecutor retorts with the following statement, also found in the ethical code: "Counselors, before engaging in sexual or romantic interactions or relationships with clients, their romantic partners, or client family members after 5 years following the last professional contact, demonstrate forethought and document (in written form) whether the interactions or relationship can be viewed as exploitive in some way and/or whether there is still potential to harm the former client; in cases of potential exploitation and/or harm, the counselor avoids entering such an interaction or relationship" (ACA, 2005, Standard A.5.b.). Although ethical codes can clearly support one's professional behavior, you can see how they can sometimes also be used against a counselor.

MALPRACTICE INSURANCE

In today's litigious society, there is little doubt that counselors need to be particularly careful, for even when they are doing everything correctly, they might still get sued. Remember, anyone can be sued by anybody! Certainly, this does not mean a counselor will lose a frivolous suit; however, if a counselor finds himself or herself in the dubious position of not having *malpractice insurance* and subsequently loses a civil suit, that counselor may be haunted by the monetary settlement for the rest of his or her life.

Although most schools and agencies generally purchase an umbrella malpractice insurance policy, it is still prudent to own additional insurance protection. And, if you do work in a setting that has purchased a malpractice policy, review it carefully, study its monetary limits, and examine any possible exclusion to the policy. For instance, are you covered if you work after hours? What if your employer lets you run a workshop for your own personal profit at the agency on the weekend? Are you still covered?

If you're interested in malpractice insurance, the ACA Insurance Trust (ACAIT) has partnered with Healthcare Providers Service Organization (HPSO) to offer professional liability insurance. This program offers malpractice insurance with rates that tend to run around $30 for students. For employed counselors, the cost can be up to a few hundred dollars for $1,000,000 worth of liability insurance, depending on your state of residence (HPSO, 2012).

AVOIDING LAWSUITS: BEST PRACTICES

As you can see from this chapter, ethical decision-making can be an arduous and potentially career-threatening process. If you are ever sued, it is essential that you show the court that you were equipped with the clinical knowledge and tools necessary to make the best decisions and that you followed *best practices* in your profession. Following one's professional association's code of ethics is one piece of evidence showing that best practices have been followed. In addition, Corey et al. (2011) suggest additional ways to ensure that one has been following best practices:

- Know relevant laws.
- Maintain good records.
- Keep your appointments.
- Stay professional with clients.
- Document treatment progress.
- Ensure the security of records.
- Maintain confidentiality of records.
- Have a sound theoretical approach.
- Preserve appropriate confidentiality.
- Obtain informed consent from clients.
- Report cases of abuse as required by law.
- Treat only within your area of competence.
- Avoid imposing your values or influence on clients.
- Obtain written permission when working with minors.
- Refer when it is in the best interest of your client to do so.
- Be attentive to your clients' needs and treat them with respect.
- Make sure that clients understand information you present to them.
- Do not engage in sexual relationships with current or former clients.
- Provide a professional disclosure statement and obtain informed consent regarding a course of treatment.
- Monitor your reactions to clients, especially when counter transference is involved.
- Assure that clients understand they can terminate counseling at any point.
- Whenever possible, obtain permission from a client to consult with others.
- Keep appropriate boundaries and know the limitations of multiple relationships (e.g., counseling a person who is a neighbor).
- Assess clients and explain diagnoses and treatment plans and their risks and benefits.
- Know how to appropriately assess clients who may pose a danger of harming themselves or others and know what to do if you think a client poses a threat.
- Know cultural and clinical issues related to bartering and accepting or giving gifts.

SUMMARY

We began this chapter by distinguishing between ethics and morality, and by underscoring the importance of our values, our professional ethics, and the role that legal issues may play when making important ethical decisions. We then identified 77 potential counselor situations and highlighted whether a random sample of counselors viewed them as ethical or unethical. We suggested that you examine those behaviors and discuss the more controversial ones in class.

As the chapter continued, we noted the relatively brief history of the development of ethical codes and identified a number of purposes and limitations of codes. We then summarized the eight sections of the ACA code (Sections A through H) and provided the names and websites of ethical codes of other counseling affiliates and organizations. We also identified related mental health professions' ethical codes (e.g., AAMFT, APA, NASW, and NOHS).

The chapter then went on to identify a number of ethical hot spots, grouped into the categories of: the counseling relationship, legal issues, social and cultural issues, relationship and boundary issues, confidentiality, informed consent, professional/ practice issues, and technology. Next, we presented ethical decision-making models, including a problem-solving model, two types of moral models: principle ethics and virtue ethics, a social constructionist model, and a developmental model. We gave an example of a difficult ethical dilemma and asked you to use the different models in coming to some conclusion about the dilemma.

Next in the chapter, we discussed the reporting of ethical violations, noting that ACA's ethical code suggests that when possible, and if no harm is likely to occur to clients or to society, an informal resolution should be attempted. We then noted that only a small percentage of complaints are actually investigated, but that the consequences to licensed professional counselors who are found to have violated an ethical guideline can be great. This section concluded with a discussion of legal issues related to ethical violations, in which we pointed out that counselors can be sued in civil or criminal court, stressed the important role that ethical codes can play in lawsuits, brought up the importance of carrying malpractice insurance, and noted how critical it is to use best practices to avoid lawsuits.

KEY TERMS

ACA Insurance Trust (ACAIT)

ACA's Ethical code

American Association for Marriage and Family Therapy (AAMFT)

American Counseling Association (ACA)

American Psychiatric Association (APA)

American Psychological Association (APA)

American School Counseling Association (ASCA)

Autonomy

Beneficence

Benevolent

Best practices

Civil liability

Civil suits

Committed in relativism

Criminal liability

Criminal violations

Developmental models

Dualistic

Ethics

Fidelity

Foundational rules

Healthcare Providers Service Organization (HPSO)

Integrity

Justice

Kegan, Robert

Kitchener, Karen

Malpractice insurance

Models of ethical decision-making

Moral models

Morality

National Association of Social Workers (NASW)

National Organization of Human Services (NOHS)

Nationally Certified Counselor (NCC)

Nonmaleficence

Post-modernist

Perry, William

Principle ethics

Problem-solving models

Prudent

Related ethical codes and standards

Reporting ethical violations

Respectful

Section A: The Counseling Relationship

Section B: Confidentiality, Privileged Communication, and Privacy

Section C: Professional Responsibility

Section D: Relationships with Other Professionals

Section E: Evaluation, Assessment, and Interpretation

Section F: Supervision, Training, and Teaching

Section G: Research and Publication

Section H: Resolving Ethical Issues

Social constructionist

Veracity

Virtue ethics

Multicultural Counseling and Social Justice Work: The Fourth and Fifth Forces

> ... cultural competency is more than a promise; it is a mandate for the counseling profession. As was the case decades ago when social activists stood up for civil rights and social justice against the forces of oppression, counselors are encouraged to stand up now for better training, more resources, less bias, and greater levels of professional proficiency. (Arredondo, Tovar-Blank, & Parham, 2008, p. 267)

Can counselors understand a client who is from a different culture from their own? Can anyone truly understand the experience of another? Is it possible to connect with a client who is from a different culture or ethnic background? What additional skills must one acquire to work effectively with clients from nondominant groups? As counselors, what is our responsibility to stand up against biases we see in our own profession and to advocate against oppressive actions that negatively impact our clients and people in general? These are some of the important questions being asked when discussing multicultural counseling and social justice work. As refinements to accreditation, credentialing, and ethical standards have increased our professional standing and our ability to work effectively with clients, identifying and embracing the attitudes, knowledge, and skills necessary to being culturally competent will increase our ability to work with all people.

DEFINING MULTICULTURAL COUNSELING AND SOCIAL JUSTICE WORK

The importance of multicultural counseling has been stressed for over 20 years, and more recently there has been a similar emphasis on social justice work. Although related, they are not the same. Multicultural counseling has been seen as

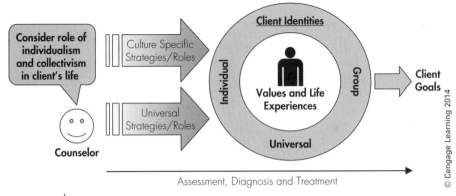

FIGURE 10.1 | ONE WAY OF UNDERSTANDING MULTICULTURAL COUNSELING

the development of counselor competencies to maximize counselor effectiveness in the counselor's work with all clients (McAuliffe, 2013). Sue and Torino (2005) suggest that multicultural counseling (see Figure 10.1):

> ... can be defined as both a helping role and process that uses modalities and defines goals consistent with the life experiences and cultural values of clients, utilizes universal and culture-specific helping strategies and roles, recognizes client identities to include individual, group, and universal dimensions, and balances the importance of individualism and collectivism in the assessment diagnosis and treatment of client and client systems. (Sue, D. W., & Torino, G. C. (2005). *Racial-cultural competences: Awareness, knowledge and skills.* In Carter, R. T. (Ed.), *Handbook of racial-cultural psychology and counseling: theory and research* (pp. 3–18). Hoboken, NJ: Wiley.)

With its focus on advocacy and taking action against oppressive forces, social justice work can be seen as a subset of multicultural counseling (Pieterse, Evans, Risner-Butner, Collins, & Mason, 2009):

> While counseling is one way to provide services to clients from oppressed groups, it is limited in its ability to foster social change. Engaging in advocacy, prevention, and outreach is critical to social justice efforts, as is grounding teaching and research in collaborative and social action processes. (Vera, E., M., & Speight, S. L. (2003). "Multicultural competence, social justice, and counseling psychology: Expanding our roles." *The Counseling Psychologist*, 31, 253–272.)

In other words, whereas multicultural counseling is mostly focused upon the development of counselor competencies in the counselor's work with all clients, social justice work focuses on (1) empowering clients so that they can take action against oppression in their lives, (2) when needed, taking action for clients who are faced with oppressive forces, and (3) taking steps to change society to assist those who are marginalized. A large part of this chapter will examine how we can broaden our *knowledge, skills, and attitudes* so that we can be better at counseling clients from non-dominant groups. Near the end of the chapter we will examine the *Advocacy Competencies*, which suggest ways that counselors can operationalize social justice work.

TABLE 10.1 | Number and Percentage of Individuals from Select Racial, Ethnic, Religious, and Sexual Identity Backgrounds in the U.S.

Ethnicity/Race*	Number (in millions)	Percentage
White	199.8	65.1
Hispanic	48.4	15.8
Black or African American	41.8	13.6
Asian	16.0	4.3
American Indian and Alaska Native (AIAN)	5.0	1.6
Native Hawaiian and other Pacific Islander (NHPI)	1.1	<1
Two or more races	5.4	1.7

SEXUAL ORIENTATION**

	Number (in millions)	Percentage
Gay		2.3
Lesbian		1.3
Bisexual		2.8
Other (not gay, lesbian, straight, or bisexual)		3.8–3.9

Religion***	Number (in millions)	Percentage
Christian	173	76.0
Christian (non-Catholic)	116	50.9
Catholic	57	25.1
Select Religions (Christian and Non-Christian)		
Baptist	36	15.8
Christian Generic	32	14.2
Mainline Christians (Methodist, Lutheran, Episcopalian, United Church of Christ)	29	12.9
Pentecostal	7.9	3.5
Mormon	3.2	1.4
Jewish	2.7	1.2
Eastern Religions (e.g., Buddhist)	2.0	0.9
Muslim	1.3	0.6
Other		2.3
Atheist/Agnostic	3.5	1.6
None	34	15.0

*Figures from U.S. Census Bureau (2009). Hispanics are treated as one group, and they identify as 92% White, 4% African-American, 1.6% AIAN, 1.5% two races, 0.6% Asian, and 0.3% NHPI. Group members may identify with more than one race. Thus, the groups add up to more than the total population of the United States. Whites listed are non-Hispanic. White including White Hispanic, equals 84% of the population.
**From: Chandra, Mosher, & Coopen (2011). Also, about 5% of males and 12% of females between ages of 15 and 44 report some same sex behavior within the past year.
***From Kosmin, B. A., & Keysar, A. (2008). Number of Jews is based on religious identification and is a smaller number than those who identify as Jewish. The number of Muslims is probably much higher, as many mosques do not officially affiliate as religious denominations.

© Cengage Learning 2014

WHY MULTICULTURAL COUNSELING?

There is little doubt that we live in a multicultural nation (see Table 10.1), and thus are called to offer counseling services to clients from many diverse backgrounds. Unfortunately, in working with diverse clients, we have not done well. In fact, it is now assumed that when clients from nondominant groups enter counseling, there is a possibility that the helper will (1) minimize the impact of social forces on the client, (2) interpret cultural differences as psychopathology, and (3) misdiagnose the client (Buckley & Franklin-Jackson, 2005; Constantine & Sue, 2005). Perhaps this is why a large body of evidence shows that nonmajority clients are frequently misunderstood, find counseling less helpful than their majority counterparts, attend counseling at lower rates, and terminate counseling more quickly than Whites (Evans, Delphin, Simmons, Omar, & Tebes, 2005; Sewell, 2009; United States Department of Health and Human Services, 2001).Why is counseling not working for a good segment of our population? Often, it is counselor incompetence, because the helper holds one or more of the following viewpoints (Buckley & Franklin-Jackson, 2005; Constantine & Sue, 2005; McAuliffe, Goméz, & Grothaus, 2013; Sue & Sue, 2008; Suzuki, Kugler, & Aguiar, 2005).

COUNSELING IS NOT WORKING FOR A LARGE SEGMENT OF OUR POPULATION

1. A belief in the *melting-pot myth*. Some helpers believe this country is a melting pot of cultural diversity and subtly pressure clients to become part of what they view as the greater whole. However, this is not the experience of many diverse clients who find themselves on the fringe of American culture, and like most people (including those from the dominant culture), find comfort in maintaining their uniqueness and special traditions. Viewing America as a *cultural mosaic* more accurately represents the essence of today's diversity.

2. *Incongruent expectations about counseling*. The Western approach to counseling emphasizes client autonomy, expression of feelings, self-disclosure, open-mindedness, insight, and cause and effect. In addition, most helpers are not bilingual, approach counseling from a nonreligious perspective, and view the mind and body as separate. Practicing a Western-only approach to counseling can create barriers that result in diverse clients entering the helping relationship with trepidation, experiencing feelings of disappointment while in counseling, and being harmed by inappropriate techniques.

3. *De-emphasis of social forces*. Although effective at attending to clients' *feelings* concerning how they have been discriminated against, helpers will often de-emphasize the actual influence that social forces have on clients. In fact, helpers often assume that most negative feelings are created by the individual, and they often have difficulty understanding the power of social influences. The helper's negation of social forces results in an inability to build a successful relationship with a client who has been considerably harmed by external factors.

4. An *ethnocentric worldview*. Ethnocentric helpers see the world only through their own lenses, tend to falsely assume that their clients view the world in a

similar manner or believe that when their clients present differing worldviews, they are emotionally disturbed, culturally brainwashed, or wrong.

5. *Ignorance of one's own racist attitudes and prejudices.* The helper who is not in touch with his or her prejudices and racist attitudes cannot work effectively with diverse clients and will often cause harm to those clients. Understanding our own stereotypes and prejudices takes a particularly vigilant effort, as many of our biases are unconscious.

6. *Misunderstanding cultural differences in the expression of symptomatology.* What is sometimes seen as abnormal in the United States may be considered quite usual and customary in another culture. The helper's lack of knowledge about cultural differences as they relate to the expression of symptoms can seriously damage a counseling relationship and result in misdiagnosis, mistreatment, and early termination of culturally diverse clients from counseling.

7. *Misjudging the accuracy of assessment and research procedures.* Over the years, assessment and research procedures have notoriously been culturally biased due to inadequate norm groups, use of language that non-native speaking Americans do not understand, and misunderstanding of differences in the expression of symptoms as a function of culture. Although strides have been made, we must continually keep our eyes open for inaccurate assessment and research procedures that can lead to the misdiagnosis of and lack of understanding of diverse clients.

8. *Ignorance of institutional racism.* Because institutional racism is embedded in society, and some would argue even within the helping professional organizations, it is likely that materials used by helpers will be biased and helpers will unknowingly have a skewed understanding of culturally different clients. No doubt there are culturally biased statements in this text of which I am not aware (see Box 10.1).

SOME DEFINITIONS

To help understand differences and to communicate effectively with others, it is important to distinguish words and terms. The following describes some of the more important ones.

CULTURE

Shared values, symbols, language, and ways of being in the world are some of the words associated with *culture*. Culture is expressed through common values, habits,

| BOX 10.1 | EXAMPLES OF WHY COUNSELING IS NOT WORKING |

Now that you've read the eight reasons why counseling may not be effective for some clients from nondominant groups, see whether you can come up with examples that illuminate each of the reasons. Share those in class.

norms of behavior, symbols, artifacts, language, and customs (McAuliffe, 2013; Sewell, 2009; Spillman, 2007).

DISCRIMINATION AND MICROAGRESSIONS

Active, harmful, conscious and unconscious acting out, such as unfair hiring practices that result in differential treatment of individuals, describes *discrimination* (Law, 2007; Lum, 2004). In recent years *microaggressions*, which are brief, subtle, sly, and common putdowns or indignities, have been identified as a type of discrimination (Constantine, Smith, Redington, & Owens, 2008; Sue, 2010). Some examples include statements like "You don't seem gay (or Black, etc.)," and "My ancestors made it in this country without anything; I don't see why your family can't."

ETHNICITY

Heritage, ancestry, and tradition are some of the words associated with *ethnicity*. When a group of people shares a common ancestry, which may include specific cultural and social patterns such as a similar language, values, religion, foods, and artistic expressions, those people are said to be of the same ethnic group (Jenkins, 2007).

MINORITY AND NONDOMINANT GROUPS

Those who are not privileged, have fewer opportunities, are viewed as different, and are systematically oppressed by people in power due to their cultural or physical characteristics are usually said to be a *minority* group. A minority group can be the numerical majority of a population, as was the case for Blacks in South Africa and as is the situation with women in the United States (Atkinson, 2004; Macionis, 2011). The counseling profession has increasingly used the term *nondominant group* because of negative connotations of the word *minority* and because the word *nondominant* suggests there are social reasons for discrimination and racism.

POWER DIFFERENTIALS

Potential abuse, force, control, and superior/underling roles are associated with the term *power differential*, which, much like differences in culture, ethnic group, race, or social class, can result in the oppression of people (Kuriansky, 2008). Power differentials can trump race or other differences so should be considered in understanding the dynamics between people. Power, which can be real or perceived, can be a function of race, class, gender, occupation, and a host of other factors.

RACE

Defined as permanent physical differences as perceived by an external authority (Arthur, 2007), *race* has traditionally been viewed as a function of genetics. However, research on the human genome shows that our genetic heritage is 99.9% the same (National Human Genome Research Project, 2010), and it is now clear

BOX 10.2	WHAT RACE ARE YOU ANYWAY?

Although most people tend to think of themselves as one race or another, take a look at what happened in one study that examined the genetic heritage of a group of students at Pennsylvania State University:

> ... about 90 students took complex genetic screening tests that compared their samples with those of four regional groups. Many of these students thought of themselves as "100 percent" white or black or something else, but only a tiny fraction of them, as it turned out, actually fell into that category. Most learned instead that they shared genetic markers with people of different skin colors. ("Debunking the Concept of Race," 2005)

that gene pools have become increasingly mixed due to migration, exploration, invasions, systematic rape as a result of wars and oppression of minorities, and intermarriage. With some sociologists saying there are no races, others saying there are three, and still others concluding there are 200, the issue of race is cloudy and perhaps doesn't matter (see Box 10.2).

RELIGION AND SPIRITUALITY

Prayer, belief systems, meditation, and inner peacefulness are sometimes associated with religion and spirituality. Whereas a *religion* is an organized or unified set of practices and beliefs which has moral underpinnings and define a group's way of understanding the world (Cipriani, 2007; McAuliffe, 2013), *spirituality* resides in a person and defines the person's understanding of self, self in relationship to others, and self in relationship to a self-defined higher power or lack thereof.

SEXISM, HETEROSEXISM, AND SEXUAL PREJUDICE

When a person denigrates, discriminates, stigmatizes, and consciously puts down another person because of his or her gender, that person is said to be *sexist*. When the same is done because of nonheterosexual behaviors, that person is said to be *heterosexist*, a term now widely used instead of *homophobic*, which implies that the negative behaviors are within the homophobic person and negates the role society plays in fostering these behaviors (Adam, 2007). Finally, *sexual prejudice* refers to negative attitudes targeted toward any individual due to his or her sexual orientation (Herek, 2000).

SEXUAL ORIENTATION

McAuliffe (2013) suggests that *sexual orientation* (in contrast to *sexual preference*) is the gender toward which a person consistently has sexual feelings, longings, and attachments. Common words describing a person's sexual orientation include *lesbian, gay, bisexual, transgender, intersex, and asexual* (*LGBTIA*). Recently, some have suggested using words like *queer* and *fag* as a means of reclaiming power and defusing the negative connotation these words have come to hold. In 1975 the American Psychological Association stated homosexuality was not a disorder. The American Counseling Association (ACA) has always supported this statement. Recently, the Association for Lesbian, Gay, Bisexual, and Transgender Issues in Counseling (ALGBTIC) endorsed Competences for Counseling LGBTIA Individuals (see www.algbtic.org and click on "resources" then "competencies").

SOCIAL CLASS (CLASS)

Money, power, status, and hierarchy are all associated with *social class*. Class is based on a person's education, income, and wealth and represents the perceived ranking of an individual within society and the amount of power an individual wields (Macionis, 2011; McAuliffe, 2013). An individual's social class may cut across a person's ethnicity, cultural identification, and/or race.

PREJUDICE, STEREOTYPES, AND RACISM

Generalizing, falsehoods, irrational fears, and anger are all associated with these words. *Prejudice* has to do with judging a person or a group based on preconceived notions or attitudes (e.g., "I hate James because he's Muslim, and Muslims are all terrorists"). *Stereotyping* is holding the belief that most or all members of a group share certain characteristics, behaviors, or beliefs (e.g., "Asians are intelligent people" or "American Indians are alcoholics") (Jennings, 2007; Lum, 2004). *Racism* has to do with believing one race is superior to another (e.g., "Whites are better than Blacks") (McAuliffe et al., 2013).

CONCEPTUAL MODELS TOWARD UNDERSTANDING CULTURAL IDENTITY

> Every person is in certain respects is like all other people, like some people, and like no other person (Kluckhohn, C., & Murray, H. A. (Eds.). (1948). *Personality in nature, society, and culture*. New York: Alfred A. Knopf.)

A number of models have been developed to help us understand a client's cultural identity as well as our own cultural development. The following briefly describes four models to help us understand how individuals come to make sense of the world relative to their cultural identities. Here, we will describe the *Respectful acronym, tripartite model of personal identity, and developmental models of cultural/racial identity*.

THE RESPECTFUL ACRONYM

If you remember, in Chapter 6 we suggested that one method of understanding clients is to address a number of areas as represented by the *RESPECTFUL acronym*. Thus, effective multicultural counselors feel comfortable asking their clients about the following: Religious/spiritual identity, Economic class background, Sexual identity, Psychological development, Ethnic/racial identity, Chronological disposition, Trauma and other threats to their personal well-being, Family history, Unique physical characteristics, and the clients' Language and location of residence (D'Andrea & Daniels, 2005).

TRIPARTITE MODEL OF PERSONAL IDENTITY

Perhaps borrowing from what has been called the existential model of cultural identity development (see Binswanger, 1963; van Deurzen, 2002), Sue and Sue (2008) suggest that we understand our clients through a tripartite model of personal identity. Clients' personal identities can be seen in three spheres: the *Individual Level*, which represents the clients' uniqueness; the *Group Level*, which is related to aspects of the person that can vary based on the cultural and ethnic groups to which the clients belong; and the *Universal Level*, which is related to common experiences, such as "(a) biological and physical similarities, (b) common life experiences (birth, death, love, sadness, etc.), (c) self-awareness, and (d) the ability to use symbols such as language" (p. 39) (see Figure 10.2).

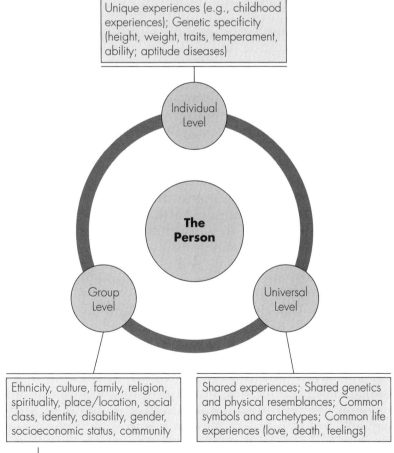

FIGURE 10.2 | THE TRIPARTITE MODEL OF PERSONAL IDENTITY

Source: Adapted from Sue, D. W., & Sue, D. (2008). *Counseling the culturally diverse: Theory and practice* (5th ed.). New York: Wiley, p. 38.

DEVELOPMENTAL MODELS OF CULTURAL/RACIAL IDENTITY

In contrast to the more static RESPECTFUL and Tripartite models of cultural identity, *developmental models* examine how specific ethnic and cultural groups pass through unique stages of development as they become increasingly aware of their cultural selves (Ponterotto, Casas, Suzuki, & Alexander, 2010; Sue & Sue, 2008).

RACIAL IDENTITY DEVELOPMENT FOR PEOPLE OF COLOR (RIDPOC)   Although culture-specific models of racial and cultural identity development have been created (e.g., African-American development, Native American development), McAuliffe, Goméz, & Grothaus (2013) offer a generic five-stage model of racial/cultural identity that synthesizes some of the more popular models. Called the Racial Identity Development for People of Color (RIDPOC), McAuliffe et al. note that a stage in the model represents a general tendency, or overall focus of behavior, relative to an individual's culture or race. Short descriptions of the five stages follow. If you are a person of color, see whether the model resonates with you as you read through the stages.

Stage 1: Conformity.   In this stage, persons of color do not see culture/race as important and tend to conform to the dominant views of culture/race. Some may denigrate their own culture/race and highly value the lifestyle, achievements, and characteristics of the dominant group. Others may simply place little importance on culture/race. These individuals tend to prefer White counselors.

Stage 2: Dissonance and Beginning Appreciation.   As individuals begin to gain positive experiences about people of color through the media, reading, and role models, they begin to question the negative views they had about their culture/race. This newfound awareness leads to confusion or dissonance about how they once viewed their culture/race and movement toward a positive experience of their culture/race. In this stage, it is suggested that counselors should offer clients positive readings, symbols, and role models from the clients' culture/race.

Stage 3: Resistance and Immersion.   As the name implies, in this stage individuals of color are immersed in their own cultural group and increasingly mistrustful of and angry at Whites. They see the dominant group as the cause of most of their problems and feel an increasing pride in their own culture/race and the struggles they have gone through. They tend to see only the positive qualities of their culture/race and are mistrustful of White counselors.

Stage 4: Introspection and Internalization.   As individuals move out of total immersion in their own culture/race, they become increasingly introspective about cultural and racial issues in general. As some encounters with Whites are positive, they begin to let go of the dualistic thinking of Stage 3 that suggested that their culture/race was good and that the White culture/race was the cause of all of their problems. Although they continue to recognize the positive qualities of their own culture/race, they can also see the positive qualities of other cultures/races. Here the counselor supports the more complex thinking and the newfound introspection of the client.

Stage 5: Universal Inclusion. This final stage is when individuals see that all people can experience oppression, even Whites. They have moved out of the black-and-white thinking that was central to the earlier stages and toward a desire to promote social justice for all individuals. They have an interest in all cultures/ races and want to embrace aspects of all cultures/races into their own understanding of the world. Counselors in this stage can work side-by-side with almost all of their clients and share complex views of the world.

WHITE IDENTITY DEVELOPMENT As with cultural/racial identity development models, *White identity development* models also suggest stage progression in that they propose specific stages that Whites are likely to pass through as they become increasingly cross-culturally aware (D'Andrea& Daniels, 1991, 1999; Helms, 1984, 1999; Helms & Cook, 1999; Sabnani, Ponterotto, & Borodovsky, 1991). Two such models presented in Table 10.2 include Helms's model, which speaks to Whites in general, and the model of Sabnani et al., which speaks specifically to White graduate students in counseling. Research has supported the notion that such models reflect the deepening awareness and understanding of multicultural issues that individuals gain as they are exposed to experiences that increase their understanding of multiculturalism (Hays, Chang, & Havic, 2005; Middleton, 2005). If you are White, see whether the models resonate with you as you read through the stages.

Sabnani and associates (1991) describe a number of variations in the ways students can move through the stages. A few examples are shown in Figure 10.3. For instance, Student A begins to move from Stage 1 to Stage 2. However, as the student is confronted with multicultural issues, perhaps in a course on multicultural counseling, he or she retreats back to Stage 1 behavior, preferring denial about racism and prejudice in society. The change process is too fearful for him or her. Student B moves through the first three stages, does not feel a strong need to retreat into his or her own culture in Stage 4, and moves on to Stage 5, where the student can feel good about his or her own culture while having an understanding of and appreciation for others. Student C, on the other hand, feels a need to retreat as he or she is rejected by some minority individuals (Stage 4). This student becomes angry, upset, and discouraged; moves away from cross-cultural contact; and needs time to reflect on his or her experiences. This student does not understand that individuals from diverse backgrounds are dealing with their own identity issues, which leads some of them to reject Whites, even Whites with good intentions. Some Stage 4 students will eventually move out of their shells and have an easy transition to Stage 5. Others, however, such as Student D, may poke their heads out as they consider moving on to Stage 5, but because they continue to struggle with feelings of rejection and anger, quickly move back to Stage 4. Keep in mind that because this is a developmental model, it is assumed that any White student, if given a conducive environment, can move to the higher stages.

TABLE 10.2 | WHITE IDENTITY MODELS

Helms (Helms, 1984, 1999; Helms & Cook, 1999)	Sabnani, Ponterotto, & Borodovsky (1991)
Stage 1: Contact. Here, Whites are unaware of themselves as racial beings, oblivious to social and cultural issues and White privilege, and naïve concerning how race impacts themselves and others.	*Stage 1: Pre-exposure.* White graduate students show naiveté and ignorance about multicultural issues and sometimes believe that racism does not exist or that, if it does, it exists only to a limited degree. Racism is generally thought of as over, and students in this stage do not understand more subtle, embedded racism.
Stage 2: Disintegration. In this stage, Whites begin to acknowledge that racism exists. Believing that society is unjust leads to a sense of confusion and disorientation as past beliefs are being challenged. Some may feel anxiety and guilt over racism and may overly identify with those from other cultures, while others may act paternalistically toward them.	*Stage 2: Exposure.* Students enter this stage when first confronted with multicultural issues, such as when students discuss in class, or take a course on, multicultural counseling. Increasing awareness of embedded racism in society leads to feelings of guilt over being White and/or depression and anger over the current state of affairs. This stage is highlighted by conflict between wanting to maintain majority views and the desire to uphold more humanistically oriented nonprejudicial views.
Stage 3: Reintegration. This stage is a backlash to the confusion and disorientation in Stage 2, and many Whites retreat back to protecting their privileged status and maintaining the status quo. Feelings of anxiety and guilt are now transformed to anger and fear of individuals from nondominant groups.	*Stage 3: Prominority/Antiracism.* Here students often take a strong prominority stance, are likely to reject racist and prejudicial beliefs, and sometimes will reject their own Whiteness in an effort to assuage the guilt felt in Stage 2. Students in this stage tend to have an intense interest in diverse cultural groups and are likely to have an increasing amount of contact with individuals from different cultures.
Stage 4: Pseudoindependence. Not comfortable with racism, these individuals have an intellectual acceptance and curiosity regarding individuals from nondominant groups. However, these individuals have not taken personal responsibility regarding their own racism and tend to see others as responsible for racism.	*Stage 4: Retreat to White Culture.* Students retreat into their own culture as they experience rejection from some individuals from nondominant groups. Intercultural contact is ended because they feel hostile toward and fearful of those from nondominant groups. The cozy home of students' culture of origin is feeling quite safe at this point in time.
Stage 5: Immersion. Whites in this stage have a need for more information about others and are eager to gain a deeper understanding of how they have been socialized to embrace racist attitudes. These individuals have a need to find a new and more compassionate definition of *White*.	*Stage 5: Redefinition and Integration.* Students develop a worldview of multiculturalism and are integrating this into their identity. They are able to feel good about their own identity and roots, and also have a deep appreciation of the culture of others. Here, they are able to expend energy toward deeply rooted structural changes in society.
Stage 6: Emersion. Whites in this stage reach out and embrace a new community of Whites that can move toward a deeper understanding of race and White identity.	
Stage 7: Autonomy. These individuals are cognitively complex, able to understand life from multiple perspectives, able to understand their White privilege, are humane and humanistic, and willing to fight all forms of racism and oppression. These individuals have a multicultural or multiracial transcendent worldview.	

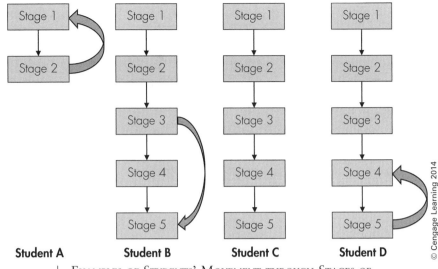

FIGURE 10.3 | EXAMPLES OF STUDENTS' MOVEMENT THROUGH STAGES OF WHITE RACIAL IDENTITY

MULTICULTURAL COUNSELING AND SOCIAL JUSTICE COMPETENCIES

In recent years, two standards have helped to drive our work with clients from non-dominant groups: the *Multicultural Counseling Competencies* and the *Advocacy Competencies*. Let's take a brief look at each of them.

THE MULTICULTURAL COUNSELING COMPETENCIES

Developed by the Association for Multicultural Counseling and Development (AMCD) and endorsed by the American Counseling Association (ACA) in 2002 (Roysircar, Arredondo, Fuertes, Ponterotto, & Toperek, 2003; Roysircar, Sandhu, & Bibbins, 2003), the Multicultural Counseling Competencies delineate *attitudes and beliefs, knowledge, and skills* in three areas: the *counselor's awareness of the client's worldview*, the *counselor's awareness of his or her own cultural values and biases*, and the *counselor's ability to use culturally appropriate intervention strategies* (Arredondo, 1999; Sue & Sue, 2008) (see Figure 10.4) (see Appendix A for a full description of the competencies).

ATTITUDES AND BELIEFS The effective cross-cultural counselor has awareness of his or her own cultural background and has actively pursued understanding his or her own biases, stereotypes, and values. This counselor can accept differing worldviews as presented by the client: "Differences are not seen as being deviant" (Sue & Sue, 2008, p. 48). Sensitivity to differences and being attuned to his or her own biases allow the culturally competent counselor to refer the client to a counselor from the client's cultural group when such a referral would benefit the client.

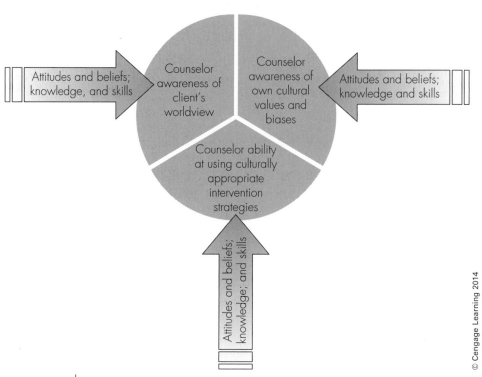

FIGURE 10.4 | FOCUS OF MULTICULTURAL COUNSELING COMPETENCIES

KNOWLEDGE The culturally competent counselor has knowledge of a client's cultural group and does not jump to conclusions about a client. In addition, he or she shows a willingness to gain a greater depth of knowledge of various cultural groups. This counselor is aware of the impact of racism, sexism, heterosexism, and other sociopolitical issues on clients from nondominant groups. In addition, this counselor knows that different counseling theories carry values that may be detrimental for some clients. Finally, this counselor understands how institutional barriers affect the willingness of minority clients to use mental health services.

SKILLS The culturally competent counselor is able to apply, when appropriate, generic interviewing and counseling skills and also has knowledge of and is able to employ specialized skills and interventions that might be effective with specific clients. This counselor has knowledge of and understands the verbal and nonverbal language of his or her clients and can communicate effectively with clients. In addition, the culturally skilled helper understands the importance of having a systemic perspective, such as understanding of the impact of family and society on clients; being able to work collaboratively with community leaders, folk healers, and other professionals; and advocating for clients when necessary.

The Advocacy Competencies

Social justice counseling includes empowerment of the individual as well as active confrontation of injustices and inequality in society because they affect clientele as well as those in their systemic contexts. (Crethar, H., Rivera, E., & Nash, S. (2008). In search of common threads: Linking multicultural, feminist, and social justice counseling paradigms. *Journal of Counseling and Development*, 86(3), 269–278.)

As I noted when we began this chapter, multicultural counseling used to focus solely on *counseling* diverse clients. However, as the multicultural paradigm unfolded, it became clear that there was a thin line between counseling a client and advocating for a client. It became evident that when clients were being mistreated, oppressed, and harassed, counselors could no longer idly stay in their offices and do nothing. With this in mind, during the 1990s and early 2000s, current and past ACA presidents focused on the importance of advocacy as a critical means of assisting clients, especially those who have been historically oppressed. As a result, a task force was formed to develop Advocacy Competencies, and in 2003 they were endorsed by ACA (see Goodman, 2009).

The Advocacy Competencies encompass three areas (*client/student, school/community*, and *public arena*), each of which is divided into two levels: whether the counselor is *acting on behalf* of the competency area or *acting with* the competency area (see Figure 10.5). For instance, in the client competency area, a counselor might *act with* a client to help the client identify his or her strengths and resources so that he or she can feel empowered and advocate for himself or herself, or, *on behalf* of the client, the counselor might assist the client in accessing needed services (Toporek, Lewis, & Crethar, 2009). The competencies run from the *microlevel* (focus on the client) to the *macrolevel* (focus on the system). In Figure 10.5 you can view the three competency areas, each divided into two levels.

This new advocacy movement shows heightened awareness amongst counselors of the real-world effects of oppression, racism, and prejudice on a large segment of society. It is only through social justice efforts that many of our clients can

Overview of ACA Advocacy Competencies

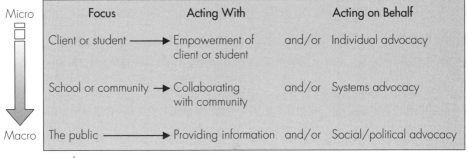

FIGURE 10.5 | The Advocacy Competencies

Source: Adapted from Crethar, Rivera, & Nash, 2008, p. 270.

| BOX 10.3 | COUNSELING VS. ADVOCACY |

It used to be that one would rarely advocate for a client outside of the counseling session. Today, it is sometimes suggested as the appropriate way to respond. When do you think such advocacy may be appropriate? Be specific. How might advocating for a client detract from the counseling relationship? How might it increase the mental health of the client?

overcome some of the external and oppressive barriers they face and subsequently feel empowered in their lives (Niles, 2009; Ratts & Hutchins, 2009) (see Box 10.3). (See Appendix B for a full description of the competencies.)

THE FOURTH AND FIFTH FORCES

> Multiculturalism is not competing with humanism, behaviorism, or psychodynamic perspectives but rather demonstrates the importance of making the cultural context central to whichever psychological theory is being applied. (Pedersen, P. B., Crethar, H., & Carlson, J. (2008). *Inclusive cultural empathy: Making relationships central in counseling and psychotherapy*. Washington, DC: American Psychological Association.)

Historically, psychodynamic approaches, behaviorism, and humanism were called the first, second, and third forces in counseling. With the more recent focus on multicultural counseling and on social justice, two new forces have emerged (Ratts, 2009). These *fourth and fifth forces* suggest that counseling theory alone cannot drive our work with our clients. Multicultural counseling and social justice work challenge counselors to understand their attitudes, knowledge, and skills relative to all people. And they dare counselors to understand their own biases and how these might affect their work with clients. In addition, they urge counselors to gain an understanding of their clients' cultures and aspects of society that actively oppress nondominant groups. Finally, they exhort counselors to advocate for their clients by empowering them, by helping them find resources, by advocating for them locally, and by advocating for systemic change nationally and internationally.

SUMMARY

This chapter examined multicultural counseling and social justice: the fourth and fifth forces in the history of counseling. The chapter began by describing one definition of multicultural counseling that suggests that multicultural counseling is the development of counselor competencies to maximize counselor effectiveness in the counselor's work with all clients, and a second definition that suggests that multicultural counseling involves the counselor considering the role of individualism and collectivism in the client's life, and in the assessment, diagnosis, and treatment process, considering the client's identities (individual, group, and universal) and applying cultural specific and universal strategies when working toward client goals.

We then went on to note that social justice work is now seen as a subset of multicultural counseling in the sense that multicultural counseling is mostly focused upon the development of counselor competencies in their work with all clients, whereas social justice work focuses on counselors empowering clients so that they can take action against oppression in their lives, and counselors taking action for clients and in society in an effort to assist those who are marginalized.

As the chapter continued, eight reasons why counseling is not effective for non-dominant clients were listed, including the fact that some counselors believe we are a melting pot, have incongruent expectations about counseling, de-emphasize the role of social forces, hold ethnocentric worldviews, are ignorant of their racist attitudes and prejudices, misunderstand cultural differences in the expression of symptomatology, misjudge the accuracy of assessment and research procedures, and are ignorant of institutional racism.

We next gave definitions of a number of words and terms, including culture; discrimination and microaggressions; ethnicity; minority and nondominant groups; power differentials; race, religion, and spirituality; sexism, heterosexism, and sexual prejudice; sexual orientation; social class; and prejudice, stereotypes, and racism.

In the interest of being effective with all clients, we examined a number of models to help us understand how individuals come to make sense of their world relative to their cultural identity, including: the RESPECTFUL acronym, the tripartite model of personal identity, the Racial Identity Development for People of Color (RIDPOC) model, Helms's White identity model, and the White identity model of Sabnani et al., who specifically looked at graduate students in counseling.

As the chapter neared its conclusion, we discussed two relatively recent standards that have helped to drive our work with clients from non-dominant groups. The Multicultural Counseling Competencies delineate attitudes and beliefs, knowledge, and skills in three areas: the counselor's awareness of the client's worldview, the counselor's awareness of his or her own cultural values and biases, and the counselor's ability to use culturally appropriate intervention strategies. Then we examined the recent advocacy competencies, noting that they encompass three areas (client/student, school/community, and public arena), each of which are divided into two levels, depending on whether the counselor is acting on behalf of the client or acting with the client. We stressed that the roots of this new advocacy movement are found in the awareness amongst counselors of the real-world effects of oppression, racism, and prejudice on a large segment of society.

KEY TERMS

Acting on behalf

Acting with

Advocacy Competencies

Association for Multicultural Counseling and Development (AMCD)

American Counseling Association (ACA)

Attitudes and beliefs, knowledge, and skills

Bisexual

Client/student

Counselor's ability to use culturally appropriate intervention strategies

Counselor's awareness of his or her own cultural values and biases

Cultural mosaic

Culture

De-emphasis of social forces

Developmental models

Developmental models of cultural/racial identity

Discrimination

Ethnicity

Ethnocentric worldview

Fag

Fourth and fifth forces

Gay

Group Level

Helms's White identity model

Heterosexist

Homophobic

Ignorance of institutional racism

Ignorance of one's own racist attitudes and prejudices

Incongruent expectations about counseling

Individual Level

Knowledge, skills, and attitudes

Lesbian

Lesbian, gay, bisexual, transgender, intersex, and asexual (LGBTIA)

Macrolevel

Melting-pot myth

Microaggressions

Microlevel

Minority

Misjudging the accuracy of assessment and research procedures

Misunderstanding cultural differences in the expression of symptomatology

Multicultural Counseling Competencies

Nondominant group

Power differential

Prejudice

Public arena

Queer

Race

Racial Identity Development for People of Color (RIDPOC)

Racism

Religion

RESPECTFUL Acronym

School/community

Sexist

Sexual orientation

Sexual preference

Sexual prejudice

Social class

Spirituality

Stereotyping

Counselor's awareness of the client's worldview

Tripartite model of personal identity

Universal Level

White Identity Development

White identity model of Sabnani et al.

Applying to Graduate School and Finding a Job

The good news is that for a career in school counseling, mental health counseling, college counseling, substance abuse counseling, rehabilitation counseling, and even genetic counseling, jobs are predicted to grow faster or much faster than average (Occupational Outlook Handbook, 2010–2011). But is this what you want to do?

Now that you've read this book, you probably have a pretty good sense of who the counselor is and what the counselor does. But maybe you need a little more information—like, how much does the average counselor earn? After all, although counselors are usually pretty selfless, they do need to make a living. So Afterword Table 1 gives you median salaries and the projected job growth for a number of different kinds of counselors, so you can make an informed decision about your future.

Still interested in the counseling profession? If you are, and if you are not already in a graduate program, this chapter will help you find one. If you are in a graduate program and may be interested in a doctoral program, this chapter will help you find such a program also. If you're in a graduate program and you're soon to be looking for a job, this chapter will also help you find a job.

SELECT ITEMS TO CONSIDER WHEN CHOOSING A PROGRAM OR FINDING A JOB

Although there are dozens of items to consider when selecting a graduate program or finding a job, the following pinpoints some critical elements. For instance, when making an informed decision about going on to graduate school, one should probably consider the following:

1. Whether or not the program is accredited
2. The kinds of counseling specialties and degrees offered
3. The philosophical orientation of the program

AFTERWORD TABLE 1 | NUMBER OF COUNSELORS/PROJECTED INCREASE, AND SALARIES

Type of Counselor	Number of Counselors (2008)	Projected Number of Additional Counselors by 2020	Percent Increase	Median Salaries*
Educational, Vocational, and School Counselors	281,800	53,400	14	$53,000
Mental Health Counselors and Marriage and Family Therapists	156,300	58,500	37	$40,000
Rehabilitation Counselor	129,800	36,6000	28	$37,000
Substance Abuse and Behavioral Disorder Counselors	85,500	23,400	27	$38,000

*These numbers are rounded to their nearest thousand. Counselors who are credentialed as Licensed Professional Counselors or Certified Rehabilitation Counselors generally earn a substantial amount more than is listed.

Source: U.S. Department of Labor, Bureau of Labor Statistics. (2012, May 25). Counselors. *Occupational Outlook Handbook, 2012–2013 Edition*. Retrieved from http://data.bls.gov/search/query/results?q=counselors

4. Entry requirements
5. The size of the program and university
6. Faculty-student ratios
7. Diversity of the student body and of the faculty
8. The cost and number of available scholarships
9. Location
10. Job placement possibilities
11. Whether the program is "on-line" and any negative ramifications if it is (for instance, some employers look down on on-line programs, even accredited ones).

Similarly, the job seeker should know the following:

1. The minimum credentials needed for the job
2. Specific requirements necessary to fulfill the job
3. The philosophical orientation of the setting
4. The number and type of clients one is expected to see
5. Other job roles and functions
6. Salary
7. Diversity of co-workers
8. Possibilities for job advancement

THE APPLICATION PROCESS

Having sat on selection committees for graduate schools and for counseling jobs in the public and private sector, I have been amazed at the number of applicants who miss the basics in their application process. The following represent some items one should address when completing such applications:

1. Complete all necessary forms, and meet all application deadlines.
2. Make sure you address each item asked of you in the graduate application or in the job advertisement.
3. Do not submit cookie-cutter applications to different jobs or different graduate schools. Make sure that your application speaks to the school or job to which you are applying.
4. Take and be prepared for any necessary tests (e.g., GREs for graduate schools, personality tests for some jobs).
5. Write a great essay or statement of philosophy.
6. Find out whether an interview is required, and prepare for it.
7. Find out about faculty members' research or be knowledgeable about your employer's background, and find an opportunity to ask questions about what they have accomplished.
8. Provide a well-written résumé.
9. Consider submitting a portfolio.
10. Use spell-check, and check your grammar.
11. Be positive, focused, and prepared.
12. Don't be negative or cynical.

THE RÉSUMÉ

Some programs and most potential employers will ask you to submit a *résumé*. Good résumés present a well-rounded picture of who you are, so it's usually a good idea to submit one even if it is not asked for. Some general guidelines when developing your résumé include:

1. Make it readable, attractive, grammatically correct, and to the point.
2. Do not use gender-biased words or phrases.
3. Do not be overly concerned about length. There has been a tendency in recent years to keep résumés under two pages. I don't agree. Whatever you decide the length of your résumé needs to be, make sure it is not hard on the eyes of the reader.
4. Do not make the résumé too wordy or too chaotic.
5. Tailor your résumé to the requirements of the program or job being pursued.
6. Do not add detail that could have you eliminated from the selection process. For instance, sometimes individuals include career goals that are at odds with the goals of the program or the job at hand.
7. Do not sell yourself short. For example, I have seen many individuals not list jobs they have had because those jobs were not in the counseling field. Don't forget that all experience is good experience and that jobs have transferable skills.
8. Brag about yourself, but don't sound narcissistic.

For a more detailed look at résumés, get a good book on résumé writing, such as *Amazing Résumés* (Bright & Earl, 2009) or *Best Résumés for College Students and New Grads* (Kursmark, 2011). In addition, today, there are some great websites to help you build a terrific résumé (see Afterword, Box 1).

THE PORTFOLIO

In addition to a résumé, a *portfolio* may increase your chances of being admitted to graduate school or obtaining a job (Cobia et al., 2005). A portfolio includes materials that demonstrate the ability of the student or counselor and can be used when applying for graduate school or for jobs. Competencies highlighted through accreditation processes (e.g., CACREP) or goals highlighted in job advertisements will often drive what is included in the portfolio.

As an example of what may be placed in a portfolio, a student who has completed a degree in school counseling may have developed a portfolio that could be used for potential employment purposes and includes: a résumé, transcripts or videos of the student's work with clients (client's identities are hidden), a supervisor's assessment of the student's work, a paper that highlights the student's view of human nature, examples of how to build a multicultural school environment, ways that the student shows a commitment to the school counseling profession, a test report written by the student, and a project that shows how the student would build a comprehensive school counseling program. Although portfolios have, in the past, been paper projects, today's portfolios are often placed on CDs or made available online (Willis & Wilkie, 2009) (see Afterword, Box 2).

LOCATING A GRADUATE PROGRAM/FINDING A JOB

You're ready to apply to a program or find a job. So where do you look? There are some specific places you can contact to find the graduate program of your choice, and there are ways to increase your chances of obtaining your dream job. The following section provides some resources for your school- or job-selection process.

FINDING A GRADUATE PROGRAM

A number of resources are available to assist potential graduate students in locating graduate schools. Some of these include the following:

- *Master's and doctoral programs in counseling:*
  Council for Accreditation of Counseling and Related Educational Programs
  1001 North Fairfax Street, Suite 510
  Alexandria, VA 22314
  Phone: 703-535-5990
  Website: www.cacrep.org
  Related association: American Counseling Association (ACA)

  Counselor Preparation: Programs, Faculty, Trends (13th ed.) (2012).
  Authors: Schweiger, W. K., Henderson, D. A., McCaskill, K., Clawson, T. W., & Collins, D. R.
  Routledge: C/O Taylor & Francis, Inc.
  7625 Empire Drive
  Florence, KY 41042-2919
  Phone: 800-634-7064
  Website: http://www.routledge.com/
  Email: orders@taylorandfrancis.com

- *Doctoral programs in counseling and clinical psychology:*
  American Psychological Association (APA)
  750 First Street NE
  Washington, D.C. 20002
  Graduate and Postdoctoral Education
  Phone: 202-336-5979
  Website: www.apa.org/education/grad/index.aspx
  Related association: American Psychological Association (www.apa.org)

- *Master's programs in rehabilitation counseling:*
  Council on Rehabilitation Education (CORE)
  1699 Woodfield Road, Suite 300
  Schaumburg, IL 60173
  Phone: 847-944-1345
  E-mail: sdenys@cpccredentialing.com
  Website: http://www.core-rehab.org/WhatisCORE.html
  Related associations:
      American Rehabilitation Counseling Association (www.arcaweb.org)
      National Rehabilitation Counseling Association (http://nrca-net.org)

- *Master's programs in marriage and family therapy:*
  Commission on Accreditation for Marriage and Family Therapy Education
  112 South Alfred Street
  Alexandria, VA 22314-3061
  Phone: 703-838-9808
  Website: www.aamft.org (click "Education and Training" and "Accreditation")
  Related association: American Association for Marriage and Family Therapy (www.aamft.org)

Council for Accreditation of Counseling and Related Educational Programs
1001 North Fairfax Street, Suite 510
Alexandria, VA 22314
Phone: 703-535-5990
Website: www.cacrep.org
Related association: International Association of Marriage and Family
    Counselors (www.iamfc.org)

- *Clinical pastoral programs:*
  Association for Clinical Pastoral Education, Inc.
  1549 Clairmont Road, Suite 103
  Decatur, GA 30033
  Phone: 404-320-1472
  Website: www.acpe.edu

- *Master's programs in social work:*
  Council on Social Work Education
  1725 Duke St., Suite 500
  Alexandria, VA 22314
  Phone: 703-683-8080
  Website: http://www.cswe.org/Accreditation.aspx
  Related associations: Council on Social Work Education (www.cswe.org)
  National Association of Social Workers (www.naswdc.org)

- *Master's programs in art therapy:*
  American Art Therapy Association
  225 North Fairfax Street
  Alexandria, VA 22314
  Phone: 888-290-0878
  Website: http://www.americanarttherapyassociation.org/aata-educational-
      programs.html
  Related association: American Art Therapy Association (www.arttherapy.org)

FINDING A JOB

There are a number of things you can do to increase your chances of finding a job. Some of these include networking, going on informational interviews, responding to ads in professional publications, interviewing at national conferences, using the services of college and university job placement services, and more.

NETWORKING You've finished your training and now are ready to find a job. What do you do? Well, if you want to get a head start on the process, you should join your local, state, and national professional associations prior to finishing your training. Networking in this manner is one of the most widely used and best methods of obtaining a job. When people see you and are impressed with you, you have gained a foot in the door. And sometimes you even get a job offered on the spot! (see Afterword, Box 3).

AFTERWORD, BOX 3

Randy was a former student of mine who was enthusiastic about the counseling field. He joined his professional associations, worked with me on research, and participated in professional activities whenever possible. Because Randy was so involved, he had the opportunity to co-present a workshop with me at a state professional association conference. His enthusiasm and knowledge so impressed one of the participants that at the end of one workshop she offered him a job—right there.

GOING ON INFORMATIONAL INTERVIEWS You have your résumé and have developed a portfolio, you're networked, you look good and sound good—now what do you do? Well, you've probably identified a few different types of jobs in the counseling field. Now it's time to find some people who have these jobs and go on some informational interviews. These interviews will allow you to get a closer look at exactly what people do and will help you make a decision regarding whether or not you really want to pursue a particular job. In fact, sometimes people will let you shadow them on the job, and sometimes informational interviews can lead you to a specific job opening.

RESPONDING TO ADS IN PROFESSIONAL PUBLICATIONS Today, there are a number of professional publications that list jobs locally, statewide, and nationally. An active counseling association in your community or state may have a job bank and list jobs in its newsletter. *Counseling Today,* the monthly ACA magazine, lists a variety of counseling-related jobs throughout the country. So does the APA newspaper, *The Monitor.* Similarly, the *Chronicle of Higher Education* lists jobs nationally, although most listed jobs are confined to the area of student affairs or doctoral-level jobs.

INTERVIEWING AT NATIONAL CONFERENCES Often, the large national conferences, such as the annual counselor conference sponsored by ACA, will offer a process whereby individuals who are looking for jobs can interview with prospective employers at the conference. Although this is generally focused on doctoral-level counselor-educator jobs, some master's-level jobs are also available.

COLLEGE AND UNIVERSITY JOB PLACEMENT SERVICES Job placement services and career management centers at colleges and universities will often have listings of local community agencies that can be helpful when conducting a job search. Sometimes these placement services will have job listings and offer job fairs that are relevant for graduate students in counseling.

OTHER JOB-FINDING METHODS Remember the tried-and-true methods for finding jobs—such as applying directly to an employer, responding to a newspaper ad, contacting a private or state employment agency, and placing an ad in a professional journal. These methods sometimes do work!

BEING CHOSEN, BEING DENIED

Counselor educators avoid saying a person is rejected from a program or a job, suggesting instead that the individual was denied admission or given other opportunities. Nevertheless, most people who are not admitted to their first-choice school or not offered their dream job often do feel rejected. If you are denied admission or not offered a desired job, ask for feedback about your application and/or the interview process. Although it is sometimes hard not to take a denial personally, this can be an opportunity to discover what you can do to improve your application. Once you know what was amiss, you can increase the chances of obtaining your next chosen graduate program or job.

MOVING AHEAD

For many of you, this is your first step toward a lifetime in the counseling profession. And, if it's anything like my career has been, it may end up a little bit like a roller coaster ride and not a straight path. However, whether you spend the rest of your years doing counseling, teaching counseling, or as a lawyer, teacher, doctor, or computer programmer, make the best of it. Remember, this is your life and you choose what you want to do. Work hard, love others, have a good support system, and have fun. A friend of mine once said, "Your life will not be complete until you have had a child, planted a tree, and written a book." So I had two children, planted a few trees, and wrote a number of books. And guess what? He was wrong, because I keep learning that my life will never be complete. I continue to find new and wondrous things to keep me interested and to keep me moving ahead!

MULTICULTURAL COUNSELING COMPETENCIES

I. Counselor Awareness of Own Cultural Values and Biases
   A. Attitudes and Beliefs
      1. Culturally skilled counselors believe that cultural self-awareness and sensitivity to one's own cultural heritage is essential.
      2. Culturally skilled counselors are aware of how their own cultural background and experiences have influenced attitudes, values, and biases about psychological processes.
      3. Culturally skilled counselors are able to recognize the limits of their multicultural competency and expertise.
      4. Culturally skilled counselors recognize their sources of discomfort with differences that exist between themselves and clients in terms of race, ethnicity, and culture.

   B. Knowledge
      1. Culturally skilled counselors have specific knowledge about their own racial and cultural heritage and how it personally and professionally affects their definitions and biases of normality/abnormality and the process of counseling.
      2. Culturally skilled counselors possess knowledge and understanding about how oppression, racism, discrimination, and stereotyping affect them personally and in their work. This allows individuals to acknowledge their own racist attitudes, beliefs, and feelings. Although this standard applies to all groups, for White counselors it may mean that they understand how they may have directly or indirectly benefited from individual, institutional, and cultural racism as outlined in White identity development models.
      3. Culturally skilled counselors possess knowledge about their social impact upon others. They are knowledgeable about communication style differences, how their style may clash with or foster the

counseling process with persons of color or others different from themselves based on the A, B, and C Dimensions, and how to anticipate the impact it may have on others.

C. Skills

1. Culturally skilled counselors seek out educational, consultative, and training experiences to improve their understanding and effectiveness in working with culturally different populations. Being able to recognize the limits of their competencies, they (a) seek consultation, (b) seek further training or education, (c) refer out to more qualified individuals or resources, or (d) engage in a combination of these.

2. Culturally skilled counselors are constantly seeking to understand themselves as racial and cultural beings and are actively seeking a non racist identity.

II. Counselor Awareness of Client's Worldview

A. Attitudes and Beliefs

1. Culturally skilled counselors are aware of their negative and positive emotional reactions toward other racial and ethnic groups that may prove detrimental to the counseling relationship. They are willing to contrast their own beliefs and attitudes with those of their culturally different clients in a nonjudgmental fashion.

2. Culturally skilled counselors are aware of the stereotypes and preconceived notions that they may hold toward other racial and ethnic minority groups.

B. Knowledge

1. Culturally skilled counselors possess specific knowledge and information about the particular group with which they are working. They are aware of the life experiences, cultural heritage, and historical background of their culturally different clients. This particular competency is strongly linked to the "minority identity development models" available in the literature.

2. Culturally skilled counselors understand how race, culture, ethnicity, and so forth may affect personality formation, vocational choices, manifestation of psychological disorders, help-seeking behavior, and the appropriateness or inappropriateness of counseling approaches.

3. Culturally skilled counselors understand and have knowledge about sociopolitical influences that impinge upon the life of racial and ethnic minorities. Immigration issues, poverty, racism, stereotyping, and powerlessness may impact self esteem and self concept in the counseling process.

C. Skills

1. Culturally skilled counselors should familiarize themselves with relevant research and the latest findings regarding mental health and mental disorders that affect various ethnic and racial groups. They

should actively seek out educational experiences that enrich their knowledge, understanding, and cross-cultural skills for more effective counseling behavior.

2. Culturally skilled counselors become actively involved with minority individuals outside the counseling setting (e.g., community events, social and political functions, celebrations, friendships, neighborhood groups, and so forth) so that their perspective of minorities is more than an academic or helping exercise.

III. Culturally Appropriate Intervention Strategies

A. Beliefs and Attitudes

1. Culturally skilled counselors respect clients' religious and/or spiritual beliefs and values, including attributions and taboos, because they affect worldview, psychosocial functioning, and expressions of distress.

2. Culturally skilled counselors respect indigenous helping practices and respect helping networks among communities of color.

3. Culturally skilled counselors value bilingualism and do not view another language as an impediment to counseling (monolingualism may be the culprit).

B. Knowledge

1. Culturally skilled counselors have a clear and explicit knowledge and understanding of the generic characteristics of counseling and therapy (culture bound, class bound, and monolingual) and how they may clash with the cultural values of various cultural groups.

2. Culturally skilled counselors are aware of institutional barriers that prevent minorities from using mental health services.

3. Culturally skilled counselors have knowledge of the potential bias in assessment instruments and use procedures and interpret findings keeping in mind the cultural and linguistic characteristics of the clients.

4. Culturally skilled counselors have knowledge of family structures, hierarchies, values, and beliefs from various cultural perspectives. They are knowledgeable about the community where a particular cultural group may reside and the resources in the community.

5. Culturally skilled counselors should be aware of relevant discriminatory practices at the social and community level that may be affecting the psychological welfare of the population being served.

C. Skills

1. Culturally skilled counselors are able to engage in a variety of verbal and nonverbal helping responses. They are able to send and receive both verbal and nonverbal messages accurately and appropriately. They are not tied down to only one method or approach to helping, but recognize that helping styles and approaches may be culture bound. When they sense that their helping style is limited and potentially inappropriate, they can anticipate and modify it.

2. Culturally skilled counselors are able to exercise institutional intervention skills on behalf of their clients. They can help clients determine whether a "problem" stems from racism or bias in others (the concept of healthy paranoia) so that clients do not inappropriately personalize problems.

3. Culturally skilled counselors are not averse to seeking consultation with traditional healers or religious and spiritual leaders and practitioners in the treatment of culturally different clients when appropriate.

4. Culturally skilled counselors take responsibility for interacting in the language requested by the client and, if not feasible, make appropriate referrals. A serious problem arises when the linguistic skills of the counselor do not match the language of the client. This being the case, counselors should (a) seek a translator with cultural knowledge and appropriate professional background or (b) refer to a knowledgeable and competent bilingual counselor.

5. Culturally skilled counselors have training and expertise in the use of traditional assessment and testing instruments. They not only understand the technical aspects of the instruments but are also aware of the cultural limitations. This allows them to use test instruments for the welfare of culturally different clients.

6. Culturally skilled counselors should attend to as well as work to eliminate biases, prejudices, and discriminatory contexts in conducting evaluations and providing interventions, and should develop sensitivity to issues of oppression, sexism, heterosexism, elitism and racism.

7. Culturally skilled counselors take responsibility for educating their clients on the processes of psychological intervention, such as goals, expectations, legal rights, and the counselor's orientation.

SOURCE: Arredondo, P., Toporek, M. S., Brown, S., Jones, J., Locke, D. C., Sanchez, J. & Stadler, H. (1996). *Operationalization of the multicultural counseling competencies*. Alexandria, VA: Association of Multicultural Counseling and Development. Retrieved from http://www.amcdaca.org/amcd/competencies.pdf

ADVOCACY COMPETENCIES

CLIENT/STUDENT EMPOWERMENT

- An advocacy orientation involves not only systems change interventions but also the implementation of empowerment strategies in direct counseling.
- Advocacy-oriented counselors recognize the impact of social, political, economic, and cultural factors on human development.
- They also help their clients and students understand their own lives in context. This lays the groundwork for self-advocacy.

EMPOWERMENT COUNSELOR COMPETENCIES

In direct interventions, the counselor is able to:

1. Identify strengths and resources of clients and students.
2. Identify the social, political, economic, and cultural factors that affect the client/student.
3. Recognize the signs indicating that an individual's behaviors and concerns reflect responses to systemic or internalized oppression.
4. At an appropriate development level, help the individual identify the external barriers that affect his or her development.
5. Train students and clients in self-advocacy skills.
6. Help students and clients develop self-advocacy action plans.
7. Assist students and clients in carrying out action plans.

CLIENT/STUDENT ADVOCACY

- When counselors become aware of external factors that act as barriers to an individual's development, they may choose to respond through advocacy.

- The client/student advocate role is especially significant when individuals or vulnerable groups lack access to needed services.

Client/Student Advocacy Counselor Competencies

In environmental interventions on behalf of clients and students, the counselor is able to:

8. Negotiate relevant services and education systems on behalf of clients and students.
9. Help clients and students gain access to needed resources.
10. Identify barriers to the well-being of individuals and vulnerable groups.
11. Develop an initial plan of action for confronting these barriers.
12. Identify potential allies for confronting the barriers.
13. Carry out the plan of action.

COMMUNITY COLLABORATION

- Their ongoing work with people gives counselors a unique awareness of recurring themes. Counselors are often among the first to become aware of specific difficulties in the environment.
- Advocacy-oriented counselors often choose to respond to such challenges by alerting existing organizations that are already working for change and that might have an interest in the issue at hand.
- In these situations, the counselor's primary role is as an ally. Counselors can also be helpful to organizations by making available to them our particular skills: interpersonal relations, communications, training, and research.

Community Collaboration Counselor Competencies

14. Identify environmental factors that impinge upon students' and clients' development.
15. Alert community or school groups with common concerns related to the issue.
16. Develop alliances with groups working for change.
17. Use effective listening skills to gain understanding of the group's goals.
18. Identify the strengths and resources that the group members bring to the process of systemic change.
19. Communicate recognition of and respect for these strengths and resources.
20. Identify and offer the skills that the counselor can bring to the collaboration.
21. Assess the effect of counselor's interaction with the community.

SYSTEMS ADVOCACY

- When counselors identify systemic factors that act as barriers to their students' or clients' development, they often wish that they could change the environment and prevent some of the problems that they see every day.

- Regardless of the specific target of change, the processes for altering the status quo have common qualities. Change is a process that requires vision, persistence, leadership, collaboration, systems analysis, and strong data. In many situations, a counselor is the right person to take leadership.

SYSTEMS ADVOCACY COUNSELOR COMPETENCIES

In exerting systems-change leadership at the school or community level, the advocacy-oriented counselor is able to:

22. Identify environmental factors impinging on students' or clients' development.
23. Provide and interpret data to show the urgency for change.
24. In collaboration with other stakeholders, develop a vision to guide change.
25. Analyze the sources of political power and social influence within the system.
26. Develop a step-by-step plan for implementing the change process.
27. Develop a plan for dealing with probable responses to change.
28. Recognize and deal with resistance.
29. Assess the effect of counselor's advocacy efforts on the system and constituents.

PUBLIC INFORMATION

- Across settings, specialties, and theoretical perspectives, professional counselors share knowledge of human development and expertise in communication.
- These qualities make it possible for advocacy-oriented counselors to awaken the general public to macro-systemic issues regarding human dignity.

PUBLIC INFORMATION COUNSELOR COMPETENCIES

In informing the public about the role of environmental factors in human development, the advocacy-oriented counselor is able to:

30. Recognize the impact of oppression and other barriers to healthy development.
31. Identify environmental factors that are protective of healthy development.
32. Prepare written and multi-media materials that provide clear explanations of the role of specific environmental factors in human development.
33. Communicate information in ways that are ethical and appropriate for the target population.
34. Disseminate information through a variety of media.
35. Identify and collaborate with other professionals who are involved in disseminating public information.
36. Assess the influence of public information efforts undertaken by the counselor.

SOCIAL/POLITICAL ADVOCACY

- Counselors regularly act as change agents in the systems that affect their own students and clients most directly. This experience often leads toward the recognition that some of the concerns they have addressed affected people in a much larger arena.

- When this happens, counselors use their skills to carry out social/political advocacy.

SOCIAL/POLITICAL ADVOCACY COUNSELOR COMPETENCIES

In influencing public policy in a large, public arena, the advocacy-oriented counselor is able to:

37. Distinguish those problems that can best be resolved through social/political action.
38. Identify the appropriate mechanisms and avenues for addressing these problems.
39. Seek out and join with potential allies.
40. Support existing alliances for change.
41. With allies, prepare convincing data and rationales for change.
42. With allies, lobby legislators and other policy makers.
43. Maintain open dialogue with communities and clients to ensure that the social/political advocacy is consistent with the initial goals.

SOURCE: Lewis, J. A., Arnold, M. S., House, R., & Toporek, R. L. (2003). *ACA advocacy competencies*. Retrieved from http://www.counseling.org/Resources/Competencies/Advocacy_Competencies.pdf

References

Adam, B. D. (2007). *Homophobia and heterosexism*. In G. Ritzer (Ed.), *Blackwell Encyclopedia of Sociology*. Retrieved from http://www. blackwellreference.com/public/

Addams, J. (1910). *Twenty years at Hull House*. New York, NY: Macmillan.

Altekruse, M. K., & Wittmer, J. (1991). Accreditation in counselor education. In F. O. Bradley (Ed.), *Credentialing in counseling* (pp. 81–85). Alexandria, VA: Association for Counselor Education and Supervision.

American Art Therapy Association. (2011). *Home page*. Retrieved from http:// aata2009.serveronline.net/aata-aboutus. html

American Association for Marriage and Family Therapists. (2001). *AAMFT code of ethics*. Retrieved from http://www. aamft.org/imis15/content/legal_ethics/ code_of_ethics.aspx

American Association for Marriage and Family Therapists. (2002–2011a). *About AAMFT*. Retrieved from http://www. aamft.org/iMIS15/AAMFT/About/ About_AAMFT/Content/About_AAMFT/ About_AAMFT.aspx?hkey=a8d047de-5bf7-40cd-9551-d626e2490a25

American Association for Marital and Family Therapy. (2002–2011b). *Commission on accreditation for marriage and family therapy education*. Retrieved from http://www.aamft.org/imis15/Content/ COAMFTE/About_COAMFTE.aspx

American Association for Marital and Family Therapy. (2002–2011c). *MFT accredited programs*. Retrieved from http://www. aamft.org/iMIS15/AAMFT/Directories/ MFT_Training_Programs/Content/ Directories/MFT_Training_Programs. aspx?hkey=7ae12d01-323a-4a36-9542-65ff4fb88b47

American Association of Pastoral Counselors. (2005–2012a). *Home page*. Retrieved from http://aapc.org/

American Association of Pastoral Counselors. (2005–2012b). Mission statement. Retrieved from http://www. aapc.org/home/mission-statement.aspx

American Association of Pastoral Counselors. (2005–2012c). *Certifications*. Retrieved from http://www.aapc.org/membership/ certifications.aspx

American Association of Pastoral Counselors. (2005–2012d). Pastoral care specialist training programs. Retrieved from http://www.aapc.org/membership/ pastoral-care-specialist-training-programs.aspx

American Association of State Counseling Boards. (2012). *Licensure and portability*.

Retrieved from http://www.aascb.org/aws/AASCB/pt/sp/licensure

American Board of Genetic Counseling. (2010). *Home page.* Retrieved from http://www.abgc.net/ABGC/AmericanBoardofGeneticCounselors.asp

American Board of Medical Specialties. (2006–2012). *What board certification means.* Retrieved from http://www.abms.org/about_board_certification/means.aspx

American Board of Professional Psychology. (2012). *Member specialty boards.* Retrieved from http://www.abpp.org/i4a/pages/index.cfm?pageid=3279

American Counseling Association. (1995a). *ACA history.* Alexandria, VA: Author.

American Counseling Association. (1995b). *Code of ethics and standards of practice* (rev. ed.). Alexandria, VA: Author.

American Counseling Association. (2005). *ACA code of ethics.* Retrieved from http://www.counseling.org/Resources/CodeOfEthics/TP/Home/CT2.aspx

American Counseling Association. (2009, August 1). *Membership report.* Alexandria, VA: Author.

American Counseling Association. (2010a). *20/20: A vision for the future of counseling: Consensus definition of counseling.* Retrieved from http://www.counseling.org/20-20/definition

American Counseling Association. (2010b). Statement of principles. Retrieved from http://www.counseling.org/20-20/principles.aspx

American Counseling Association. (2011a). *2011 statistics on mental health professions.* Retrieved from http://www.counseling.org/PublicPolicy/PDF/Mental_Health_Professions%20_Statistics_2011.pdf

American Counseling Association. (2011b). *Who are licensed professional counselors?* Retrieved from http://www.counseling.org/PublicPolicy/WhoAreLPCs.pdf

American Counseling Association. (2012a). *About us.* Retrieved from http://www.counseling.org/AboutUs/

American Counseling Association. (2012b). *ACA divisions.* Retrieved from http://www.counseling.org/AboutUs/DivisionsBranches AndRegions/TP/Divisions/CT2.aspx

American Counseling Association. (2012c). *ACA encourages state licensure boards to facilitate licensure portability.* Retrieved from http://www.counseling.org/PressRoom/PressReleases.aspx?AGuid=201c676f-afc9-468b-aaf1-fc805336ea15

American Counseling Association. (2012d). *Licensure and certification.* Retrieved from http://www.counseling.org/Counselors/LicensureAndCert.aspx

American Counseling Association. (2012e). *Public policy.* Retrieved from http://www.counseling.org/PublicPolicy/

American Mental Health Counselors Association. (2010). *Principles for AMHCA Code of ethics.* Retrieved from https://www.amhca.org/assets/news/AMHCA_Code_of_Ethics_2010_w_pagination_cxd_51110.pdf

American Nurses Credentialing Center. (2012). *Home page.* Retrieved from http://www.nursecredentialing.org/

American Psychiatric Association. (2000). *Diagnostic and statistical manual of mental disorders* (4th ed., text revision). Washington, DC: Author.

American Psychiatric Association. (2009). *The principles of medical ethics: With annotations especially applicable to psychiatry.* Retrieved from http://www.psych.org/MainMenu/PsychiatricPractice/Ethics/ResourcesStandards/PrinciplesofMedicalEthics.aspx

American Psychiatric Association. (2010). *DSM-5 development.* Retrieved from http://www.dsm5.org/Pages/Default.aspx

American Psychiatric Association. (2012). *About APA.* Retrieved from http://www.psych.org/FunctionalMenu/AboutAPA.aspx

American Psychiatric Nurses Association. (n.d.). *Home page.* Retrieved from http://www.apna.org/

American Psychoanalytic Association. (2008). *Principles and standards for education in psychoanalysis.* Retrieved from http://www.apsa.org/Portals/1/docs/Training/Standards_rv_06_08.pdf

American Psychological Association. (2010). *Ethical principles of psychologists and code of conduct: 2010 amendments.* Retrieved from http://www.apa.org/ethics/code/index.aspx

American Psychological Association. (2011). *Careers in psychology.* Washington, DC: Author.

American Psychological Association. (2012a). *About APA*. Retrieved from http://www.apa.org/about/index.aspx

American Psychological Association. (2012b). *Accreditation*. Retrieved from http://www.apa.org/ed/accreditation/

American School Counselor Association. (2005). *The ASCA National Model: A framework for school counseling programs* (2nd ed.). Arlington, VA: Author.

American School Counselor Association. (2006–2012). *State certification requirements*. Retrieved from http://www.schoolcounselor.org/content.asp?contentid=242

American School Counselor Association. (2010). *Ethical standards for school counselors*. Retrieved from http://asca2.timberlakepublishing.com//files/EthicalStandards2010.pdf

Anderson, T., Lunnen, K. M., & Ogles, B. M. (2010). Putting models and techniques in context. In B. L. Duncan, S. D. Miller, B. E. Wampold, & M A. Hubble (Eds.), *The heart and soul of change* (2nd ed., pp. 143–166). Washington, DC: American Psychological Association.

Appignanesi, R., & Zarate, O. (2007). *Introducing Freud*. Royton, England: Icon Books.

Arredondo, P. (1999). Multicultural counseling competencies as tools to address oppression and racism. *Journal of Counseling and Development, 77*, 102–108.

Arredondo, P., Toporek, R., Brown, S. P., Jones, J., Locke, D. C., Sanchez, J., & Stadler, H. (1996). Operationalization of the multicultural counseling competencies. *Journal of Multicultural Counseling and Development, 24*(1), 42–78.

Arredondo, P., Tovar-Blank, Z., & Parham, T. (2008). Challenges and promises of becoming a culturally competent counselor in a sociopolitical era of change and empowerment. *Journal of Counseling and Development, 86*, 261–268.

Art Therapy Credentials Board. (2007). *Welcome to the art therapy credentials board, Inc.!* Retrieved from http://www.atcb.org/

Arthur, M. M. L. (2007). *Race*. In G. Ritzer (Ed.), *Blackwell Encyclopedia of Sociology*. Retrieved from http://www.blackwellreference.com/subscriber/tocnode?id=g9781405124331_chunk_g978140512433124_ss1-1

Asay, T. P., & Lambert, M. J. (1999). The empirical case for common factors in therapy: Quantitative findings. In M. A. Hubble, B. L. Duncan, and S. D. Mioller (Eds.), *The heart and soul of change: What works in therapy* (pp. 23–55). Washington, DC: American Psychological Association.

Association for Specialists in Group Work. (2007). *ASGW best practice guidelines*. Retrieved from http://www.asgw.org/PDF/Best_Practices.pdf

Atkinson, D. R. (2004). Defining populations and terms. In D. R. Atkinson (Ed.), *Counseling American minorities* (6th ed., pp. 3–26). Boston, MA: McGraw-Hill.

Attridge, W. C. (2000). *Ethical considerations for internet counseling*. Retrieved from ERIC database. (ED448369)

Attridge, W. C. (2004). *Current practices & future implications for internet counseling*. Retrieved from ERIC database. (ED448369)

Aubrey, R. F. (1977). Historical development of guidance and counseling and implications for the future. *Personnel and Guidance Journal, 55*, 288–295.

Aubrey, R. F. (1982). A house divided: Guidance and counseling in twentieth-century America. *Personnel and Guidance Journal, 61*, 198–204.

Baker, S. & Gerler, E. (2008). *School counseling for the twenty-first century* (5th ed.). Upper Saddle River, NJ: Merrill.

Baldwin, S. A., Wampold, B. E., & Imel, Z. E. (2007). Untangling the alliance-outcome correlation: Exploring the relative importance of therapist and patient variability in the alliance. *Journal of Consulting and Clinical Psychology, 75*(6), 842–852. doi:10.1037/0022-006X.75.6.842

Bandura, A. T. (1969). *Principles of behavior modification*. New York, NY: Holt, Rinehart & Winston.

Barber, C. (2008, February). The medicated Americans: Antidepressant prescriptions on the rise. *Scientific American*, Retrieved from http://www.scientificamerican.com/article.cfm?id=the-medicated-americans

Bauman, S. (2008). To join or not to join: School counselors as a case study in professional membership. *Journal of Counseling and Development, 86,* 164–177.

Baxter, W. E. (1994). American psychiatry celebrates 150 years of caring. *The Psychiatric Clinics of North America, 17*(3), 683–693.

Beers, C. W. (1948). *A mind that found itself* (7th ed.). Garden City, NY: Doubleday.

Belgium, D. (1992). Guilt. In M. T. Burker & J. G. Miranti (Eds.), *Ethical and spiritual values in counseling.* (pp. 53–66). Alexandria, VA: American Association for Counseling and Development.

Belkin, G. S. (1988). *Introduction to counseling* (3rd ed.). Dubuque, IA: William C. Brown.

Bent, R. J., Packard, R., & Goldberg, R. (2009). *Who we are: A brief history of the American Board of Professional Psychology.* In C. M. Nezu, A. J. Finch, & N. P. Simon (Eds.), Becoming board certified by the American board of professional psychology (pp. 3–26). New York, NY: Oxford.

Berne, E. (1964). *Games people play.* New York, NY: Simon & Schuster.

Beutler, L. E., Malik, M., Alimohamed, S., Harwood, T. M., Talebi, H., Noble, S., & Wong, E. (2004). Therapist variables. In M. J. Lambert (Ed.), *Bergin and Garfield's handbook of psychotherapy and behavior change* (5th ed.) (227–306). New York, NY: Wiley.

Biggerstaff, M. A. (1995). Licensing, regulation, and certification. In R. L. Edwards (Ed.), *Encyclopedia of social work* (19th ed., Vol. 2, 1616–1624). Washington, DC: NASW Press.

Bike, D. H., Norcross, J. C., & Schatz, D. M. (2009). Process and outcomes of psychotherapists' personal therapy: Replication and extension 20 years later. *Psychotherapy: Theory, Research, Practice, Training, 46*(1), 19–31. doi:10.1037/a0015139

Binswanger, L. (1963). *Being-in-the-world: Selected papers.* New York, NY: Basic Books.

Birky, I. & Collins, W. (2011). Facebook: Maintaining ethical practice in the cyberspace age. *Journal of College Student Psychotherapy, 25*(3), 193–203.

Bloom, J. (1996). *Credentialing professional counselors for the 21st Century.* Retrieved from ERIC database. (ED399498)

Bloom, J., Gerstein, L., Tarvydas, V., Conaster, J., Davis, E., Kater, D., ... Esposito, R. (1990). Model legislation for licensed professional counselors. *Journal of Counseling and Development, 68,* 511–523.

Bohart, A. C., Elliot, R., Greenberg, L. S., & Watson, J. C. (2002). Empathy. In J. C. Norcross (Ed.), *Psychotherapy relationships that work: Therapist contributions and responsiveness to patients* (pp. 89–108). New York, NY: Oxford University Press.

Bradley, L. J. (1995). Certification and licensure. *Journal of Counseling and Development, 74,* 185–186.

Bradley, L. J., Hendricks, B., & Kabell, D. R. (2011). Postmortem confidentiality: An ethical issue. *Family Journal: Counseling and Therapy for Couples and Families, 19,* 417–420.

Braun, S. A., & Cox, J. A. (2005). Managed mental health care: Intentional misdiagnosis of mental disorders. *Journal of Counseling and Development, 83,* 425.

Breasted, J. H. (1930). *The Edwin Smith surgical papyrus.* Chicago: University of Chicago Press.

Breasted, J. H. (1934). *The dawn of conscience.* New York, NY: Scribner's.

Brewer, J. M. (1932). *Education as guidance.* New York, NY: Macmillan.

Briddick, W. C. (2009a). Frank findings: Frank Parsons and the Parson family. *Career Development Quarterly, 57*(3), 207–214.

Briddick, W. C. (2009b). Frank Parsons on interests. *Journal of Vocational Behavior, 24*(2), 230–233.

Bright, J., & Earl, J. (2009). *Amazing resumes: What employers want to see— and how to say it* (2nd ed.). Indianapolis, IN: JIST works.

Brooks, D. K., & Gerstein, L. H. (1990). Counselor credentialing and interprofessional collaboration. *Journal of Counseling and Development, 68,* 477–484.

Brown, K. (2008). Genetic counseling. *Journal of Legal Medicine, 29,* 345–361.

Buckley, T. R., & Franklin-Jackson, C. F. (2005). Diagnosis in racial-cultural practice. In R. T. Carter (Ed.), *Handbook of racial-cultural psychology and counseling: Theory and research* (Vol. 2, pp. 286–296). Hoboken, NJ: John Wiley.

Burger, W. (2011). *Human services in contemporary America* (8th ed.). Belmont, CA: Brooks/Cole.

Campbell, D. P. (1968). The Strong Vocational Interest Blank: 1927–1967. In P. McReynolds (Ed.), *Advances in psychological assessment*, (Vol. 1, pp. 105–130). Palo Alto, CA: Science and Behavior Books.

Capshew, J. H. (1992). Psychologists on site: A reconnaissance of the historiography of the laboratory. *American Psychologist*, 47(2), 132–142. doi:10.1037/0003-066X.47.2.132

Carkhuff, R. (1969). *Helping and human relations* (Vol. 2). New York, NY: Holt, Rinehart & Winston.

Carson, A. D., & Altai, N. M. (1994). 1000 years before Parsons: Vocational psychology in classical Islam. *The Career Development Quarterly*, 43, 197–206.

Chandra, A., Mosher, W. D., & Copen, C. (2011). Sexual behavior, sexual attraction, and sexual identity in the United States: Data from the 2006–2008 national survey of family growth. *National Health Statistics Reports, 36.* Retrieved from http://www.cdc.gov/nchs/data/nhsr/nhsr036.pdf

Chaplin, J. P. (1975). *Dictionary of psychology* (2nd ed.). New York, NY: Dell.

Cipriani, R. (2007). Religion. In G. Ritzer (Ed.), *Blackwell Encyclopedia of Sociology.* Retrieved from http://www.blackwellreference.com/public/

Claiborn, C. D. (Ed.). (1991). *Multiculturalism as a fourth force in counseling* [Special issue]. *Journal of Counseling and Development*, 70(1).

Clarkin, J. F., & Levy, K. N. (2004). The influence of client variables on psychotherapy. In M. J. Lambert (Ed.), *Bergin and Garfield's handbook of psychotherapy and behavior change* (5th ed., pp. 195–226). New York, NY: Wiley.

Clawson, T., Henderson, D. A., Schweiger, W. K., & Collins, D. R. (2008). *Counselor Preparation: Programs, faculty, trends* (12th ed.). New York, NY: Brunner-Routledge.

Cobia, C. D., Carney, J. S., Buckhalt, J. A., Middleton, R. A., Shannon, D. M., Trippany, R., & Kunkel, E. (2005). The doctoral portfolio: Centerpiece of a comprehensive system of evaluation. *Counselor Education and Supervision, 44*, 242–254.

Commission on Rehabilitation Counselor Certification. (2010). *Code of professional ethics for rehabilitation counselors.* Retrieved from https://www.crccertification.com/filebin/pdf/CRCC_COE_1-1-10_Rev12-09.pdf

Commission on Rehabilitation Counselor Certification. (2011). *About CRCC.* Retrieved from http://www.crccertification.com/pages/about_crcc/112.php

Conn, S. R., Roberts, R. L., & Powell, B. M. (2009). Attitudes and satisfaction with a hybrid model of counseling supervision. *Educational Technology & Society*, 12, 298–306.

Constantine, M. G., Smith, L., Redington, R. M., & Owens, D. (2008). Racial microaggressions against Black counseling and counseling psychology faculty: A central challenge in the multicultural counseling movement. *Journal of Counseling and Development*, 86, 348–355.

Constantine, M. G. & Sue, D. W. (2005). *Strategies for building multicultural competence in mental health and educational settings.* Hoboken, NJ: John Wiley.

Corey, G. (2013). *Theory and practice of counseling and psychotherapy* (9th ed.). Belmont, CA: Brooks/Cole.

Corey, G., Corey, M. S., Callanan, P. (2011). *Issues and ethics in the helping professions* (8th ed.). Belmont, CA: Brooks/Cole.

Cottone, R. R. (2001). A social constructivism model of ethical decision making in counseling. *Journal of Counseling and Development*, 79, 39–45.

Cottone, R. (2004). Displacing the psychology of the individual in ethical decision-making: The social constructivism model. *Canadian Journal of Counseling*, 38(1), 5–13.

Cottone, R. R., & Claus, R. E. (2000). Ethical decision-making models: A review of the literature. *Journal of Counseling and Development, 78,* 275–283.

Council for Accreditation of Counseling and Related Educational Programs. (2009). *2009 standards.* Retrieved from http://www.cacrep.org/doc/2009% 20Standards%20with%20cover.pdf

Council for Accreditation of Counseling and Related Educational Programs. IRCEP: Weclome and history. (2012a). Retrieved from http://www.ircep.org/ircep/template/index.cfm

Council for Accreditation of Counseling and Related Educational Programs. (2012b). IRCEP: Vision, mission and core values. Retrieved from http://www.ircep.org/ircep/template/page.cfm?id=93

Council for Accreditation of Counseling and Related Educational Programs. CACREP Programs on IRCEP Registry. (2012c). Retrieved from http://www.ircep.org/ircep/index.cfm/cacrep-programs-on-ircep-registry

Council for Accreditation of Counseling and Related Educational Programs. (2012d). *Home page.* Retrieved from http://www.cacrep.org

Council for Accreditation of Counseling and Related Educational Programs. (2012e). *Programs in process.* Retrieved from http://www.cacrep.org/directory/directory.cfm

Council for Standards in Human Service Education. (2010). *Home page.* Retrieved from http://www.cshse.org/

Council on Rehabilitation Education. (2011). *Home page.* Retrieved from http://www.core-rehab.org/

Council on Social Work Education. (2012). *Home page.* Retrieved from http://www.cswe.org/

Crethar, H., Rivera, E., & Nash, S. (2008). In search of common threads: Linking multicultural, feminist, and social justice counseling paradigms. *Journal of Counseling and Development, 86,* 269–278.

Cummings, N. A. (1990). The credentialing of professional psychologists and its implications for the other mental health disciplines. *Journal of Counseling and Development, 68,* 45–490.

D'Andrea, L. M., & Liu, L. (2009, March). *The CACREP standards: How much do students know?* Paper based on a program presented at the American Counseling Association Annual Conference and Exposition, Charlotte, NC. Retrieved from http://counselingoutfitters.com/vistas/vistas09/DAndrea-Liu.doc

D'Andrea, M., & Daniels, J. (1991). Exploring the different levels of multicultural counseling training in counselor education. *Journal of Counseling and Development, 70,* 78–85.

D'Andrea, M., & Daniels, J. (1999). *Exploring the psychology of White racism through naturalistic inquiry. Journal of Counseling and Development, 77,* 93–101.

D'Andrea, M., & Daniels, J. (2005). A socially responsible approach to counseling, mental health care. *Counseling Today, 48*(1), 36–38.

Davis, L. E. (Ed.). (2011). Racial disparity in mental health services: Why race still matters. London: Routledge and Psychology Press.

Deal, H. D. (2003). The relationship between critical thinking and interpersonal skills: Guidelines for clinical supervision. *The Clinical Supervisor, 22*(2), 3–19. doi:10.1300/J001v22n02_02

Dodgen, D., Fowler, R. D., & Williams-Nickelson, C. (2003). Getting involved in professional organizations: A gateway to career advancement. In M. J. Prinstein & M. D. Patterson (Eds.), *The portable mentor: Expert guide to a successful career in psychology* (pp. 221–233). New York, NY: Springer/Kluwer Academic/Plenum.

Dolgoff, R., Loewenberg, F. M., & Harrington, D. (2009). *Ethical decisions for social work practice* (8th ed.). Belmont, CA: Brooks/Cole.

Donaldson v. O'Connor, 422 U.S. 563 (1975).

Douthit, K. Z. (2006). The convergence of counseling and psychiatric genetics: An essential role for counselors. *Journal of Counseling and Development, 84,* 16–28.

Doyle, A. C., Sir. (1922). *Tales of terror and mystery* [eBook]. Retrieved from http://www.bookrags.com/ebooks/537/15.html

Dyeson, T. B. (2004). Social work licensure: A brief history and description. *Home*

Health Care Management & Practice, 16, 408–411. doi:10.1177/108482230 4264657

Debunking the concept of race. [Editorial] (2005, July 30). *New York Times*, A28.

Egan, G. (1975). *The skilled helper: A model for systematic helping and interpersonal relating*. Pacific Grove, CA: Brooks/Cole.

Egan, G. (2010). *The skilled helper: A problem management and opportunity-development approach to helping* (9th ed.). Belmont, CA: Brooks/Cole.

Ellis, A., & Harper, R. A. (1961). *A guide to rational living*. Englewood Cliffs, NJ: Prentice Hall.

Ellwood, R. S., & McGraw, B. A. (2009). *Many peoples, many faiths: Women and men in the world religions* (9th ed.). Boston, MA: Pearson.

Eriksen, K. P., & McAuliffe, G. J. (2006). Constructive development and counselor competence. *Counselor Education and Supervision, 45*, 180–192.

Erikson, E. H. (1950). *Childhood and society*. New York, NY: Norton.

Evans, A. C., Delphin, M., Simmons, R., Omar, G., & Tebes, J. (2005). Developing a framework for culturally competent systems care. In R. T. Carter (Ed.), *Handbook of racial-cultural psychology and counseling: Theory and research* (Vol. 2, pp. 492–513). Hoboken, NJ: John Wiley.

Evans, K. M., & Larrabee, M. J. (2002). Teaching the multicultural counseling competencies and revised career counseling competencies simultaneously. *Journal of Multicultural Counseling and Development, 30*(1), 21–39.

Eysenck, H. J. (1952). The effects of psychotherapy: An evaluation. *Journal of Consulting Psychology, 16*, 319–324.

Feldman, M. (2010). *Comparison of school counselors and school social workers: Performance of tasks and perceived preparedness*. Retrieved from Proquest dissertations and thesis database. (AAT 3401428).

Frankl, V. (1963). *Man's search for meaning*. Boston, MA: Beacon.

Freedman, J., & Combs, G. (1996). *Narrative therapy: The social construction of preferred realities*. New York, NY: W. W. Norton and Company.

Gabbard, G. O. (1995a). Are all psychotherapies equally effective? *The Menninger Letter, 3*(1), 1–2.

Garcia, A. (1990). An examination of the social work profession's efforts to achieve legal regulation. *Journal of Counseling and Development, 68*, 491–497.

Gelso, C. J., & Carter, J. A. (1994). Components of the psychotherapy relationship: Their interaction and unfolding during treatment. *Journal of Counseling Psychology, 41*(3), 296–306. doi:10.1037/0022-0167.41.3.296

Gelso, C. J., Kelley, F. A., Fuertes, J. N., Marmarosh, C., Holmes, S. E., Costa, C., & Hancock, G. R. (2005). Measuring the real relationship in psychotherapy: Initial validation of the therapist form. *Journal of Counseling Psychology, 52*, 640–649. doi:10.1037/0022-0167.52.4.640

Ginzberg, E., Ginsburg, S. W., Axelrad, S., & Herma, J. (1951). *Occupational choice: An approach to a general theory*. New York, NY: Columbia University Press.

Gladding, S. T. (2013). *Counseling: A comprehensive approach* (7th ed.). Upper Saddle River, NJ: Pearson.

Glasser, W. (1961). *Mental health or mental illness?* New York, NY: Harper & Row.

Glasser, W. (1965). *Reality therapy: A new approach to psychiatry*. New York, NY: Harper & Row.

Glosoff, H., & Freeman, L. T. (2007). Report of the ACA ethics committee: 2005–2006. *Journal of Counseling and Development, 85*, 251–254.

Gompertz, K. (1960). The relation of empathy to effective communication. *Journalism Quarterly, 37*, 535–546.

Goodman, J. (2009). (Ed.). (2009). Advocacy competence [Special section]. *Journal of Counseling and Development, 87*, 259–294.

Goodyear, R. K. (1984). On our journal's evolution: Historical developments, transitions, and future directions. *Journal of Counseling and Development, 63*, 3–9.

Goss, S. S., & Anthony, K. K. (2009). Developments in the use of technology in counselling and psychotherapy. *British Journal of Guidance & Counselling, 37*(3), 223–230.

Gould, S. J. (1982, May, 6). A nation of morons. *New Scientist, 84.* 349–352.

Graham, L. B. (2010). *Implementing CACREP disaster/crisis standards for counseling students.* Retrieved from http://counselingoutfitters.com/vistas/vistas10/Article_90.pdf

Granello, D. (2010). Cognitive complexity among practicing counselors: How thinking changes with experience. *Journal of Counseling and Development, 88,* 92–100.

Green, C. D. (2009). Darwinian theory, functionalism, and the first American psychological revolution. *American Psychologist, 64*(2), 75–83. doi:10.1037/a0013338

Guterman, J. T., & Rudes, J. (2008). Social constructionism and ethics: Implications for counseling. *Counseling and Values, 52,* 136–144.

Haberstroh, S., Parr, G., Bradley, L., Morgan-Fleming, B., & Gee, R. (2008). Facilitating online counseling: Perspectives from counselors in training. *Journal of Counseling and Development, 86,* 460–470.

Hackney, H., & Cormier, L. S. (2013). *The professional counselor: A process guide to helping* (7th ed.). Boston, MA: Pearson.

Hayes, B. (2008). The use of multimedia instruction in counselor education: A creative teaching strategy. *Journal of Creativity in Mental Health, 3,* 243–253.

Hayes, R. A. (2005). Introduction to evidence-based practices. In C. E. Stout & R. A. Hayes (Eds.), *The evidence-based practice: Methods, models, and tools for mental health professionals* (pp. 1–9). Hoboken, NJ: Wiley.

Hays, D., Chang, C. Y., & Havic, P. (2005) White racial identity statuses as predictors of white privilege awareness. *Journal of Humanistic Counseling, Education & Development, 47,* 234–246.

Healthcare Providers Service Organization. (2012). *Home page.* Retrieved from http://www.hpso.com/

Helms, J. E. (1984). Toward a theoretical model of the effects of race on counseling: A black and white model. *The Counseling Psychologist, 12*(4), 153–165. doi:10.1177/0011000084124013

Helms, J. E. (1999). Another meta-analysis of the White Racial Identity Attitude Scale's Cronbach alphas: Implications for validity. *Measurement and Evaluation in Counseling and Development, 32,* 122–137.

Helms, J. E., & Cook, D. A. (1999). Using race and culture in counseling and psychotherapy: theory and process. Needham Heights, MA: Allyn & Bacon.

Herek, G. M. (2000). The psychology of sexual prejudice. *Current Directions in Psychological Science, 9*(1), 19–22. doi:10.1111/1467-8721.00051

Herlihy, B., & Dufrene, R. L. (2011). Current and emerging ethical issues in counseling: A delphi study of expert opinions. *Counseling and Values, 56*(1–2), 10–24.

Herr, E. L. (1985). *Why counseling?* (2nd ed.). Alexandria, VA: American Association for Counseling and Development.

Herr, E. L., Cramer, S. H., & Niles, S. G. (2004). *Career guidance and counseling through the life span: Systematic approaches* (6th ed.). Boston, MA: Pearson/Allyn & Bacon.

Hinkle, J. S., & O'Brien, S. (2010). The human services—board certified practitioner: An overview of a new national credential. *Journal of Human Services, 30,* 23–28.

Hollis, J. W., & Dodson, T. A. (2000). *Counselor preparation 1999–2001: Programs, faculty, trends* (10th ed.). Philadelphia, PA: Taylor & Francis.

Hosie, T. (1991). Historical antecedents and current status of counselor licensure. In F. O. Bradley (Ed.), *Credentialing in counseling* (pp. 23–52). Alexandria, VA: Association for Counselor Education and Supervision.

Iannone, A. P. (2001). *Dictionary of world philosophy.* New York, NY: Routledge.

International Association of Marriage and Family Counseling (n.d.a). *Welcome to IAMFC.* Retrieved from http://www.provisionsconsultingcms.com/~iamfc/

International Association of Marriage and Family Counselors (n.d.b). *IAMFC Ethical Code.* Retrieved from http://www.iamfconline.com/PDFs/Ethical%20Codes.pdf

Ivey, A. E. & Gluckstein, N. (1974). *Basic attending skills: An introduction to microcounseling and helping*. N. Amherst, MA: Microtraining Associates.

Jenkins, R. (2007). *Ethnicity*. In G. Ritzer (Ed.), *Blackwell Encyclopedia of Sociology*. Retrieved from http://www.blackwellreference.com/public/

Jennings, L. (2007). *Prejudice*. In G. Ritzer (Ed.), *Blackwell Encyclopedia of Sociology*. Retrieved from http://www.blackwellreference.com/public/

Johnson, J. (2009). Whether states should create prescription power for psychologists. *Law and psychology review*, *33*, 167–178.

Jones, K. D. (2010). The Unstructured Clinical Interview. *Journal of Counseling and Development*, *88*, 220–226.

Jones, L. K. (1994). Frank Parsons' contribution to career counseling. *Journal of Career Development*, *20*, 287–294. doi:10.1177/089484539402000403

Kalat, J. W. (2009). *Biological psychology* (10th ed.). Belmont, CA: Wadsworth.

Kaplan, D. (2012, January). Licensure reciprocity: A critical public protection issue that needs action. *Counseling Today*, Retrieved from http://ct.counseling.org/2012/01/licensure-reciprocity-a-critical-public-protection-issue-that-needs-action/

Kaplan, D. M., Kocet, M. M., Cottone, R. R., Glosoff, H. L., Miranti, J. G., Moll, E. C., ... Tarvydas, V. M. (2009). New mandates and imperatives in the revised ACA code of ethics. *Journal of Counseling and Development*, *87*, 241–256.

Kaplan, M., & Cuciti, P. L. (Eds.). (1986). *The Great Society and its legacy: Twenty years of U.S. social policy*. Durham, NC: Duke University Press.

Keferl, J. E. (2011, October). *Thank you for your leadership efforts ...* Retrieved from http://www.arcaweb.org/wp-content/uploads/ARCA_letter_to_CORE_Board_October_2011.pdf

Kegan, R. (1982). *The evolving self*. Cambridge, MA: Harvard University Press.

Kegan, R. (1994). *In over our heads*. Cambridge, MA: Harvard University Press.

Keith-Spiegel, P., & Wiederman, M. W. (2000). *The complete guide to graduate school admission: Psychology, counseling and related professions* (2nd ed.). Mahwah, NJ: Erlbaum.

Kitchener, K. S. (1984). Intuition, critical evaluation and ethical principles: The foundation for ethical decisions in counseling psychology. *The Counseling Psychologist*, *12*(3), 43–45. doi:10.1177/0011000084123005

Kitchener, K. S. (1986). Teaching applied ethics in counselor education: An integration of psychological processes and philosophical analysis. *Journal of Counseling and Development*, *64*, 306–311. doi:10.1177/0011000084123005

Klein, M. H., Kolden, G. G., Michels, J. L., & Chisholm-Stockard, S. (2001). Congruence or genuineness. *Psychotherapy*, *38*, 396–400. doi:10.1037/0033-3204.38.4.396

Kleinke, C. L. (1994). *Common principles of psychotherapy*. Pacific Grove, CA: Brooks/Cole.

Kleist, D., & Bitter, J. R. (2009). Virtue, ethics, and legality in family practice. In J. Bitter, *Theory and practice of family therapy and counseling* (pp. 43–65). Belmont, CA: Brooks/Cole.

Kluckhohn, C., & Murray, H. A. (Eds.). (1948). *Personality in nature, society, and culture*. New York, NY: Alfred A. Knopf.

Kocet, M. (2006). Ethical challenges in a complex world: Highlights of the 2005 ACA Code of Ethics. *Journal of Counseling and Development*, *84*, 228–234.

Kornetsky, C. (1976). *Pharmacology: Drugs affecting behavior*. New York, NY: Wiley.

Kosmin, B. A., & Keysar, A. (2008). *American religious identification survey*. Hartford, CO: Trinity College.

Kottler, J. (2011). *Introduction to counseling: Voices from the field* (7th ed.). Belmont, CA: Brooks/Cole.

Krumboltz, J. D. (1966a). Promoting adaptive behavior. In J. D. Krumboltz (Ed.), *Revolution in counseling* (pp. 3–26). Boston, MA: Houghton Mifflin.

Krumboltz, J. D. (Ed.). (1966b). *Revolution in counseling*. Boston, MA: Houghton Mifflin.

Kuriansky, J. (2008). A clinical toolbox for cross-cultural counseling and training. In U. P. Gielen, J. G. Draguns, &

J. M. Fish (Eds.), *Principles of multicultural counseling and therapy.* New York, NY: Routledge.

Kursmark, L. M. (2011). *Best resumes for college students and new grads: Jump-start your career* (3rd ed.). Indianapolis, IN: JIST Works.

Lambie, G. W., Hagedorn, W. B., & Ieva, K. P. (2010). Social-cognitive development, ethical and legal knowledge, and ethical decision making of counselor education students. *Counselor Education and Supervision, 49,* 228–246.

Lambie, G. W., & Williamson, L. L. (2004). The challenge to change from guidance counseling to professional school counseling: A historical proposition. *Professional School Counseling, 8,* 124–131.

Law, I. (2007). *Discrimination.* In G. Ritzer (Ed.), *Blackwell Encyclopedia of Sociology.* Retrieved from http://www.blackwellreference.com/public/

Lawson, G. (2007). Counselor wellness and impairment: A national survey. *Journal of Humanistic Counseling, Education and Development, 46,* 20–34.

Lawson, G., & Myers, J. E. (2011). Wellness, Professional Quality of Life, and Career-Sustaining Behaviors: What Keeps Us Well? *Journal of Counseling and Development, 89,* 163–171.

Layne, C. M., & Hohenshil, T. H. (2005). High-tech counseling revisited. *Journal of Counseling and Development, 83,* 222–227.

Leary, D. (1992). William James and the art of human understanding. *American Psychologist, 47*(2), 152–160. doi:10.1037/0003-066X.47.2.152

Leiby, J. (1978). *A history of social welfare and social work in the United States.* New York, NY: Columbia University Press.

Linstrum, K. S. (2005). The effects of training on ethical decision making skills as a function of moral development and context in master-level counseling students. *Dissertation Abstracts International Section A: Humanities & Social Sciences,* Vol. 65(9-A), 3289. U.S.: University Microfilms International.

List of psychotherapies. (2012). *The Wikipedia free encyclopedia.* Retrieved from http://en.wikipedia.org/wiki/List_of_psychotherapies

Livingston, R. (1979). The history of rehabilitation counselor certification. *Journal of Applied Rehabilitation Counseling, 10,* 111–118.

Lovell, C. (1999) Empathic-cognitive development in students of counseling. *Journal of Adult Development, 6*(4), 195–203. doi:10.1023/A:1021432310030

Lum, C. (2010). *A guide to state laws and regulations on professional school counseling.* Alexandria, VA: American Counseling Association.

Lum, D. (2004). *Social work practice and people of color: A process-stage approach* (5th ed.). Pacific Grove, CA: Brooks/Cole.

Macionis, J. J. (2011). *Sociology* (14th ed.). Upper Saddle River, NJ: Prentice Hall.

Malchiodi, C. A. (Ed.). (2005). *Expressive therapies.* New York, NY: Guilford Press.

Marmarosh, C. L., Markin, R. D., Gelso, C. J., Majors, R., Mallery, C., & Choi, J. (2009). The real relationship in psychotherapy: Relationships to adult attachments, working alliance, transference, and therapy outcome. *Journal of Counseling Psychology, 56,* 337–350. doi:10.1037/a0015169

Martin, W. E., Easton, C., Wilson, S., Takemoto, M., & Sullivan, S. (2004). Salience of emotional intelligence as a core characteristic of being a counselor. *Counselor Education and Supervision, 44,* 17–30.

May, R. (1950). *The meaning of anxiety.* New York, NY: Ronald Press.

McAuliffe, G. (2013). Culture and diversity defined. In G. McAuliffe (Ed.), *Culturally alert counseling: A comprehensive introduction* (2nd ed., pp. 3–21). Los Angeles: Sage Publications.

McAuliffe, G., & Eriksen, K. (Eds.). (2010). *Handbook of Counselor Preparation.* Thousand Oaks, CA: Sage and Alexandria, VA: Association for Counselor Education and Supervision.

McAuliffe, G., Grothaus, T., & Gomez, E. (2013). Conceptualizing race and racism. In G. McAuliffe (Ed.), *Culturally alert counseling: A comprehensive introduction* (2nd ed., pp. 89–124). Los Angeles: Sage Publications.

McDaniel, S. H. (2005). The psychotherapy of genetics. *Family Process, 44,* 25–44.

McDaniels, C., & Watts, G. A. (Eds.). (1994). Frank Parsons: Light, information, inspiration, cooperation [Special issue]. *Journal of Career Development, 20*(4).

McGlothlin, J. M., & Davis, T. E. (2004). Perceived benefit of CACREP (2001) core curriculum standards. *Counselor Education and Supervision, 43,* 274–285.

Meara, N. M., Schmidt, L. D., & Day, J. D. (1996) Principles and virtues: A foundation for ethical decisions, policies, and character. *The Counseling Psychologist, 24,* 4–77. doi:10.1177/0011000096241002

Mehr, J. J. & Kanwischer, R. (2011). *Human services: Concepts and intervention strategies* (11th ed.). Boston, MA: Pearson.

Middleton, R. A., Stadler, H. A., Simpson, C., Yuh-Jen, G., Brown, M. J., Crow, G., ... Lazarte, A. A. (2005). "Mental health practitioners: The relationship between white racial identity attitude and self-reported multicultural counseling competencies. *Journal of Counseling and Development 83,* 444–456.

Milliken, T. F. (2004). The impact of cognitive development on White school counselor interns' perspectives and perceived competencies for addressing the needs of African American students. (Doctoral dissertation, College of William and Mary, 2003). *Dissertation Abstracts International, 65*(02A), 420.

Minuchin, S. (1974). *Families and family therapy.* Cambridge, MA: Harvard University Press.

Morales, A. T., Sheafor, B. W., & Scott, M. E. (2007). *Social work: A profession of many faces* (11th ed.). Boston, MA: Allyn & Bacon.

Myers, J., & Sweeney, T. J. (2008). Wellness counseling: The evidence base and practice. *Journal of Counseling and Development, 86,* 482–493.

National Association of School Psychologists. (n.d.a). *What is a school psychologist?* [Brochure]. Bethesda, MD: Author.

National Association of School Psychologists. (n.d.b). *National certification.* Retrieved from http://www.nasponline.org/certification/index.aspx

National Association of School Psychologists. (2007). *Vision, Mission, and Goals section.* Retrieved from http://www.nasponline.org/about_nasp/strategicplan.pdf

National Association of Social Workers. (2008). *Code of ethics.* Retrieved from http://www.socialworkers.org/pubs/code/code.asp

National Association of Social Workers. (2012a). *About NASW.* Retrieved from http://www.naswdc.org/nasw/default.asp

National Association of Social Workers. (2012b). *NASW credentialing center.* Retrieved from http://www.naswdc.org/credentials/credentials/acsw.asp

National Association of Social Workers. (2012c). *NASW credentialing center.* Retrieved from http://www.naswdc.org/credentials/list.asp

National Board for Certified Counselors. (2005). *Code of ethics.* Retrieved from http://www.nbcc.org/Assets/Ethics/nbcc-codeofethics.pdf

National Board for Certified Counselors. (2011a). *Understanding NBCC's national certifications.* Retrieved from http://www.nbcc.org/OurCertifications

National Board for Certified Counselors. (2011b). *About NBCC.* Retrieved from http://www.nbcc.org/about

National Board for Certified Counselors. (2011c). *Application options for the national certified counselor (NCC) certification.* Retrieved from http://www.nbcc.org/Professional/Options#OptC

National Board for Certified Counselors. (2011d). *National certification and state licensure.* Retrieved from http://www.nbcc.org/Certification-Licensure

National Board for Certified Counselors. (2012). List of counseling programs nationally. Greensboro, NC: Author.

National Credentialing Academy. (n.d.a). *Overview and general information.* Retrieved from http://www.natlacad.4t.com/overview.html

National Credentialing Academy. (n.d.b). *Welcome to the national credentialing academy.* Retrieved from http://nationalcredentialingacademy.com/

National Credentialing Academy. (n.d.c). *NCA certification criteria.* Retrieved from http://nationalcredentialingacademy.com/certification.html/

National Human Genome Research Project. (2010). *From blueprint to you.* Retrieved from http://www.genome.gov/Pages/

Education/Modules/BluePrintToYou/ BlueprintCoverto2.pdf

National Organization of Human Services. (1996). Ethical standards for human service professionals. Retrieved from http://www.nationalhumanservices.org/ ethical-standards-for-hs-professionals

National Organization of Human Services. (2009). *Home page.* Retrieved from http://www.nationalhumanservices.org/

National Rehabilitation Counseling Association. (2012). *Home page.* Retrieved from http://nrcanet.org/

Neukrug, E. (1980). The effects of supervisory style and type of praise upon counselor trainees' level of empathy and perception of supervisor. (Doctoral dissertation, University of Cincinnati, 1980). *Dissertation Abstracts International, 41*(04A), 1496.

Neukrug, E. (2001). Medical breakthroughs: Genetic research and genetic counseling, psychotropic medications, and the mind-body connection. In T. McClam & M. Woodside (Eds.), *Human service challenges in the twenty-first century.* (pp. 115–132). Birmingham, AL: Ebsco Media.

Neukrug, E. (2011). *Counseling theory and practice.* Belmont, CA: Brooks/Cole.

Neukrug, E. S., & Fawcett, R. C. (2010). *Essentials of testing and assessment: A practical guide for counselors, social workers, and psychologists* (2nd ed.). Belmont, CA: Brooks/Cole.

Neukrug, E., Lovell, C., & Parker, R. (1996). Employing ethical codes and decision-making models: A developmental process. *Counseling and Values, 40,* 98–106.

Neukrug, E., & Milliken, T. (2011). Counselors' perceptions of ethical behaviors. *Journal of Counseling and Development, 89,* 206–217.

Neukrug, E., Milliken, T., & Walden, S. (2001). Ethical practices of credentialed counselors: An updated survey of state licensing boards. *Counselor Education and Supervision, 41,* 57–70.

Neukrug, E. & Schwitzer, A. M. (2006). *Skills and tools for today's counselors and psychotherapists: From natural helping to professional counseling.* Pacific Grove, CA: Brooks/Cole.

Niles, S. (Ed.). (2009). Special section: Advocacy competencies. *Journal of Counseling and Development, 87*(3).

Norcross, J. C. (2010). The therapeutic relationship. In B. L. Duncan, S. D. Miller, B. E. Wampold, & M A. Hubble (Eds.), *The heart and soul of change* (2nd ed., pp. 113–142). Washington, DC: American Psychological Association.

Norcross, J. C., Beutler, L. E., & Levant, R. (2006). *Evidenced-based practices in mental health: Dialogue on the fundamental questions.* Washington, DC: American Psychological Association.

Norcross, J. C., Bike, D. H., Evans, K. L., & Schatz, D. M. (2008). Psychotherapists who abstain from personal therapy: Do they practice what they preach? *Journal of Clinical Psychology, 64,* 1368–1376. doi:10.1002/jclp.20523

Nugent, F. A., & Jones, K. D. (2009). *Introduction to the profession of counseling* (5th ed.). Boston, MA: Pearson.

O'Brien, P. (Ed.). (2009). Accreditation: Assuring and enhancing quality [Special issue]. *New Direction for Higher Education,* 145.

Occupational Outlook Handbook (2010–2011). *Counselors.* Retrieved from http://www.bls.gov/oco/ocos067.htm

O'Leary, E. (2006). The need for integration. In E. O'Leary & M. Murphy (Eds.), *New approaches to integration in psychotherapy* (pp. 3–12). New York, NY: Routledge.

Oppenheimer, J. R. (1954). *In the matter of J. Robert Oppenheimer.* Washington, DC: United States Atomic Energy Commission, Personnel Security Board.

Orlinsky, D. E., Ronnestad, M. H., & Willutzki, U. (2004). Fifty years of psychotherapy process outcome research: Continuity and change. In M. J. Lambert (Ed.), *Bergin and Garfield's handbook of psychotherapy and behavior change* (5th ed., 307–389). New York, NY: Wiley.

Parsons, F. (1989). *Choosing a vocation.* Garrett Park, MD: Garrett Park. (Original work published 1909)

Patterson, C. H. (1973). *Theories of counseling and psychotherapy* (2nd ed.). New York, NY: Harper & Row.

Patterson, C. H. (1986). *Theories of counseling and psychotherapy* (4th ed.) New York, NY: HarperCollins.

Patterson, J. (2008, December). Counseling vs. life coaching. *Counseling Today,* 32–37.

Patureau-Hatchett, M. (2009). Counselors' perceptions of training, theoretical orientation, cultural and gender bias, and use of the "Diagnostic and Statistical Manual of Mental Disorders-IV-Text Revision." *Dissertation Abstracts International, 69,* 10A.

Pedersen, P. B., Crethar, H., & Carlson, J. (2008). *Inclusive cultural empathy: Making relationships central in counseling and psychotherapy.* Washington, DC: American Psychological Association.

Pence, G. E. (2004). *Classic cases in medical ethics: Accounts of the cases that have shaped medical ethics, with philosophical, legal, and historical backgrounds* (4th ed.). New York, NY: McGraw Hill.

Pence, G. (2010). *Medical ethics: Accounts of ground-breaking cases.* Columbus, OH: McGraw Hill.

Pepinsky, H. B. (2001). Counseling psychology: History. In W. E. Crawford & C. B. Nemeroff (Eds.), *The Corsini encyclopedia of psychology and behavioral science* (Vol. 1, pp. 375–379). New York, NY: Wiley.

Perls, F. (1969). *Gestalt therapy verbatim.* Moab, UT: Real People Press.

Perry, W. G. (1970). *Forms of intellectual and ethical development in the college years: A scheme.* New York, NY: Holt, Rinehart, & Winston.

Phillips, S. J. (2007). A comprehensive look at the legislative issues affecting advanced nursing practice. *Nurse Practitioner, 32*(1), 14–17. doi:10.1097/00006205-200701000-00006

Piaget, J. (1954). *The construction of reality in the child.* New York, NY: Basic Books.

Pieterse, A. L., Evans, S. A., Risner-Butner, A., Collins, N. M., & Mason, L. B. (2009). Multicultural and social justice training in counseling psychology and counselor education: A review and analysis of a sample of course syllabi. *The Counseling Psychologist, 37,* 93–115. doi:10.1177/0011000008319986

Ponterotto, J. G. (1988). Racial consciousness development among White counselor trainees: A stage model. *Journal of Multicultural Counseling and Development, 16*(4), 145–156.

Ponterotto, J. G., Casas, J. M., Suzuki, L. A., & Alexander, C. M. (Eds.). (2010). *Handbook of multicultural counseling* (3rd ed., Section IV). Thousand Oaks, CA: Sage.

Ponton, R., & Duba, J. (2009). The "ACA Code of Ethics": Articulating counseling's professional covenant. *Journal of Counseling and Development, 87,* 117–121.

Pope, M. (2004, February). Your professional responsibility: It's a good thing. *Counseling Today,* 5–6.

Pope, M., & Sveinsdottir, M. (2005). Frank, we hardly knew ye: The very personal side of Frank Parsons. *Journal of Counseling and Development, 83,* 105–115.

Preston, J. D., O'Neal, J. H., & Talaga, M. C. (2010). *Handbook of clinical psychopharmacology for therapists* (6th ed.). Oakland, CA: New Harbinger Publications.

Purton, C. (1993). Philosophy and counseling. In B. Thorne and W. W. Dryden (Eds.). *Counseling: Interdisciplinary perspectives* (pp. 152–161). Philadelphia, PA: Open University Press.

Ratts, M. J. (2009). Social justice counseling: Toward the development of a fifth force among counseling paradigms. *Journal of Humanistic Counseling, Education, and Development, 48,* 160–172.

Ratts, M. J., & Hutchins, A. M. (2009). ACA advocacy competencies: Social justice advocacy at the client/student level. *Journal of Counseling and Development, 87,* 269–275.

Remley, T. P., & Herlihy, B. (2010). *Ethical, legal, and professional issues in counseling* (3rd ed.). Upper Saddle River, NJ: Prentice Hall.

Ritchie, M., & Bobby, C. (2011, February). CACREP vs. the Dodo bird: How to win the race. *Counseling Today, 53*(8), 51–52.

Ritter, J. A., Vakalahi, H. F. O., & Kiernan-Stern, M. (2009). *101 careers in social work.* New York, NY: Springer Publishing.

Roach, L. F., & Young, M. E. (2007). Do counselor education programs promote wellness in their students? *Counselor Education and Supervision, 47*, 29–45.

Roberts, S. A., Kiselica, M. S., & Fredrickson, S. A. (2002). Quality of life of persons with medical illnesses: Counseling's holistic contribution. *Journal of Counseling and Development, 80*, 422–432.

Rockwell, P. J., & Rothney, W. M. (1961). Some social ideas of pioneers in the guidance movement. *Personnel and Guidance Journal, 40*, 349–354.

Rogers, C. R. (1942). *Counseling and psychotherapy: New concepts in practice.* Boston, MA: Houghton Mifflin.

Rogers, C. R. (1951). *Client-centered therapy: Its current practice, implications and theory.* Boston, MA: Houghton Mifflin.

Rogers, C. R. (1957). The necessary and sufficient conditions of therapeutic personality change. *Journal of Consulting Psychology, 21*, 95–103. doi:10.1037/h0045357

Rogers, C. R. (1989). A client-centered/person-centered approach to therapy. In H. Kirschenbaum (Ed.), *The Carl Rogers reader* (pp. 135–152). Boston, MA: Houghton Mifflin. (Original work published in 1986.)

Routh, D. K. (2000). Clinical psychology: History of the field. In A. E. Kazdin (Ed.), *Encyclopedia of psychology* (Vol. 2, pp. 113–118). New York, NY: Oxford University Press.

Roysircar, G., Arredondo, P., Fuertes, J. N., Ponterotto, J. G., & Toporek, R. L. (Eds). (2003). *Multicultural counseling competencies 2003: Association for Multicultural Counseling and Development.* Alexandria, VA: Association for Multicultural Counseling and Development.

Roysircar, G. Sandhu, D. S., & Bibbins, V. E. (Eds.). (2003). *Multicultural competencies: A guidebook of practices.* Alexandria, VA: Association for Multicultural Counseling and Development.

Sabnani, H. B., Ponterotto, J. G., & Borodovsky, L. G. (1991). White racial identity development and cross-cultural counselor training: A stage model. *The Counseling Psychologist, 19*, 76–102. doi:10.1177/0011000091191007

Sabshin, M. (1990). Turning points in twentieth-century American psychiatry. *The American Journal of Psychiatry, 147*, 1267–1274.

Satir, V. (1967). *Conjoint family therapy.* Palo Alto, CA: Science and Behavior Books.

Schatzberg, A. F., & Nemeroff, C. B. (Eds.). (2009). *The American psychiatric publishing textbook of psychopharmacology* (4th ed.). Washington, DC: American Psychiatric Press.

Schmidt, J. J. (1999). Two decades of CACREP and what do we know? *Counselor Education and Supervision, 39*, 34–45.

Schmidt, L. D. (2000). Counseling psychology: History of the field. In A. E. Kazdin (Ed.), *Encyclopedia of psychology* (Vol. 2, pp. 317–320). New York, NY: Oxford University Press.

Scoville, E., & Newman, J. S. (2009, May). A very brief history of credentialing. *ACP Hospitalist.* Retrieved from http://www.acphospitalist.org/archives/2009/05/newman.htm

Sewell, H. (2009). *Working with ethnicity, race and culture in mental health.* Philadelphia, PA: Jessica Kingsley Publishers.

Shallcross, L. (2011, March). Breaking away from the pack. *Counseling Today, 53*(9), 28–36.

Sheridan, E. P., Matarazzo, J. D., & Nelson, P. D. (1995). Accreditation of psychology's graduate professional education and training programs: An historical perspective. *Professional Psychology, Research and Practice, 26*, 386–392. doi:10.1037/0735-7028.26.4.386

Sokal, M. M. (1992). Origins and early years of the American Psychological Association, 1890–1906. *American Psychologist, 47*(2), 111–122. doi:10.1037/0003-066X.47.2.111

Solomon, M. (1918). The increasing importance of the biological viewpoint in psychopathology and psychiatry. *The Journal of Abnormal Psychology, 13*, 168–171. doi:10.1037/h0070702

Spillman, L. (2007). *Culture.* In G. Ritzer (Ed.), *Blackwell Encyclopedia of*

Sociology. Retrieved from http://www.blackwellreference.com/public/

Stout, C. E., & Hayes, R. A. (Eds.). (2005). *The evidence-based practice: Methods, models, and tools for mental health professionals.* Hoboken, NJ: Wiley.

Sue, D. W. (2010). *Microaggressions in everyday life: Race, gender, and sexual orientation.* New York, NY: Wiley.

Sue, D. W., & Sue, D. (2008). *Counseling the culturally diverse: Theory and practice* (5th ed.). New York, NY: Wiley.

Sue, D. W., & Torino, G. C. (2005). Racial-cultural competences: Awareness, knowledge and skills. In Carter, R. T. (Ed.), *Handbook of racial-cultural psychology and counseling: theory and research* (pp. 3–18). Hoboken, NJ: Wiley.

Suzuki, L. A., Kugler, J. F., & Aguiar, L. J. (2005). Assessment practices in racial-cultural psychology. In R. T. Carter (Ed.), *Handbook of racial-cultural psychology and counseling: Theory and research* (Vol. 2, pp. 297–315). Hoboken, NJ: John Wiley.

Sweeney, T. J. (1991). Counselor credentialing: Purpose and origin. In F. O. Bradley (Ed.), *Credentialing in counseling* (pp. 81–85). Alexandria, VA: Association for Counselor Education and Supervision.

Sweeney, T. J. (1992). CACREP: Precursors, promises, and prospects. *Journal of Counseling and Development, 70,* 667–672.

Sweeney, T. J. (1995). Accreditation, credentialing, professionalization: The role of specialties. *Journal of Counseling and Development, 74,* 117–125.

Swenson, L. C. (1997). *Psychology and law for the helping professions* (2nd ed.). Belmont, CA: Brooks/Cole.

The benefits of joining a professional association (2010, August). *GradSchools. com: The #1 graduate school directory on the planet.* Retrieved from http://www.gradschools.com/article-detail/professional-association-1569

The CACREP Connection. (2007, Fall). *CACREP/CORE merger fails.* Alexandra, VA: CACREP.

The top 10: The most influential therapists of the past quarter-century. (2007,

March/April). *Psychotherapy Networker.* Retrieved from http://www.psychotherapynetworker.org/component/content/article/81-2007-marchapril/219-the-top-10

Todd, J., & Bohart, A. C. (2006). *Foundations of clinical and counseling psychology* (4th ed.). Long Grove, IL: Waveland Press.

Toporek, R. L., & Lewis, J. A., & Crethar, H. C. (2009). Promoting systemic change through the ACA advocacy competencies. *Journal of Counseling and Development, 87,* 260–268.

Trepal, H., Haberstroh, S., Duffey, T., & Evans, M. (2007). Considerations and strategies for teaching online counseling skills: Establishing relationships in cyberspace. *Counselor Education and Supervision, 46,* 266–279.

Turkington, C. (1985). Analysts sued for barring non-MDs. *APA Monitor, 16*(5), 2.

Tyler, L. E. (1969). *The work of the counselor* (3rd ed.). Englewood Cliffs, NJ: Prentice Hall.

U.S. Bureau of Labor Statistics. *O*NET OnLine: Summary report for genetic counselors.* Retrieved from http://www.onetonline.org/link/summary/29-9092.00

U.S. Census Bureau. (2009). *Annual Estimates of the Resident Population by Sex, Race, and Hispanic Origin for the United States: April 1, 2000 to July 1, 2009 (NC-EST2009-03).* Retrieved from http://www.census.gov/popest/national/asrh/NC-EST2009-srh.html

U.S. Department of Commerce. (2000). *Percent of U.S. households with a computer and Internet access.* Retrieved from http://www.ntia.doc.gov/ntiahome/fttn00/chartscontents.html

U.S. Department of Commerce. (2011). *Exploring the digital nation: Computer and Internet use at home.* Retrieved from http://www.ntia.doc.gov/files/ntia/publications/exploring_the_digital_nation_computer_and_internet_use_at_home_11092011.pdf

U.S. Department of Health and Human Services. (2001). *Mental health: Culture, race, and ethnicity: A supplement to mental health: A report of the surgeon general*. Retrieved from http://www.ncbi. nlm.nih.gov/books/NBK44243/

U.S. Department of Health and Human Services. (2010). *Health, United States, 2010: With special feature on death and dying*. Retrieved from http://www.cdc. gov/nchs/data/hus/hus10.pdf#095

Urofsky, R., Engels, D., & Engebretson, K. (2008). Kitchener's principle ethics: Implications for counseling practice and research. *Counseling and Values, 53(1)*, 67.

Vaccaro, N., & Lambie, G. W. (2007). Computer-based counselor-in-training supervision: Ethical and practical implications for counselor educators and supervisors. *Counselor Education and Supervision, 47*, 46–57.

van Deurzen, E. (2002). *Existential counseling and psychotherapy in practice* (2nd ed.). London: Sage publications.

Vera, E. M., & Speight, S. L. (2003). Multicultural competence, social justice, and counseling psychology: Expanding our roles. *The Counseling Psychologist, 31*, 253–272. doi:10.1177/001100000 3031003001

Virginia Board of Counseling. (2011). *Laws governing counseling*. Virginia board of counseling: Laws and regulations. Retrieved from http://www.dhp.virginia. gov/counseling/counseling_laws_regs. htm#law

Visconti, R. (n.d.). *Develop your career by joining a professional association*. Retrieved from http://www.jobscareers. com/articles/developingyourcareer.html

Wadeson, H. (2004). To be or not to be licensed: Is that the question? *Art Therapy, 21(4)*, 182–183.

Wampold, B. E. (2010a). *The basics of psychotherapy: An introduction to theory and practice*. Washington, DC: American Psychological Association.

Wampold, B. E. (2010b). *The great psychotherapy debate: Models, methods, and findings*. Mahwah, NJ: Lawrence Erlbaum Associates.

Wampold, B. E. (2010c). The research evidence for common factors models: A historically situated perspective. In B. L. Duncan, S. D. Miller, B. E. Wampold, & M. A. Hubble (Eds.), *The heart and soul of change* (2nd ed.,

pp. 49–82). Washington, DC: American Psychological Association.

Watts, G. A. (1994). Frank Parsons: Promoter of a progressive era. *Journal of Career Development, 20*, 265–286. doi:10.1007/BF02106300

Weissmann, G. (2008). Citizen Pinel and the madman at Bellevue. *The Journal of the Federation of American Societies for Experimental Biology. 22*, 1289–1293. doi:10.1096/fj.08-0501ufm

Welfel, E. R. (2010). *Ethics in counseling and psychotherapy: Standards, research, and emerging issues* (4th ed.). Pacific Grove, CA: Brooks/Cole.

Wendler, A. E. (2009). Universal-diverse orientation, cognitive complexity, and sociopolitical Advocacy in counselor trainees. *Journal of Multicultural Counseling & Development, 37(1)*, 28–39.

Wertheimer, M. (2000). *A brief history of psychology* (4th ed.). New York, NY: Harcourt College Publishers.

Whiston, S. C., & Coker, J. K. (2000). Reconstructing clinical training: Implications from research. *Counselor Education and Supervision, 39*, 228–253.

Wilcoxon, S., Magnuson, S., & Norem, K. (2008). Institutional values of managed mental health care: Efficiency or oppression? *Journal of Multicultural Counseling and Development, 36(3)*, 143.

Wilczenski, F. L., & Cook, A. L. (2011). Virtue Ethics in school counseling: A framework for decision making. *Journal of School Counseling, 9(7)*. Retrieved from ERIC database. (EJ933173)

Williams, R. (2010). Atonement. In D. A. Leeming, K. Madden, & S. Marlan (Eds.), *Encyclopedia of psychology and religion* (Vol. 1, pp. 83–84), New York, NY: Springer.

Williamson, E. G. (1950). *Counseling adolescents*. New York, NY: McGraw-Hill.

Williamson, E. G. (1958). Value orientation in counseling. *Personnel and Guidance Journal, 37*, 520–528.

Williamson, E. G. (1964). An historical perspective of the vocational guidance movement. *Personnel and Guidance Journal, 42*, 854–859.

Willis, L., & Wilkie, L. (2009). Digital career portfolios: Expanding institutional opportunities. *Journal of Employment Counseling, 46*(2), 73.

Wolpe, J. (1958). *Psychotherapy by reciprocal inhibition.* Stanford, CA: Stanford University Press.

Your investment + our commitment = your member benefits and services! *Counseling Today, 51*(10), 60.

Zwelling, S. S. (1990). *Quest for a cure: The public hospital in Williamsburg, Virginia, 1773–1885.* Williamsburg, VA: The Colonial Williamsburg Foundation.

Zytowski, D. G. (1972). Four hundred years before Parsons. *Personnel and Guidance Journal, 50,* 443–450.

INDEX